FROMMER'S

BUDGET TRAVEL GUIDE

BERLIN '94-'95 ON $50 A DAY

Y0-BPY-175

by Beth Reiber

PRENTICE HALL TRAVEL

NEW YORK • LONDON • TORONTO • SYDNEY • TOKYO • SINGAPORE

FROMMER BOOKS

Published by Prentice Hall General Reference
A division of Simon & Schuster Inc.
15 Columbus Circle
New York, NY 10023

ISBN 0-671-84915-8
ISSN 1055-5366

Design by Robert Bull Design
Maps by Geografix Inc.

FROMMER'S BERLIN ON $50 A DAY '94-'95

Frommer's Editorial Staff

Vice President/Editorial Director: Marilyn Wood
Senior Editor/Editorial Manager: Alice Fellows
Senior Editor: Lisa Renaud
Editors: Charlotte Allstrom, Thomas F. Hirsch, Peter Katucki, Sara Hinsey
Raveret, Theodore Stavrou
Assistant Editors: Margaret Bowen, Christopher Hollander, Alice Thompson, Ian Wilker
Editorial Assistants: Gretchen Henderson, Bethany Jewett
Managing Editor: Leanne Coupe

Special Sales

Manufactured in the United States of America

CONTENTS

LIST OF MAPS

INVITATION TO THE READERS

In researching this book, I have come across many wonderful establishments, the best of which I have included here. I am sure that many of you will also come across appealing hotels, inns, restaurants, guest houses, shops, and attractions. Please don't keep them to yourself. Share your experiences, especially if you want to comment on places that have been included in this edition that have changed for the worse. You can address your letters to:

Beth Reiber
Frommer's Berlin on $50 a Day '94–'95
c/o Prentice Hall Travel
15 Columbus Circle
New York, NY 10023

A DISCLAIMER

Readers are advised that prices fluctuate in the course of time, and travel information changes under the impact of the varied and volatile factors that affect the travel industry. Neither the author nor publisher can be held responsible for the experiences of readers while traveling. Readers are invited to write to the publisher with ideas, comments, and suggestions for future editions.

SAFETY ADVISORY

Whenever you're traveling in an unfamiliar city or country, stay alert. Be aware of your immediate surroundings. Wear a moneybelt and keep a close eye on your possessions. Be particularly careful with cameras, purses, and wallets, all favorite targets of thieves and pickpockets.

INTRODUCING BERLIN

Once again the capital of a united Germany, Berlin mirrors its nation's history more vividly than any other city. The seat of 19th-century Prussian imperialism under Bismarck, it blossomed culturally in the twenties, only to fall under the shadow of Hitler's Third Reich. Almost totally destroyed during World War II, Berlin then became both victim and symbol of the Cold War. Isolated and surrounded by East Germany, Berlin was a divided city, a division made concrete with the erection of the Wall. A hideous structure more than 100 miles long and 13 feet high, it was constructed to stop the mass exodus of East Germans into West Berlin that was draining East Germany of its youngest, brightest, and best-educated. No one dreamed that in 1989, another exodus would trigger the fall of the Wall and the end of East Germany's Communist regime.

Today Berlin is the most popular travel destination in Germany, receiving more than 10 million visitors a year. Now that the Wall is history, visitors are discovering the treasures Berlin has harbored all along, including some of the world's great museums, housing such gems as the bust of Nefertiti and the magnificent Pergamon Altar. Having been divided for so many decades, Berlin has two of almost everything: two major opera houses, two museums for primeval and early history, two Egyptian museums, two historical museums, two museums of modern art, two museums of European masterpieces, one sculpture collection and one sculptural gallery. And that's only the beginning.

No German city has been more acutely affected by reunification than Berlin. Not only did it suddenly become the country's capital, but it also faced the formidable task of integrating two separate systems that had 40 years to develop, each with its own political, social, economic, cultural, and ideological values. Everything from bus lines to telephone lines had to be coordinated and changed; streets severed by the Wall had to be rejoined. The differences between eastern and western Berlin are still rather shocking. Although there is no longer a physical barrier between the two halves, there is still a psychological one, and Berliners still speak of "east" or "west" Berlin as though they were two separate entities.

Although the core of former East Berlin is showing signs of

WHAT'S SPECIAL ABOUT BERLIN

Museums

- ☐ The Pergamon Museum in eastern Berlin, with the Pergamon Altar, the Market Gate of Miletus, and the Babylonian Processional Street.
- ☐ The Gemäldegalerie in Dahlem, with about 20 paintings by Rembrandt.
- ☐ The Ägyptisches Museum, with the bust of Nefertiti.
- ☐ The Neue Nationalgalerie and Nationalgalerie, with Berliner impressionist and expressionist artists.
- ☐ Museums filled with art from around the world.
- ☐ Museum Haus am Checkpoint Charlie, documenting the history of the Wall and nonviolent revolutions around the world.

Diversity

- ☐ Colorful neighborhoods, reflecting the ethnic/social mix—Kreuzberg with its large Turkish population, working-class Köpenick, and middle-class Dahlem.
- ☐ Restaurants featuring Greek, Turkish, Italian, Japanese, Chinese, Indian, and Thai cuisine.

Shopping

- ☐ KaDeWe, the largest department store on the Continent, famous for its food floor.
- ☐ The fashionable Ku'damm, a great place for window-shopping.
- ☐ Wilmersdorfer Strasse, a pedestrian lane lined with boutiques.
- ☐ The Europa-Center, a large mall.
- ☐ More than 100 art galleries.
- ☐ Outdoor and indoor markets, a treasure trove for antiques, junk, and crafts.

Festivals

- ☐ International Film Festival, held every February.
- ☐ Jazz-Fest Berlin in autumn, a colorful mix of avant-garde and classical jazz.
- ☐ Weihnachtsmarkt, an annual Christmas market, held around the Ku'damm.

Nightlife

- ☐ Famous opera houses and concert halls, including the Deutsche Oper Berlin and the Philharmonie.
- ☐ Cabarets, a Berlin tradition.
- ☐ Live-music houses, bars, and discos.

revitalization, much of it is in economic shambles, with high unemployment and many businesses closed down, waiting for private buyers. Buildings are decaying, pockmarked with shrapnel as though World War II ended only yesterday.

But Berliners are tough, and years of living with the Wall have taught them to survive adversity. Always Germany's least provincial city—liberal and tolerant—Berlin attracts artists, writers, students, and those in search of alternative lifestyles. Its rich culture—museums, opera, theater, symphony, jazz, international film premieres, rock concerts, and nightlife that never shuts down—makes Berlin one of the most interesting destinations in Europe. With the sweeping curves of its art nouveau architecture, its tree-lined streets, and the refinement of its old-style cafés, Berlin is graceful, but it also has the weird, the wired, and the energy of the avant-garde. Even young Europeans—who generally skip Germany for the more liberal climes of Paris, Amsterdam, or Copenhagen—are flocking to Berlin. Berlin also serves as a perfect gateway to Eastern Europe. Suddenly, Berlin is in. This is a great time to be visiting, as Berlin forges ahead in its new—and old—role as capital of Germany.

1. CULTURE, HISTORY & BACKGROUND

GEOGRAPHY & PEOPLE

Located in northeast Germany, Berlin occupies the geographical center of Europe, about halfway between Moscow and Lisbon. It shares the same latitude with London and Vancouver, Canada, and has the same longitude as Naples, Italy. With almost 3.5 million people and a total area of 340 square miles, it is Germany's largest and most densely populated city. In fact, it's larger in area than New York City, and could easily accommodate the cities of Atlanta, Boston, Cleveland, and San Francisco within its boundaries. Its boundaries are so encompassing, that the western half of Berlin alone has close to 60 square miles of woods, lakes, rivers, and parks— which served as an important breathing space for West Berliners during the decades of the Wall. After the division of Germany following World War II, Berlin was closer to Poland (60 miles) than it was to West Germany (100 miles). Berlin is 184 miles from Hamburg, 343 miles from Frankfurt, and 363 miles from Munich.

Not surprisingly, Berlin's years as a divided city and its physical isolation from the West have played a major role on the psyche and character of Berliners. They are survivors, having suffered almost total destruction of their city during World War II, followed by decades of crises sparked by the Cold War.

The differences between East and West Berliners remain. West Berliners, after years of living with the uncertainty posed by the Wall and an encircling hostile regime, developed a distinct "live for today" lifestyle, much more Bohemian and liberal than their compatriots in other German cities. Berlin's liberal climate was further enhanced by policies of the West German government. In an effort to encourage young West Germans to live in this metropolitan outpost, residents were granted generous housing subsidies and exemption from military service, thereby attracting artists, activists, rebels, and others in search of an alternative lifestyle. Because of their isolation, West Berliners were as apt to identify themselves with the citizens of Paris or New York as they were with fellow Germans.

Thus, when the Wall came down and the initial jubilation wore off, East Berliners came as something of a shock to the liberal West Berliners. Unmistakable in their tiny, squat, Trabant automobiles and the dull sameness of Eastern-Bloc clothing, East Germans seemed so serious, so naive, so obedient to authority—so German. But West Berlin was no less shocking to East Berliners, with its decadent nightlife, availability of drugs, unabashed pursuit of capitalism, and all the ills of the Western world. West Berliners were seen as arrogant

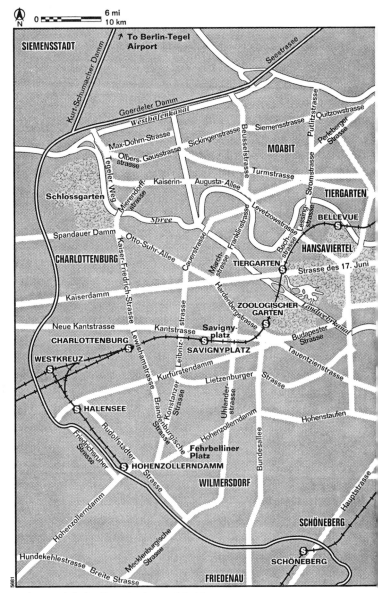

and materialistic; East Berliners felt like second-class citizens and suffered a loss of self-esteem.

It hasn't been easy resolving the differences between East and West, and although it will take time the process has begun and differences are shrinking daily. Even now, it's not always easy to tell what side of the city a Berliner hails from, and surely the day will come when a Berliner is once again simply a Berliner.

After all, Berliners are bound together by certain characteristics that are thoroughly and unmistakably German—not to mention

WEDDING

PRENZLAUER BERG

Fennstrasse

Chausseestrasse

Heidestrasse

NORDBAHNHOF

Invalidenstrasse

Schönhauser Allee

Prinzenstrasse

Greifswalder Strasse

HRTER TADTBAHNHOF

Invalidenstrasse

Wilh.-
Pieck-

Rosenthaler Strasse

Oranienburger Strasse

Spree

BERLIN-MITTE

HACKESCHER MARKT

Mollstrasse

Alexander-
platz

Karl-Marx-Allee

FRIEDRICHSTRASSE

Karl-Liebknecht-

Alexander Strasse

Pariser
Platz

Unter den Linden

Marx
Engels
Platz

Mühlendamm

JANOWITZ-
BRÜCKE

UNTER DEN LINDEN

Gertrauden-
strasse

Brücken-
strasse

Spree

Tiergarten

Leipziger Strasse

Heinrich-Heine Strasse

Leipziger
Platz

Friedrichstrasse

Lindenstrasse

POTSDAMER
PLATZ

Stresemann-

Oranienstrasse

Schöneberger Ufer

ANHALTER
BAHNHOF

Gitschiner Strasse

Potsdamer Strasse

Bülow
strasse

Tempelhofer Ufer

Landwehrkanal

ORCKSTRASSE

Yorckstrasse

Gneisenaustrasse

Urbanstrasse

KREUZBERG

Hasenheide

Kolonnenstrasse

Katzbachstrasse

Dudenstrasse

Columbiadamm

Boelckestrasse

Flughafenstrasse

To Berlin-
Schönefeld
Airport

Berlin-Tempelhof
Airport

S-Bahn — S

Prussian, which means that they take pleasure in orderliness, precision, and the established order of things. But Berliners are also known for their dry wit and humor, and their penchant for nicknaming everything in sight: They call the Kongresshalle the "pregnant oyster," while the new church next to the Gedächtniskirche is known as the "lipstick and powder puff." The large global fountain in front of the Europa-Center is the "wet dumpling," while the TV tower on Alexanderplatz is the "tele-asparagus."

Berliners also have what's called "schnauze," a cocky attitude that makes them say that everything is bigger and better in Berlin. It's a trait that they share with Bavarians and fellow Munchners and in fact, there's a story that goes like this: A Bavarian boasted to a Berliner that Bavaria was superior to Berlin because of its Alps. He then smugly asked the Berliner if Berlin had any comparable mountains.

"No," answered the Berliner calmly, "but if we did, you can be sure they'd be higher than yours."

Of all German cities, Berlin also has the largest non-German population—Poles, Silesians, East Prussians, Turks, Yugoslavs, and Greeks. The first to arrive were the Huguenots, invited by Friedrich Wilhelm II (the "Great Elector") to Berlin in the 17th century; and traces of their influence can still be found today. For example, the Berlin meatball specialty, "boulette," was introduced to Berlin by them.

In Imperial times, Poles, Silesians, and East Prussians were drawn to Berlin. In the twenties, artists and bohemians chose Berlin as their home. After World War II, Turkish, Yugoslavian, Greek, and Polish immigrants found homes and ready employment in Berlin, and rebellious students from West Germany were attracted to the city in the 1960s. Most recently, newcomers to Berlin have included refugees from former Eastern-Bloc countries.

Today, one in 10 residents is a foreigner, and one out of five children under age six have parents with foreign passports. Turks are the largest minority in Berlin, numbering more than 100,000 and living mainly in the western precincts of Kreuzberg, Neukölln, and Wedding. Although problems occasionally arise because of differences in customs and cultural backgrounds, escalating in recent times to animosity and violence toward foreign workers and their families, on the whole Berlin enjoys greater racial harmony than many parts of Germany. Decades of isolation helped forge a sense of community spirit; years of living with the Wall have bred tolerance and determination.

DATELINE

- **1200** Two settlements, Berlin and Cölln, founded on the Spree River.
- **1307** Berlin and Cölln unite and build a joint town hall.
- **1415** Count Friedrich von Nürnberg becomes Friedrich I, Prince Elector of Brandenburg.
- **1470** Berlin becomes the official residence of the

(continues)

HISTORY/POLITICS

As with any city, Berlin's atmosphere, architecture, and cultural life have been shaped by its past. For a more thorough understanding of Berlin and its history, refer to the books in the recommended reading list at the end of this chapter.

MEDIEVAL TOWN TO ROYAL CAPITAL As ironic as it now seems, Berlin began life as a divided city 800 years ago, when two Wendish settlements were founded on the Spree River: Berlin, on a bank of the river, and Cölln (or Kölln), on a nearby island in the river. Located about halfway between the established fortresses of Spandau and Köpenick, the two small settlements developed as trading towns, spreading along the banks of the Spree in what is now Berlin-Mitte. A convenient stopover on a much-traveled trade route,

Berlin-Cölln cleverly required all traveling tradesmen who passed through to stay several days and offer their merchandise for sale: This gave the towns' merchants an opportunity to purchase rye, wool, oak, hides, furs, and other goods and then to export them as far afield as Hamburg, Flanders, and even England. Both towns grew and prospered, and although their citizens were not particularly interested in unifying, eventually it became inevitable. In 1307 they merged under the name of Berlin and built a joint town hall. Berlin also joined the powerful Hanseatic League, a protective and commercial federation of free towns along the Baltic Sea.

During the next century, Berlin fell under the rule of various dynasties and was repeatedly attacked by robber barons and roving bandits. In desperation, Berlin finally appealed to the Holy Roman Emperor in 1411 for protection against the robber barons. To the rescue came Count Friedrich from the Hohenzollern house in Nuremberg, and by 1414 he had defeated the most notorious robber barons of the day. Shortly thereafter he proclaimed himself the Prince Elector of Brandenburg, thereby gaining control of Berlin and surrounding Brandenburg.

Although the people revolted against the Hohenzollern takeover, the rebellion was easily quashed. In 1470 Berlin became the official residence of the Elector of Brandenburg. (The German word for *Elector,* by the way, is *Kurfürst* which literally means "Choosing Prince," one who had the right to elect the emperor.) Berlin lost the freedom it had enjoyed as an independent trading town.

The Hohenzollerns ruled from Berlin for the next 500 years, during which time Berlin changed from a town of merchants to a city of civil servants and government administrators. The tone of urban life was set by the Elector's courtiers and officials, who had a fondness for lavish festivities and feasts. Noblemen and jurists moved to this new city of opportunity, and the demand for luxury goods drew many craftspeople. In an attempt to curb the wild consumption of alcohol and loose morals that had filtered down from the privileged class to the lower classes, the authorities issued decrees against drunkenness and disturbing the peace; they

DATELINE

Elector of Brandenburg.

- **1539** Prince Elector Joachim II converts to Protestantism and the Reformation comes to Berlin.
- **1618–48** The Thirty Years' War reduces Brandenburg's population by half.
- **1640–88** Friedrich Wilhelm, the "Great Elector," reigns.
- **1685** The Great Elector invites 6,000 persecuted Huguenots from France to settle in Berlin.
- **1701** Elector Friedrich III crowns himself first king of Prussia, Friedrich I.
- **1709** Friedrich I names Berlin the royal residence.
- **1713–40** Friedrich Wilhelm I, the "Soldier King," reigns. He enlarges the army and fortifies Berlin.
- **1735** Berlin's population: 60,000.
- **1740–86** Friedrich II, "Frederick the Great," reigns. He builds Sanssouci Palace in Potsdam, makes Berlin a European capital, and builds the Prussian army.
- **1770** Unter den Linden constructed.
- **1791** Brandenburger Tor erected.
- **1806** Napoléon marches into Berlin.

(continues)

DATELINE

occupying the city for two years.

- **1862** Bismarck becomes Chancellor of Prussia.
- **1871** Berlin becomes capital of German Reich.
- **1918** End of World War I; Kaiser Wilhelm II abdicates and Germany becomes a Republic.
- **1920** Greater Berlin formed and subdivided into 20 precincts with almost 4 million inhabitants.
- **1933** Hitler and Nazis seize power; Third Reich begins.
- **1936** XIth Summer Olympics held in Berlin; black athlete Jesse Owens wins four gold medals.
- **1939** Hitler invades Poland, World War II begins.
- **1945** German army surrenders. Berlin divided into four zones occupied by the Four Powers.
- **1948** 11-month Berlin Blockade. Berlin Airlift supplies West Berlin.
- **1949** DDR formed, with East Berlin as capital.
- **1953** Uprising in East Berlin on June 17 spreads over DDR repressed with Soviet troops.
- **1958** USSR issues the Berlin Ultimatum, demanding that Western Allies *(continues)*

even divided the residents of Berlin into four distinct classes, each with its own restrictions on the type, price, and material of dress. As might be expected, such decrees were hard to enforce, especially as the population grew. From 1450 to 1600, residents of Berlin increased from 6,000 to 12,000.

But then came the plague, smallpox, and the Thirty Years' War (1618–48), a religious confrontation between Protestants and Catholics. By the end of the war, half of Berlin's citizens had lost their lives and much of the city lay in ruins. Luckily for Berlin, however, Friedrich Wilhelm had come to power in 1640. One of Berlin's most able rulers, he enjoyed great popularity for his defeat of the Swedes in the decisive battle of Fehrbellin during the Thirty Years' War; to this day he is still fondly known as the Great Elector. To bolster the town's economy and rebuild its population, in 1685 he invited 6,000 Huguenots, French Protestants who were forced to flee because of religious persecution, to settle in Berlin. By 1700, nearly one Berliner in five was of French lineage.

In 1701 the Great Elector's son, Elector Friedrich III, crowned himself the first king of Prussia and became Friedrich I. Up until then, Prussia had been only a duchy under the rule of electors. In 1709, he merged Berlin and several surrounding towns into one community, declaring Berlin his royal residence and the royal capital of Brandenburg-Prussia. On the whole, however, Friedrich I was an unpopular and unloved king. Mocked for his vanity, he nevertheless did have the insight to marry Sophie Charlotte, a beautiful and intelligent woman adored by the masses. An ardent advocate of intellectual and spiritual growth, she built a small summer residence where she could entertain some of the great minds of the age, holding lively discussions and debates. Upon nearing death at age 36, she said she was ready to see what the afterlife had in store. As for her husband, she predicted that her death and subsequent funeral would give him another "opportunity to demonstrate his magnificence." She was right; he enlarged the palace and named it for her. Today Schloss Charlottenburg remains the finest example of baroque architecture in Berlin.

During the 18th century, Berlin became the most important political, economic, and cultural center of the area. The town blossomed under the talents of architects Andreas Schlüter, Karl Friedrich Schinkel, and Georg Wenzeslaus von Knobelsdorff: In a flurry of activity, the Berlin Palace (destroyed in World War II) was enlarged, the boulevard of Unter den Linden was laid, the Brandenburger Tor (Brandenburg Gate) and 12 other city gates were erected, and the Supreme Court (now the Berlin Museum), the Opera, and the Arsenal were completed.

But the man credited with elevating Berlin to one of Europe's premier capitals was Friedrich II, better known as Frederick the Great, who reigned from 1740 to 1786. At first he rebelled at the idea of becoming king and tried to flee to England with an army officer. But Friedrich's father, known as the strict "soldier king," punished his disobedient son by making him watch the beheading of his friend (who, so the story goes, was also Friedrich's lover). That, perhaps more than anything, convinced Friedrich that he wanted to be king after all, and during his long reign he doubled the size of the Prussian army and made Prussia the greatest military power in Europe. He also built a charming summer residence in nearby Potsdam, Schloss Sanssouci, where he could escape the rigors and worries of an administrative life.

Under Frederick the Great's rule, Berlin became a mecca of the Enlightenment, attracting such greats as the philosopher Moses Mendelssohn, author Gotthold Ephraim Lessing, and publisher Friedrich Nicolai. Voltaire came to Potsdam as the king's guest and stayed three years. In 1763, Frederick the Great took over a failing porcelain company, banned all imports, and granted it a monopoly. The company, the Königliche Porzellan-Manufaktur (KPM) is still well-known today. By 1800, Berlin boasted 200,000 inhabitants, making it the third-largest city in Europe after London and Paris.

On October 27, 1806, Napoléon marched into the capital of a defeated Prussia, entering triumphantly through Brandenburger Tor. Knowing that it would strike at the very heart of the proud Prussians, Napoléon removed the Quadriga—a chariot drawn by four horses, and the symbol of Berlin—from the top of the gate and carted it off to Paris as part of the spoils of war. When the Prussians finally managed to rout the French a couple years later, they recovered their Quadriga—adding an Iron Cross and a Prussian Eagle—and returned it to its perch on Brandenburger Tor.

During the Industrial Revolution of the 19th century, Berlin

DATELINE

leave Berlin, but Allies ignore the order.

• **1961** Wall constructed August 13; seals off Western Sectors.

• **1963** President Kennedy gives "Ich bin ein Berliner' speech at Rathaus Schöneberg.

• **1971** Allies sign Four-Powers Agreement on Berlin.

• **1972** West Berliners again allowed to visit DDR.

• **1987** 750th Anniversary of Berlin.

• **1988** Berlin declared "Cultural City" of Europe.

• **1989** East Germans flee to West through Hungary. Nov 9 the Wall opened by DDR.

• **1990** Demolition of Wall begun; Germany reunified Oct. 3; Berlin once again becomes capital.

emerged as a center of trade and industry, producing silk, woolens, porcelain, and machinery. For many of the working class, industrialization brought increasing poverty and destitution. Despite the abolition of serfdom and reforms in education, peasants who flocked to Berlin to find work—including women and children—were exploited in dismal factories under harsh conditions. The middle class, meanwhile, demanded more political power to keep abreast with their newly acquired social status. Although the people rose in revolt several times—notably in the March Revolution of 1848—few concessions were gained. By the 1870s there were 70,000 homeless in Berlin out of a population of 826,000. But even those with a roof over their head often lived in gloomy and depressing flats that never saw the light of day. As many as one-tenth of the total population lived in basements; one-third lived in one-room apartments that averaged 4.3 occupants. Thus, Berlin had the dubious distinction of being the world's largest tenement city.

FROM THE GERMAN REICH TO THE THIRD REICH In 1871, Prussian Chancellor Otto von Bismarck succeeded in uniting all of Germany with a nationalistic policy under the slogan "iron and blood." As Bismarck was Prussian, Berlin naturally became capital of this new German Reich, attracting even more industry and settlers so that by 1906 the city had two million inhabitants. After the turn of the century, Berlin supplanted Munich as Germany's cultural capital, attracting such artists as Max Liebermann, Lovis Corinth, and Max Slevogt. Ornate apartment dwellings lined the streets, graced with the curvilinear lines of art nouveau. Max Reinhardt came to Berlin to direct the Deutsches Theater, and Richard Strauss became conductor of the Royal Opera.

In 1920, Berlin incorporated seven formerly autonomous towns, 59 rural communities, and 27 landed estates to form a Greater Berlin, which it then divided into 20 precincts. This made Berlin the biggest industrial giant on the Continent, the nucleus of the North German railway network, as well as a commercial-banking and stock-exchange center. Through the twenties, Berlin flourished as an intellectual and cultural center, and such architectural greats as Martin Gropius and Hans Scharoun left their marks upon the city. In 1926, a young playwright named Bertolt Brecht scored a huge success with the premiere of his *Threepenny Opera,* in this city that had 35 theaters, several opera houses, and more than 20 concert halls. Berlin's university gained a reputation as one of the best in the country, and Einstein, who was director of physics at what would later become the Max-Planck Institute, received the Nobel Prize in 1921. As many as 150 daily and weekly newspapers were published in Berlin. The city rivaled Paris as one of the most exciting cities in Europe.

But behind the facade of greatness, trouble was brewing: The woes of the working class had become increasingly acute, a despair and hopelessness captured by such artists as Käthe Kollwitz and Heinrich Zille and writer Kurt Tucholsky, but otherwise largely ignored. Like the rest of Germany, Berlin had suffered hardships during World War I, with weekly rationings of one egg, 20 grams of butter, and 80 grams of meat per person. Heating fuel, lighting, and clothing were rationed as well. But the end of the war brought little relief, even though the German emperor abdicated and Germany was proclaimed a German Republic. In the winter of 1918–19, 300,000

? DID YOU KNOW . . . ?

- In 1700, one Berliner in five was of French extraction.
- In 1800, Berlin was the third-largest city in Europe after London and Paris.
- In the 1920s, Berlin boasted 35 theaters, several opera houses, more than 20 concert halls, and 150 daily and weekly newspapers.
- Founded in 1844, Berlin's Tiergarten zoo housed 10,000 animals in 1939, but only 91 survived the war.
- Berlin is closer to Poland (60 miles) than it is to any city in former West Germany.
- Berlin has more students than any other German university city, and more students than Boston.
- Berlin has about 1,000 bridges— more than the city of Venice.
- Berlin has more than 480 miles of hiking and biking trails.
- A landlocked city, Berlin has more than 30,000 registered boats.

Berliners were out of work. And yet Germany was saddled with huge war reparations, and parts of the country had been sliced off and given to the victors. Runaway inflation had made the currency virtually worthless: it took barrelfuls just to buy a loaf of bread and 600 marks just to ride the trolley. In 1921, one dollar equalled 75 marks; by November 20, 1923, one dollar was worth 4,200,000,000,000 marks. When new banknotes were finally issued, one new banknote was equal to 1,000 billion of the worthless old paper marks.

The political situation also deteriorated. There were struggles between extreme rightists and leftists that often resulted in street fights, militant strikes, and bloody riots. In 1929 the economic crisis went from bad to worse, with 636,000 unemployed in Berlin by the end of 1932. Many families lost their homes, some people committed suicide.

During this upheaval an obscure political party called the National Socialists used the social/economic situation and the harshness of the World War I treaty to gain followers with promises of making Germany great again. On January 30, 1933, Adolf Hitler became Chancellor of Germany. Hitler knew he was not a popular figure in Berlin—his Nazi party had been consistently defeated in elections here—so one of his first moves was to rid "Red Berlin" of its leftist majority. First Berlin's Communist party headquarters was raided by police on the pretense of a planned coup d'etat. Second, on the night of February 27, 1933, the Reichstag building was mysteriously set ablaze. Although no one ever proved who set the fire— indeed, many believe it was the Nazis themselves—hundreds of Communists, Social Democrats, trade unionists, and intellectuals were rounded up, imprisoned, tortured, and murdered.

The reign of terror had only begun: After a massive book burning near the Staatsoper in May 1933, most of the country's best writers fled the country—scientists soon followed. In 1936 the Olympics were staged in Berlin, and Hitler hoped to showcase his Third Reich. Although the Germans won the most gold medals, it was a black American athlete, Jesse Owens, who stole the show by winning four gold medals.

But the Olympics could not gloss over the fact that the Nazi party reigned by terror, with much of that terror directed towards its Jewish citizens. Although the Nazi's anti-Semitic campaign had been muted during the Olympics, it resumed once the games were over. Anti-Semitic posters were put up once again, and out came more notices barring Jews from public places. On November 9, 1938, Berlin was the scene of the so-called *Kristallnacht* (Crystal Night), a night of terror directed against Jews, during which synagogues and Jewish businesses were burned to the ground. During the next years, as many as 50,000 Berliners of Jewish faith died in concentration camps. By the time Germany invaded Poland in 1939 and catapulted Europe into another world war, it had rid itself of virtually all opposition.

FROM 1945 TO 1989 On May 8, 1945, the German army surrendered. In Berlin, the legacy of the "Thousand Year Reich" was a wasteland of ruin and destruction. Of the 245,000 buildings in Berlin before the war, 50,000 were destroyed. As many as 80,000 Berliners had lost their lives. Of the 160,000 Jews who had lived in Berlin before 1933, only 7,247 remained. There were food shortages and fuel shortages, and everyone who had anything to sell resorted to the black market. Berliners laden with furs and jewelry headed for farms in the country to barter luxuries for food. Even drinking water had to be brought in from the country, and there was no electricity or gas. When winter came, fuel was so scarce that the Berliners cut down all their trees for firewood.

Soon Berliners were at work clearing away the rubble, too busy trying to survive and create a livable world to worry about tomorrow. But their fate had been sealed even before the end of the war: The Allies had divided Germany and Berlin into occupation zones to be governed by Great Britain, the United States, the Soviet Union, and later, France. Although each Allied Power had supreme authority in its own sector, Berlin was to be ruled jointly. This proved easier said than done.

In the summer of 1945, Churchill, Truman, and Stalin met at Potsdam, where they agreed to disarm and demilitarize Germany. There was never any intention to split the country in half or change Berlin's role as capital. Rather, they agreed that Nazism must be abolished and that local self-government should be set up on a democratic basis. Unfortunately, they had no plans for how things should proceed and harbored differing ideas of what constituted a democracy. As time went on, ideological differences and political aims created chasms between the Western and Soviet powers.

Already the Soviets had been at work setting up a Communist party in Berlin and appointing a municipal council. But when elections were held for the city parliament (Municipal Assembly) in October 1946, the Social Democrats (SPD) won almost half of the votes while the Communist party, the Socialist Unity Party, garnered

---

IMPRESSIONS

An immense responsibility rests upon the German people for this subservience to the barbaric idea of autocracy. This is the gravamen against them in history—that, in spite of all their brains and courage, they worship Power, and let themselves be led by the nose.
—SIR WINSTON CHURCHILL, 1937

only 19.8% of the votes. The Communists clearly did not have the majority.

In 1948 the Western Powers introduced the Deutsche Mark in West Berlin, thus financially separating it from East Germany and strengthening its ties with West Germany. As far as the Soviets were concerned, Berlin, with a growing democratic following, was becoming a dangerous thorn in the Soviet side. In retaliation, the Soviets introduced their own currency, declaring it legal tender throughout all of Berlin. They then imposed a road blockade of Berlin. Since food, raw materials, and necessities for two million people came from the Western Zones, there was no alternative but to organize an Allied airlift. Gen. Lucius D. Clay, who organized the lift, said the blockade "was one of the most brutal attempts in recent history to use mass starvation as a means of applying political pressure."

The largest airlift in history began on June 26, 1948. Within weeks, 4,000 tons of supplies were being flown into Berlin daily; in only 3 months, Tegel Airport was built. At the peak of the airlift, a plane was landing every 1 to 2 minutes, and, in April 1949, a record was set when nearly 13,000 tons of supplies were flown in on a single day. During the 11 months that the airlift lasted, more than 200,000 flights had brought in 1.7 million tons of supplies.

Although the Soviets had hoped the blockade would end Western influence in Berlin, instead it drew the Western Powers together, formed a bond of friendship between Berliners and the West, and convinced the Western Powers that they must remain in Berlin to defend their concept of freedom. Soon thereafter, the Municipal Assembly and the City Council—which had had their seats in the Eastern Sector—moved to the Western Sector. The Communists responded by appointing their own City Council. The city was now divided, politically and ideologically. From then on, both sectors followed their own course of development. In 1949, East Berlin became the capital of the German Democratic Republic (DDR). In 1952, telephone communications between the two cities were cut off, tram and bus lines were severed, and West Berliners were no longer allowed into the surrounding East German countryside. However, there was still unrestricted movement throughout Berlin, with many East Berliners working in the Western sectors. In 1955, West Germany became a member of NATO; East Germany, a member of the Warsaw Pact. The Cold War was on.

And yet, few could imagine that a divided Germany was anything but temporary. As far as West Germany was concerned, its goal was reunification—with the reestablishment of Berlin as its capital. An uprising of East German workers on June 17, 1953, brutally quashed by Soviet soldiers, only reconfirmed West Germany's commitment.

Meanwhile, Berlin began to regain prosperity. In 1950, there were 300,000 unemployed Berliners; seven years later it was down to 90,000. Since Berliners could still travel freely through the city, many East Berliners flocked to factories in West Berlin. Housing estates mushroomed, replacing homes that had been destroyed in the war. In 1957, West Berlin hosted a worldwide architectural competition that brought 48 leading architects from around the world to design housing for the Hansaviertel (Hansa Quarter). Clearly, West Berlin was recovering much more rapidly than East Germany, making it a popular attraction for East Germans eager for a look at the new and prosperous Berlin. Many of them liked what they saw so much that they decided to stay. Before long, East Germany was losing many of its brightest, best-educated, and most-skilled workers to the West, a resource needed if the country was ever to get its feet on the ground.

In November 1958, Soviet Prime Minister Nikita Kruschchev issued the Berlin Ultimatum, demanding that the Western Powers withdraw from West Berlin. Since Berlin was seen as strategic in the "domino theory" of Communist takeovers, the Western Powers refused. Refugees continued to pour into the West. From 1949 to 1961, approximately three million East Germans fled their country. From the East German point of view, something clearly had to be done.

On August 13, 1961, East Germany began erecting a wall between East and West Berlin, tearing up streets and putting up posts and barbed wire. A few days later, the wall was reinforced with concrete and brick. Movement between the two Berlins was now forbidden, leaving families and friends separated by what was soon known around the world simply as the Wall. Measuring 13 feet high and approximately 100 miles long, the Wall was backed by hundreds of guardhouses, 293 sentry towers, patrol dogs, and a vast swath of a no-man's-land that was brightly illuminated. And yet that didn't stop some East Germans willing to risk their lives for freedom. Approximately 5,000 East Germans managed to escape to West Berlin, most of them during the early years when the Wall was not yet perfected. But 78 people lost their lives trying to flee to West Berlin, most shot by East German guards.

For 28 years, the Wall stood as a constant reminder of Germany's forced division. Even for visitors, seeing the Wall for the first time was both chilling and unsettling, a feeling that intensified when crossing into East Berlin at Checkpoint Charlie. Mirrors were shoved under cars to make sure no one was hiding underneath; travelers on foot were shuttled through doors that clanged shut behind them, as though they were entering a high-security prison. Entering into East Berlin was eerie and 1984ish, as the differences between the two Berlins had became so radical with the passage of time. West Berlin was a capitalist's dream—intense, aggressive, and chaotic—a whirling blend of traffic, people, neon, and noise. East Berlin was conservative and subdued, sterile and quiet, with soldiers everywhere.

In 1971, the Four Powers signed an agreement that confirmed political and legal ties between West Berlin and West Germany. Telephone communications between the two Berlins were restored, and West Berliners were allowed to visit East Germany. For the next 18 years, conditions between East and West steadily improved, although Westerners were required to exchange a minimum amount of Western currency into East German marks, and travel into East Germany was still complicated and difficult for non-Germans.

In autumn of 1989, Hungary opened its borders to the West and allowed East Germans to pass through. This prompted tens of thousands of East Germans to journey to freedom. This exodus was accompanied by pro-reform demonstrations throughout East Germany, which finally led to the ouster of hard-line East German leader Erich Honecker on October 18. By November 1989, approximately 175,000 East German refugees had fled, almost 1% of the total population.

On the evening of November 9, 1989, East German authorities announced that it was permanently lifting travel restrictions on its citizens, granting them freedom of movement for the first time since the Wall was built in 1961. That evening, 50,000 East Berliners streamed into West Berlin and were welcomed on the other side with embraces and tears. Many Berliners climbed on top of the Wall to dance and celebrate.

With a story similar to others in Berlin at the time, a teacher working in West Berlin recalled what it was like in those first heady days of the Wall's opening.

"On Friday [November 10] I went to the school where I work, and the director decided to cancel all classes, because history was being made in the streets and the children should see it. So I went to Potsdamer Square, and the whole experience was so emotional, so strange, that I had goosebumps several times that day. We watched the East Berliners come through the opening in the Wall. The first ones seemed very unsure of themselves, as though they still didn't believe they could. They came slowly, with big eyes. Some of them, especially the older ones, wept. It was like they were being let out of prison after so many years."

FROM 1990 TO THE PRESENT Soon after the Wall came down, the West German government reiterated its dedication to reunification. On March 18, 1990, democratic elections were held in East Germany that signaled the official demise of the Communist regime. Reunification of the two Germanys followed on October 3, 1990. Berlin became Germany's capital, with the seat of government remaining in Bonn.

As the jubilation of reunification wore off, new problems began to surface, and there were fears about the future in both East and West. After all, by March 1990, as many as 500,000 East Germans had settled in the West, entitling them to "adjustment money," household compensation, housing subsidies, and job retraining. (A policy established years before entitled any East German coming to West Germany for the first time—even for a day—to a welcoming token of 100 DM [$62.50]; but Bonn hadn't foreseen every East German receiving it.) Many West Germans began worrying about the financial burdens of reunification, especially the cost of East German economic development. Some West Berliners—irritated by the long queues of East Germans in shops and restaurants and the soaring cost of real estate—grumbled that they wished the Wall had never come down at all. Some said that East Germans expected too much too soon, and that if East Germans wanted a more affluent lifestyle, they should have to work hard to achieve it, just as the West Germans had.

East Germans, on the other hand, were concerned about their ability to compete in a capitalist society, the impact of materialism on their youth, the appearance of a drug culture, and being treated economically and socially as second-class citizens. They worried about the loss of the old regime's benefits like controlled rents, job security, and old-age pensions. Many, especially those who had envisioned reunification as an opportunity to combine the best of socialism and democracy, felt powerless in the wave of new laws and reforms that eroded the very values they thought worth saving. Some went so far as to describe reunification as a hostile takeover.

With the closing of noncompetitive, formerly subsidized enterprises, unemployment skyrocketed. By the end of 1991, unemployment in former East Germany had risen to 11%. Many are still jobless, especially East Germany's youths. The problem has been compounded by waves of foreign asylum-seekers entering Germany (their numbers climbed from 57,000 in 1987 to 500,000 in 1992), some of whom have been the victims of attacks by right-wing extremists.

No German city has been and will be more affected by the reunification than Berlin. It faces the formidable challenge of integrating two very different systems and all of the attendant social upheavals. Besides the actual integration of East Berlin it also has to slay the ghost of its past as the capital of the Third Reich in order to take its place once again as one of Europe's great capitals. A compelling, exciting challenge for this intense, extraordinary city.

FAMOUS BERLINERS

Otto von Bismarck (1815–98) Known as the Iron Chancellor, Bismarck was a brilliant politician who succeeded in uniting all of Germany in 1871 and became the empire's first chancellor. Dismissed from office by Kaiser Wilhelm II in 1890, Bismarck remained popular.

Willy Brandt (1913–92) From 1957 to 1966, Brandt served as mayor of Berlin, weathering the construction of the Wall. A prominent and popular member of the Social Democratic Party (SPD), Brandt became Chancellor of West Germany in 1969 and received the Nobel Peace Prize in 1971, but in 1974 resigned after scandal in which his close personal aide and confidant, Günter Guillaume, was unmasked as a spy for DDR.

Bertolt Brecht (1898–1956) A well-known playwright, Brecht came to Berlin in 1920, and worked with Max Reinhardt at the Deutsches Theater. An ardent Marxist, Brecht wrote epic dramas that scorned the materialistic self-absorption of the upper class and underscored the plight of the poor and the working class. In 1928 he achieved fame with *The Threepenny Opera*. Other well-known plays include *Mother Courage and Her Children* and *The Good Woman of Szechuan*. In 1933 Brecht left Berlin but returned after the war to East Berlin and founded the famous Berliner Ensemble, which continues to stage his works.

Friedrich II, "Frederick the Great" (1712–86) The third and most well-known king of Prussia, he built the charming Sanssouci Palace in Potsdam where he could retreat to meditate and pursue philosophy. Frederick the Great was an advocate of the Enlightenment, a composer and a musician, and a friend to Voltaire.

Walter Gropius (1883–1969) Born in Berlin, Gropius studied architecture in Munich and Berlin. In 1919 he was named director of the Weimar School of Art, which became the legendary Bauhaus. From 1928 to 1934 he worked as an architect in Berlin, immigrating in 1934 to England, and then to the United States in 1937, where he was a professor at Harvard until 1952. See the

---

IMPRESSIONS

Berlin is a city for artists, for the young, for the creative. Not for idyllic artists, who wish to sit on the bank of a pond, dreaming; but for those to whom a melody can come from the struggles of life . . . Berlin has taken a massive step toward becoming a center, if not the center of artistic force in Germany.
—PAUL WESTHEIM, 1929

Gropius apartment building in the Hansaviertel and the Bauhaus-Archiv, built after his death according to his designs.

Heinrich von Kleist (1777–1811) Kleist, who served for a time in the Prussian army, wrote a number of short stories and plays, including *The Broken Pitcher* and *Prinz Friedrich von Homburg*. Throughout his life, Kleist was plagued with depression and restlessness, leaving and returning to Berlin many times. He took his own life on the shores of Wannsee Lake on the outskirts of Berlin.

Georg Wenzeslaus von Knobelsdorff (1699–1753) After studying in Italy, Paris, Spain, and Dresden, Knobelsdorff actualized sketches drawn by Frederick the Great for Sanssouci Palace in Potsdam, which remains the rococo architect's greatest achievement. He also designed the Deutsche Staatsoper (destroyed by fire in 1843) on Unter den Linden, as well as several buildings in the Sanssouci park.

Käthe Kollwitz (1867–1945) A Berliner, Kollwitz was a gifted graphic artist, painter, and sculptress who expressed strong emotion in her studies of working-class Berliners. See her works at the Käthe-Kollwitz Museum on Fasanenstrasse near the Ku'damm.

Peter Josef Lenné (1789–1866) A landscape gardener, Lenné was instrumental in shaping Berlin's most important royal grounds. Among his works are the city's central Tiergarten park and Park Sanssouci in Potsdam.

Max Liebermann (1847–1935) Liebermann was founder and president of the Secession movement, a group of artists concerned with developing their own approach and impressionist style. His works are on display in the Neue Nationalgalerie in Tiergarten and the Nationalgalerie on Museum Island.

Adolph von Menzel (1815–1905) A self-taught painter, graphic artist, draftsman, and illustrator, Menzel is credited with anticipating impressionism in his paintings done in the 1840s and 1850s. He gained fame in Berlin with his portraits and was known to frequent the city's lively cafés. The Neue Nationalgalerie in Tiergarten has the world's largest collection of his work.

Otto Nagel (1894–1967) Nagel is known for his realistic portraits of Berlin's working class. His works, most from the 1920s and 1930s, are on display at the Otto-Nagel-Haus in Berlin-Mitte.

Max Reinhardt (1873–1943) Born in Vienna, Reinhardt is legendary in German theater and is credited with introducing it to the rest of the world. He served as director of the Deutsches Theater in Berlin from 1905 to 1920, and again from 1924 to 1932. Reinhardt also served as director of the Festspielhaus in Salzburg and founded the world-renowned Salzburg Festival.

Karl Friedrich Schinkel (1781–1841) A gifted architect who received his training in Berlin, Schinkel is to Berlin what Haussmann is to Paris: the man most responsible for the city's architectural style and continuity. His works, mainly neoclassical, include the Neue Wache (New Guardhouse) on Unter den Linden, which today houses a memorial to victims of fascism; Das Alte Museum on Museumsinsel; the Schauspielhaus on Gendarmenmarkt; and the Schlossbrücke bridge over the Spree. Particularly delightful is his summerhouse behind Schloss Charlottenburg, built in the style of an Italian villa and known today as the Schinkel Pavilion. The Friedrichwerdersche Kirche in Berlin-Mitte, which he also designed, contains a museum of the architect's work and life. Schinkel also worked as a landscape painter and stage designer.

Andreas Schlüter (1660–1714) Schlüter was Berlin's top baroque architect and is credited with giving Berlin a royal appearance. Also a sculptor and influenced by Michelangelo, Schlüter is best known for his 21 masks of dying warriors in the courtyard of the Arsenal on Unter den Linden (undergoing renovation at presstime) and his equestrian statue of the Great Elector now in the forecourt of Schloss Charlottenburg. As the court architect, he also rebuilt the Berlin Palace (no longer in existence) but fell out of favor when a tower he designed collapsed.

Heinrich Zille (1858–1929) A popular graphic artist and caricaturist, Zille was a chronicler of turn-of-the-century life in Berlin, which he depicted with compassionate humor. He is particularly known for his sketches of the poor and working class. Having an eye for the absurd, he contributed regularly to satirical journals. His works are on display at the Berlin Museum in Kreuzberg.

ART, ARCHITECTURE & CULTURAL LIFE

With more than 80 museums and home to the Deutsche Oper, the Staatsoper, and the Berlin Philharmonic Orchestra, not to mention a thriving and vibrant nightlife, there is no question that Berlin is the reunified country's cultural capital.

Visually, much of Berlin is a new city, with little from before World War II remaining. In my opinion, it's hard to rave about the aesthetic charm of the Kurfürstendamm or fall in love with the sterility of Alexanderplatz, and even the city's oldest buildings such as the Nikolaikirche and the Marienkirche are usually reconstructions. The Berlin Palace, a sumptuous Renaissance residence for the Prussian kings, was deemed irreparable after World War II by the DDR and was torn down to make way for East Berlin's hideously modern Palace of the Republic with its concert halls and restaurants.

Fortunately, not all of Berlin is new. There's Schloss Charlottenburg—which served as a summer residence for Prussian kings— considered Berlin's most beautiful baroque building. There are also fine, turn-of-the-century patrician homes throughout the city, with rich art nouveau stucco facades, projecting balconies, recessed arched windows, sweeping staircases, and high ceilings. Built during prosperous times, they sit on broad tree-lined streets that give them an even grander appearance. Fasanenstrasse and other side streets off the Kurfüstendamm boast a number of these beautiful buildings.

There are also many public buildings from previous centuries, such as the 17th-century Arsenal on Unter den Linden, the museums on Museumsinsel, and the Staatsoper built by Georg Wenzeslaus von Knobelsdorff in the mid-1700s (although the original Staatsoper burned in 1843, the present building is a faithful reconstruction of Knobelsdorff's design). From the same period is Berlin's most famous landmark, the Brandenburger Tor, completed in 1786 as one of 13 city gates that used to mark the entrance to Berlin.

Perhaps the most credit for Berlin's architectural greatness should be given to Karl Friedrich Schinkel (1781–1841), a protomodernist in his structural engineering who used mainly neoclassical but also Gothic, Byzantine, and Renaissance designs in his creations. His works include the Alte Museum on Museum Island and the delightful Schinkel Pavilion on the grounds of Schloss Charlottenburg.

The most famous new quarter of postwar Berlin is the Hansaviertel, a residential area created by 48 leading architects from around the world, each of whom was asked to design one building. Among the participants were Alvar Aalto, Walter Gropius, Oscar Niemeyer, and Arne Jacobsen. Walter Gropius also left his mark on the Bauhaus-Archiv, a light and airy building housing a museum dedicated to the principles of the Bauhaus school of design.

And of course, there's also a lot of empty land waiting for development—notice the snaking scar left from the removal of the Wall. Potsdamerplatz, once the lively heart of prewar Berlin, became a wasteland of weeds and vacant lots after the Wall went up. Bordered on the west end by Hans Scharoun's impressive Philharmonie with its golden, tentlike roof, Potsdamerplatz became the focus of hot debate following the demise of the Wall as different interest groups presented their own plans for development. Some thought it should become a park; others thought it should go to the highest bidder. Today it's a maze of construction sites as Sony and Daimler-Benz construct new office buildings. More construction is taking place in former East Berlin, especially in Berlin-Mitte and along Friedrichstrasse. The Berlin of tomorrow depends heavily on decisions made by today's city planners.

For the most part, Berlin's artistic heritage lives on in its museums. Berlin's love affair with museums can be traced back to the 1820s, when construction of a museum complex was begun by King Friedrich Wilhelm III, who wished to make his collection of masterpieces available to the public. Located on an island in the middle of the Spree River in the heart of the city (known today as Museumsinsel, or "Museum Island"), the complex grew through the next century, as German archeologists searched the world for artifacts and treasures from Persia, Greece, and Egypt. Berlin today is home of the famous bust of Nefertiti, the incredible Pergamon Altar, and the breathtaking Gate of Ishtar. Throughout Berlin there is an array of art museums, history museums, collections of applied arts, and special interest museums. But the majority of museums is concentrated in four areas of Berlin: Dahlem, Tiergarten, Charlottenburg, and Museum Island.

Of course, it would be wrong to assume that all Berlin's treasures originated someplace else, for Berlin was home to a great many artists in the past century. One of the earliest to gain fame was Adolph von Menzel (1815–1905), a painter who was largely self-taught and became known for his portraits. Menzel sought company in coffeehouses and is considered a forerunner of the impressionists. He was followed by a group of artists who in 1892 founded the Secession movement, headed by Max Liebermann, which was concerned with developing its own stylistic approach to impressionism. Liebermann, Lovis Corinth, and Max Slevogt are considered foremost among German impressionists.

After the turn of the century a new generation of painters flocked to Berlin. Prominent among them was a group from Dresden known as Die Brücke (The Bridge) who arrived 1910–1911. Horrified by the industrialized urban society and rejecting traditional subjects and style, they painted images expressing their feelings of fear, longing, unrest, and doom: Thus was born German expressionism. Numbered among Die Brücke was Ernst Ludwig Kirchner, Emil Nolde, Max Pechstein, and Oskar Kokoschka. Two other important artists were Käthe Kollwitz and Heinrich Zille, who portrayed the city's growing army of the poor. Visit the Brücke-Museum in Dahlem, the Käthe-Kollwitz Museum near the Ku'damm, and the Neue Nationalgalerie (New National Gallery) in the Tiergarten. The Neue Nationalgalerie, in particular, has an outstanding collection of works by Berlin's artists, including Menzel, Max Beckmann, Lovis Corinth, Oskar Kokoschka, and Ernst Ludwig Kirchner. Another great museum for Berliner art is the Alte Nationalgalerie (Old National Gallery) with works by Max Liebermann, Max Slevogt, Ernst Ludwig Kirchner, Emil Nolde, Oskar Kokoschka, and Käthe Kollwitz.

In addition, works by contemporary Berlin artists are shown regularly in special exhibitions in the Neue Nationalgalerie and the Berlinische Galerie. And there are more than 120 galleries in Berlin, many conveniently located near the Ku'damm. Although prices are out of range for most of us, it costs nothing to look. For affordable art and crafts, there's the weekend market held on Strasse des 17. Juni, where Berliners sell everything from sketches and handmade toys to tie-dyed scarves and jewelry.

As for Berlin's performance art scene, it has a rich tradition of the stage as well. Much of Germany's theatrical history stems from Berlin, for it was here that playwrights Hauptmann, Ibsen, Strindberg, and Brecht made their first major breakthroughs. Max Reinhardt, recognized as the man who introduced German theater to the world, directed the Deutsches Theater from 1905 to 1920 and again from 1924 to 1932. (Reinhardt also founded the world-famous Salzburg Festival.) In the 1920s, Berlin had approximately 35 theaters, several opera houses, and more than 20 concert halls.

Today Berlin is still famous for its theater, including the Schiller Theater and the Berlin Ensemble and cabaret—although not as intense or in the same form as before World War II. Berlin is home to three well-known opera houses, the International Film Festival, the Philharmonic Orchestra, and a number of concert halls and live-music houses. Rock stars make regular concert appearances in Berlin, and there's a strong jazz and avant-garde scene in bars and smaller music houses. As many bars remain open all night, Berlin is a mecca for nightlife revelers.

2. FOOD & DRINK

If you love pork, you're in the right country. Surely the Germans have invented more ways to serve pork than any other people: from simple pork sausages with a dab of mustard and a hard roll to pig's knuckle served with sauerkraut and potatoes. Berlin's KaDeWe department store, famous for its massive food floor, features 1,000 different kinds of sausage alone—most of them pork. You could have a variety of pork dishes for breakfast, lunch, and dinner.

Portions in a German restaurant are huge, consisting of a main course served with a couple of side dishes on the same plate—accompanied by the almost obligatory rounds of beer. In other words, German food is not a weight-reducing cuisine. It seems to me that few worry about calories in Germany: witness the coffee shops packed at 4pm—the unofficial coffee break around the country—when everyone downs cups of coffee and tortes and cakes.

DINING CUSTOMS

Although there are refined Berlin restaurants where dining is quiet and elegant, more typical is the neighborhood place—popular for its beer, camaraderie, and no-nonsense cuisine. They're usually crowded and lively, especially during lunchtime when most Germans eat their big meal or after work.

Except for the more expensive restaurants where customers are seated by the management, it's acceptable to take any free seat—even if the rest of the table is occupied: But ask first whether the seat is free and whether your fellow diners object. Although increasingly rare, in some restaurants, especially those in former East Berlin, you may be expected to first give your coat or jacket to the coat clerk at the *Garderobe,* for which the clerk expects a small tip of a mark (60¢).

As for dining etiquette, Germans use a fork and knife for almost everything, including french fries, sandwiches, pizza, chicken, and other foods that Americans are more likely to eat with their fingers. Historically, it wasn't until 1846 that forks were produced for the masses; before that, Germans ate with their fingers, too. Fifteenth-century etiquette called for using three fingers to pick up meat from plates but frowned upon stuffing food into one's mouth with both hands or keeping one's hands resting on plates for too long.

Today, Germans hold their fork in their left hand and keep the knife in their right. Once you've mastered this technique, you'll find it makes a lot more sense than switching your fork from hand to hand everytime you want to cut that piece of pork.

Drinking also has its rules. If you're among German acquaintances, don't take a sip until your host raises his glass. Quite often you'll bash your beer mugs or clink your wine glasses together before taking your first sip. This custom grew out of a superstition that the devil could enter the body of a person who was drinking: the clashing together of glasses was meant to create a colossal noise and scare the devil away.

If you're taking a breather from your meal and don't wish the waiter to clear your plate, lay your fork and knife down in the same position as you held them: that is, the fork on the left side of the plate and your knife on the right. If you place your knife and fork together, side by side on the plate, it's a signal to the waiter that you've finished your meal. When you get up to leave, it's considered good etiquette to say good-bye to the other diners at your table, even if they're strangers and you didn't talk to them the whole meal.

THE CUISINE

BREAKFAST   The typical German breakfast consists of bread or rolls topped with marmalade, cheese, or sausage. Unlike American

---

IMPRESSIONS

Think of the man who first tried German sausage.
—JEROME K. JEROME, 1889

sandwiches, which are stuffed as much as possible, in Germany it's customary to place only a single slice of cheese or sausage upon each slice of bread. Germans eat these open bread sandwiches with a knife and fork, the fork turned upside down. A soft-boiled egg—left in its shell and served in an egg cup—often accompanies these. Breakfast buffets in hotels may include cereals, such as *Muesli* (a grain cereal similar to granola) or cornflakes, fruit, juices, and coffee. German coffee is much stronger than American coffee—there's rarely a bottomless cup in Germany, though some hotels do serve extra coffee during breakfast. In some expensive hotels, breakfast buffets will also include scrambled eggs, bacon, and hash browns. At the other end is a continental breakfast, consisting simply of coffee or tea and rolls with marmalade.

If your hotel doesn't serve breakfast, choose from the many famous coffeehouses along the Ku'damm. And there are many breakfast cafés, many of which are open not only during the day but all night as well.

LUNCH & DINNER   For lunch or dinner, your choice ranges from the neighborhood *Gaststätte* (simple restaurants/pubs) to restaurants with cuisine from around the world. Since most Germans have their big meal of the day at lunch and restaurants may be crowded, you might want to consider eating during the off-hours.

In a traditional German restaurant, start your meal with a hearty bowl of soup, which can be quite filling. One of my favorites is *Linsensuppe* (lentil soup, often with pieces of sausage). *Leberknödelsuppe* (a dumpling soup made with beef liver, onions, and garlic) and *Kartoffelsuppe* (potato soup) are other common choices. *Gulaschsuppe,* borrowed from Hungary, is a spicy soup featuring beef, paprika, and potatoes. Appetizers include *Hackepeter* (raw minced meat, like a steak tartare) and *Soleier* (pickled eggs). There is almost an endless selection of bread: from rye to pumpernickel, and various hard rolls called *Brötchen*.

For the main dish, one of Berlin's most well-known specialties is *Eisbein* (pig's knuckle), usually served with sauerkraut and *Kartoffelpuree* (mashed potatoes) or *Erbspuree* (puréed peas), *Kasseler Rippenspeer* is smoked pork chops, created long ago by a butcher in Berlin named Kassel. A *Boulette,* introduced by the French Huguenots, is a type of cold meatball served with mustard. For pork lovers there's *Schweinebraten* (pot-roasted pork) and *Spanferkel* (suckling pig). If you come across a *Schweinshaxen,* it's grilled knuckle of pork. A *Schlachteplatte* is only for the adventuresome (roughly translated, it's "butcher's platter"), consisting of fresh blood sausage, liverwurst, pig's kidneys, and boiled pork. You'll find *Würste,* or "sausages," on almost every menu, as well as at *Imbisse* (food stands), where they're served with a hard roll and mustard. Berlin's specialty sausage is the *Bockwurst,* a superlong boiled sausage, often served with *Erbensuppe* (split-pea soup). Another favorite is grilled *Bratwurst* from Nürnberg, often prepared with beer, and the *Wiener.* A *Currywurst* is a sausage served with a curry-flavored sauce.

For something other than pork, there's *Sauerbraten* (marinated beef in a thick sauce), *Schnitzel* (breaded veal cutlet), *Brathering* (grilled herring), *Brathuhn* (roast chicken), *Aal grün* (boiled eel in a dill sauce), and *gebratene Kalbsleber Berliner Art* (sautéed calves' liver with onions and apples). Other main courses you may come across include *Tafelspitz* (boiled beef with vegetables), *Leberkäs* (a type of German meat loaf, common to southern Germany), and *Sülze* (jellied meat). Vegetarians should look for a *Gemüseplatte,* a dish of assorted vegetables.

In addition to traditional German fare, Berlin boasts an astounding assortment of international cuisines, thanks, in part, to the Wall. In order to attract businesses to pre-unification Berlin, the West German government offered generous subsidies that induced immigrants from Turkey, Greece, Italy, Asia, and other countries to open up shop. With time, Berliners have grown more and more appreciative of and interested in foreign food. With the largest Turkish population of any city outside Istanbul, Berlin is especially known for its Turkish restaurants. There are Imbisse all over town offering *doner kebab* (pita bread filled with grilled lamb, lettuce, and garlic sauce), and restaurants serving everything from lamb in a spicy sauce to shish kebab. Italian eateries—especially those specializing in inexpensive pizzas—seem to be on every street corner. Beware, however, that if you order a *peperoni pizza,* you'll get one with hot jalapeño peppers; order a *salami* pizza if you want an American-style pepperoni pizza.

DRINK

Germany is known for its wines and beers, both of which are plentiful in Berlin. Berlin itself, however, is not a wine-producing region. Frederick the Great tried his hand at winemaking at Sanssouci, but the rows of grapevines are all that remain of his efforts. When in Berlin, you should try wines from other regions in Germany, such as the Rhine (Rheingau, Rheinhessen, and Rheinpfalz), Baden-Württemberg, and Franken. Wines range from the Riesling (white wine) to *Sekt* (a sparkling wine), from dry (*trocken*) to sweet (*süss*). Unless you know your German wines or simply want to experiment, ask your sommelier or waiter for a recommendation.

As for beer, Berlin's most famous brew among tourists is the *Berliner Weisse,* a draft wheat beer served with a shot of raspberry or a green woodruff syrup—a summertime drink. Strangely enough, Berliners rarely drink the stuff. If you simply order *ein Bier,* you'll get either a draft beer (*vom Fass*) or bottled beer (*eine Flasche*). An *Export* is slightly stronger but is still considered light; a *Bock* beer is dark and rich. A *Pils* or *Pilsener* is light and slightly bitter. One of my favorites is *Hefe-Weizen,* a wheat beer.

Although it's considered safe, Germans don't drink their tap water, preferring bottled water. A *Mineralwasser* is bottled mineral water, usually carbonated; if you don't like the bubbly stuff, add the words "ohne Kohlensäure."

3. RECOMMENDED BOOKS & FILMS

BOOKS

POLITICS & HISTORY In *Before the Deluge: A Portrait of Berlin in the 1920s* (Harper & Row, 1986), Otto Friedrich captures life in the city in the 1920s, when it was home to Dietrich, Einstein, Garbo, Brecht, Gropius, Kandinsky, and Klee.

Bertolt Brecht's Berlin (Anchor Press/Doubleday, 1975) by Wolf Von Eckardt and Sander L. Gilman covers the years of the Weimar Republic, from 1918 to 1933, describing everything from nightlife and the underworld to the media and architecture along with the personalities that influenced each. With more than 280 photographs.

Norman Gelb's *The Berlin Wall: Kennedy, Khruschchev, and a Showdown in the Heart of Europe* (Times Books, 1988) explains Berlin's pivotal role in the Cold War.

Living with the Wall: West Berlin 1961–1985 (Duke Publishing Co., 1985) is Richard and Anna Merritt's description of the divided city. Similarly, Peter Wyden's *Wall—The Inside Story of Divided Berlin* (Simon & Schuster, 1989) is a documentation of the Wall based on eyewitness accounts and interviews with intelligence agents and government officials. Wyden's account is a gripping human drama, complete with stories of people who escaped East Germany, those who died in the attempt, and families ripped apart by Berlin's division.

Events leading up to and after the fall of the Wall are chronicled by Ken Smith in *Berlin: Coming in from the Cold* (Penguin, 1990), which provides an insider's view of what it was like to be in Berlin before and during those joyous days of celebration following the fall of the Wall.

Those celebrations are also vividly captured in Jerry Bornstein's pictorial presentation *The Wall Came Tumbling Down: The Berlin Wall and the Fall of Communism* (Arch Cape Press, 1990). With an introduction by Willy Brandt and more than 100 photographs.

Berlin's history is documented in Alexander Reissner's *Berlin 1675–1945: The Rise and Fall of a Metropolis* (Oswald Wolff, London, 1984).

Berlin Diary The Journal of a Foreign Correspondent 1934–1941 (Little, Brown, 1988) is a personal account by correspondent William L. Shirer, who also wrote the definitive *The Rise and Fall of the Third Reich* (Simon & Schuster, 1960).

Ann and John Tuna's *The Berlin Airlift* (Atheneum, 1988) re-creates those 11 months in 1948.

Berlin's very recent history is captured in John Borneman's thought-provoking *After the Wall: East Meets West in the New Berlin* (Basic Books, 1991). Borneman addresses the realities of a unified Berlin, especially the disorientation and disillusionment experienced by former East Berliners who had hoped that East Germany would survive as a new type of democracy but instead watched its disintegration as it became absorbed by the materialistic West. Also by Borneman is *Belonging in the Two Berlins: Kin, State, Nation* (Cambridge University Press, 1992), which examines the social, economic, and political life of today's Berliners.

We Were the People: Voices from East Germany's Revolutionary Autumn of 1989 (Duke, 1992) by Dirk Philipsen is an oral history of dissidents in former East Germany who dared petition and demonstrate against a monolithic police state, contributing to its demise; most of these former East Germans also express disappointment with the results of unification.

FICTION   Christopher Isherwood lived in Berlin from 1929 to 1933, and his impressions are expressed in *The Berlin Stories* (New

Directions, 1954) and the famous *Goodbye to Berlin,* a fictionalized account of the last days of the Weimar Republic, which was later adapted into the stage play and movie *Cabaret.*

A more recent depiction of life in Berlin is provided by Ian Walker in his colorful *Zoo Station: Adventures in East and West Berlin* (Atlantic Monthly Press, 1987), which explores the alternative and underground cultural life of former divided Berlin.

FILMS

Berlin Alexanderplatz (1980) by Rainer Werner Fassbinder is the story of working-class life in Berlin from 1927 to 1978.

Berlin Express (1948) is an espionage thriller with documentary overtones that uses actual footage of bombed-out Berlin; Merle Oberon and Paul Lukas star.

Berlin, Symphony of a Great City (1927) is one of the first impressionist documentaries and offers a look at life in old Berlin.

Der Blaue Engel (The Blue Angel, 1930) is the tragic story of an elderly professor seduced by a cabaret singer; it launched Marlene Dietrich to international fame and captured the atmosphere of Berlin in the '20s.

The dawn of the Nazi era is the backdrop for Bob Fosse's *Cabaret* (1972), a highly effective musical set in the Berlin of 1931. It is based on Christopher Isherwood's *The Berlin Stories* and stars Liza Minnelli and Joel Grey.

Wings of Desire (1989) by Wim Wenders is set in contemporary Berlin and deals with a race of angels who can observe but not help humanity; with Peter Falk and Bruno Ganz.

CHAPTER 2

PLANNING A TRIP TO BERLIN

Read this chapter before leaving home, and you'll be ahead of the game when it comes to preparing for your trip, packing, and getting the most for your money. However, don't stop here. By reading the other chapters, you'll be familiar with Berlin before you even arrive and may already know what you want to see and do. Knowing that Berlin has many lakes great for swimming may prompt you to pack your swimsuit; on the other hand, learning that there are many nude beaches may prompt you to leave your suit at home.

1. INFORMATION, ENTRY REQUIREMENTS & MONEY

INFORMATION The **German National Tourist Office (GNTO)** publishes a wealth of free, colorful brochures available for travelers, including a map of Germany, general information about travel in Germany, a brochure on Berlin itself, and a pamphlet on Berlin's hotels.

If you'd like information and literature before leaving home, contact one of the GNTO offices:

United States: GNTO, 122 E. 42nd St., 52nd floor, New York, NY 10168 (tel. 212/661-7200).

GNTO, 11766 Wilshire Blvd., Suite 750, Los Angeles, CA 90025 (tel. 310/575-9799).

Canada: GNTO, Office National Allemand du Tourisme, 175 Bloor St. E., North Tower, Suite 604, Toronto, Ontario M4W 3R8 (tel. 416/968-1570).

England: GNTO, Nightingale House, 65 Curzon St., London W1Y 7PE (tel. 071/495-3990).

Australia: GNTO, Lufthansa House, 9th floor, 143 Macquarie St., Sydney 2000, Australia (tel. 02/367-3890).

Additionally, information on Berlin is available in the United

IMPRESSIONS

All free men, wherever they live, are citizens of Berlin, and
therefore, as a free man. I take pride in the words, Ich bin ein
Berliner.
—JOHN F. KENNEDY, 1963

States by calling the Berlin Desk in New York at 212/705-1371. For
free brochures, request the Berlin Travel Kit by calling toll free
800/248-9539; a packet containing a hotel brochure, city map, a
program of current exhibitions and happenings, and other information on Berlin will be sent free of charge in seven to ten days.

ENTRY REQUIREMENTS Citizens of the United States, Canada, Australia, and New Zealand need only a valid passport for entry
to Germany and stays up to three months. Visitors from the United
Kingdom need only an identity card.

Students should be sure to bring an International Student Identification Card as well; if you plan to rent a car, be sure to bring a valid
driver's license (a U.S. license is fine).

If you are a citizen of a country outside Europe, you can bring
duty-free into Germany 400 cigarettes or 100 cigars or 500 grams of
tobacco, 1 liter of spirits, and 2 liters of wine. If you are an American
or Canadian residing in Europe, however, your allowance is only half
that given above for tobacco products. You may bring gifts into
Germany totaling 620 DM ($387.50), including a maximum of 155
DM ($97) in gifts from non-Common Market countries.

Since Customs regulations may change, it would be wise to
confirm German Customs requirements before your trip.

A Note on Customs for British Citizens On January 1,
1993, the borders between European countries were relaxed as the
European markets united. When you're traveling within the EC, this
will have a big impact on what you can buy and take home with you
for personal use.

If you buy your goods in a duty-free shop, then the old rules still
apply—you're allowed to bring home 200 cigarettes and 2 liters of
table wine, plus 1 liter of spirits or 2 liters of fortified wine. If you
don't want the fortified wine, you can take an extra 2 liters of table
wine. The perfume allowance is 60 ml, and you can take home £36
worth of other assorted goodies.

But now you can buy your wine, spirits, or cigarettes in an
ordinary shop in France or Belgium, for example, and bring home
almost as much as you like. U.K. Customs and Excise does set
theoretical limits: 10 liters of spirits, plus 110 liters of beer, 20 liters of
fortified wine, 90 liters of ordinary wine (no more than 60 liters of
this can be sparkling wine), 800 cigarettes, 400 cigarillos, 200 cigars,
and 1 kilo of tobacco. But remember, this only applies to goods
bought in ordinary shops. If you buy in duty-free shops, these new
rules don't apply to you.

If you are returning home from a non-EC country, the allowances
are the standard ones from duty-free shops. You must declare any
goods in excess of these allowances.

You cannot buy goods and take them with you to sell to others.

This is a criminal offense in the U.K., and customs officers claim to be looking out for those making repeated trips or those laden down with goods.

MONEY   The basic unit of currency in Germany is the **Deutsche Mark (DM).** One DM equals 100 Pfennig. Coins come in denominations of 1, 2, 5, 10, and 50 Pfennig, and 1, 2, and 5 DM. Bills are issued in denominations of 5, 10, 20, 50, 100, 200, 500, and 1,000 DM. Note that new banknotes were issued in 1991 that are valid along with the older ones.

Although rates fluctuate continually, all conversions in this book are based on a rate of 1.60 DM to U.S. $1 (and then rounded off to the nearest nickel). To help you with money in Germany, see "The Mark & The Dollar" chart in Section D of the Appendix of this book. At presstime, the pound sterling exchanged at the rate of £1 = 2.40 DM. Keep in mind that the rates may have changed, so plan your budget accordingly.

In addition, keep in mind that prices themselves will change in Berlin during the lifetime of this book—which means that they will

WHAT THINGS COST IN BERLIN	U.S. $
Taxi from Tegel Airport to Bahnhof Zoo train station	15.50
Underground from Kurfürstendamm to Dahlem	2.00
Local telephone call (for three minutes)	.20
Double room at the Hotel Tiergarten Berlin (deluxe)	103.10
Double room at Hotel-Pension Dittberner (moderate)	81.25
Double room at Pension Fischer (budget)	50.00
Lunch for one at Café Hardenberg (moderate)	9.00
Lunch for one at Rogacki (budget)	5.00
Dinner for one, without wine, at Fofi's (deluxe)	30.00
Dinner for one, without wine, at Hardtke (moderate)	18.00
Dinner for one, without wine, at Athener Grill (budget)	5.00
Half-liter of beer	2.80
Glass of wine	3.10
Coca-Cola in a restaurant	1.80
Cup of coffee	2.05
Roll of ASA 100 Kodacolor film, 36 exposures	5.60
Admission to Dahlem Gemäldegalerie	2.50
Movie ticket	5.60
Theater ticket to Berlin Philharmonic Orchestra	7.50

go up. Prices for hotels, for example, rose dramatically after the Wall came down and people flocked to Berlin, simply because there was more demand than there was supply. Real estate prices also skyrocketed, resulting in higher rents. Since most proprietors of Berlin's budget restaurants and pensions are renters rather than landowners, some of the increased costs have been passed on to customers. Prices given in this book, therefore, should be used only as a guideline.

Instead of traveling with large amounts of cash, convert most of your money to traveler's checks. Traveler's checks issued in U.S. dollars and other foreign currencies can be exchanged only in banks, major hotels, some large department stores, and the American Express office. If you plan to spend all your time in Germany, you may wish to buy traveler's checks in German marks, available through American Express or MasterCard traveler's checks. Be aware, however, that such traveler's checks are not commonly used in Europe and will probably not be accepted as payment at small stores or restaurants.

In any case, buy traveler's checks in both small and large denominations (commission fees are charged per transaction, not on the total number of checks cashed at any one time). Similarly, be sure to include large and small denominations in the cash you bring. I always carry at least $10 worth of $1 bills when I travel, for tips and small favors.

As for credit cards, American Express, Diners Club, MasterCard, and VISA are the ones most readily accepted (and JCB, of course, in case you happen to have a Japanese credit card). All major hotels and many shops and restaurants accept credit cards, particularly in Western Berlin. In eastside Berlin, however, credit cards are usually accepted only in places frequented by international tourists, such as hotel restaurants. In addition, smaller locales in both east and west are not equipped to deal with credit cards, including the majority of budget establishments listed in this book. Make sure you have enough cash on hand, therefore, or you may find yourself in the ridiculous position of having to spend more money at upper-end establishments that accept credit cards. Take what you need for the day, keeping most of it secured in a money belt. Leave the rest of your cash and traveler's checks at your hotel's safe-deposit box.

And how much money should you bring with you? Plan on a minimum of $50 a day per person for lodging in a shared double room and meals. A much more comfortable allowance is $60 a day, including transportation costs, admission to museums and attractions, and drinks in a neighborhood pub. To be on the safe side, bring a bit more in traveler's checks than you think you'll need—you can always use them later when you return home.

2. WHEN TO GO — CLIMATE, HOLIDAYS & EVENTS

Berlin is a tourist destination throughout the year. In fact, now that it's become one of the hottest destinations in Europe, it can be as lively and crowded in February as in August.

CLIMATE Berlin is at the same latitude as Vancouver and enjoys the changes of the four seasons. Its summers are generally mild and even pleasantly cool, which accounts for the fact that very few hotels and establishments in Berlin bother with air conditioning. Spring and autumn can be glorious times of the year—my favorite time of year is October. Winters, on the other hand, can be quite severe, though not as bad as the northern regions of the United States. I've been to Berlin in April when it snowed; I've also been to Berlin in February when it was so warm that plants and grass started turning green. In other words, be prepared for all kinds of weather, since temperatures and the amount of rainfall seem to vary from year to year. However, the following averages may help you plan your trip.

Berlin's Average Daytime Temperature & Rainfall

	Jan	Feb	Mar	Apr	May	June	July	Aug	Sept	Oct	Nov	Dec
Temp. F	30	32	40	48	53	60	64	62	56	49	40	34
C	−1	0	4	9	12	16	18	17	13	9	4	1
Rainfall Inches	2.2	1.6	1.2	1.6	2.3	2.9	3.2	2.7	2.2	1.6	2.4	1.9

HOLIDAYS Because Berlin is predominantly Protestant instead of Catholic, it doesn't have nearly as many holidays as Germany's Catholic regions such as Bavaria. However, there are a few official bank holidays to keep in mind. Some museums and restaurants are closed certain holidays of the year. State museums, for example, are closed on New Year's Day, May 1, and December 24, 25, and 31. To avoid disappointment, be sure to telephone in advance if you wish to visit a certain establishment on a holiday.

Holidays in Berlin are New Year's (January 1), Good Friday, Easter Sunday and Monday, Ascension Day, Whit Sunday and Monday, Labor Day (May 1), German Reunification Day (October 3), Day of Prayer and Repentance (third Wednesday in November), and Christmas (both December 25 and 26).

THE YEAR IN BERLIN If you're lucky, your trip may coincide with one of Berlin's cultural events. But if you do arrive in Berlin during any of the major events described below, it's a good idea to reserve a room in advance. For other events that may be happening, including sporting events, art exhibits, or other one-time happenings, contact the German National Tourist Organization nearest you. In Berlin, the organization in charge of arranging all of Berlin's major festivals is the **Berliner Festspiele GmbH,** near the Europa-Center at Budapester Strasse 50 (tel. 030/25 48 90). You can also purchase tickets here. The **Verkehrsamt Berlin** (tourist office), located in the Europa-Center on Budapester Strasse (tel. 030/262 60 31), is another invaluable source of information.

BERLIN
CALENDAR OF EVENTS

FEBRUARY

✪ *INTERNATIONAL FILM FESTIVAL* *The calendar year starts off with a bang with this festival, which attracts stars, directors, movie critics, and film lovers from all over the world. Established back in 1951, it lasts almost two weeks and usually features about 700 films from some 20 countries at the main showing. In addition, there are other movies shown round the clock under such headings as the "International Forum of Young Filmmakers" and "New German Movies."*

Where: Various theaters. When: Late Feb. How: Tickets, 10 DM to 15 DM ($6.25–$9.35), can be purchased at the box offices or at a special booth set up on the first floor of the Europa-Center.

MAY

☐ **Theatertreffen.** This drama festival, or "Theater Meeting," features German-language productions from throughout the German-speaking world, including Austria and Switzerland. It serves as a workshop for new forms of expression and performance. You have to understand German, therefore, to appreciate the various offerings. If you do and you love theater, you'll be in heaven.

JUNE/JULY

☐ **Serenade concerts in Charlottenburg Palace.** Call Verkehrsamt Berlin (tel. 26/2 60 31) for information.

SEPTEMBER

✪ *BERLINER FESTWOCHEN* *The Berlin Festival Weeks is one of the biggest events of the year and recognizes excellence in all fields of the arts: opera, theater, music, and art.*

Where: Various theaters. When: End of Aug. through Sept. How: Ticket cost depends on the venue, and may be purchased at the box offices or Berliner Festspiele, Budapester Strasse 50.

OCTOBER/NOVEMBER

✪ *JAZZ-FEST BERLIN* *A colorful mix of avant-garde and classical jazz musicians from around the world, a must for jazz fans. There's everything from blues and swing to bebop, cool jazz, and free jazz.*

Where: Philharmonie, Delphi and Musikinstrumenten Museum. **When:** End of Oct. or Nov. **How:** Tickets, costing between 10 DM ($6.25) and 45 DM ($28.10), may be purchased at the box offices and Berliner Festspiele.

DECEMBER

☐ **Weihnachtsmarkt.** The traditional Christmas market is the number-one attraction in Berlin during December. Although there are several markets held around the city, the most popular, and most convenient is at the heart of the city—from the Gedächtniskirche all the way to Wittenbergplatz. It's open daily from 11am to 9pm, and features more than 150 stalls selling cookies, candied apples, mulled wine, Christmas ornaments, candy, and more. Other Christmas markets include those in the Spandau Altstadt, open only on weekends in December from 10am to 7pm with some 500 market stands set up in the Old City district; and Marx-Engels-Platz in Berlin-Mitte, which features children's rides in addition to market stalls. It takes place Sunday to Friday from 1 to 9pm and Sunday from 1 to 10pm from the end of November to Christmas Eve.

3. HEALTH & INSURANCE

No shots or inoculations are required for entry to Germany. If you need special medications, however, it's a good idea to bring them with you. Otherwise German pharmacies are well-equipped with their own brands of medicine. If a pharmacy cannot fulfill your American prescription, it will give you a German substitution.

Medical and hospital services are not free in Germany, so ask your insurance company before leaving home if you are covered for medical treatment abroad. If not, you may wish to take out a short-term traveler's medical policy that covers medical costs and emergencies. If an emergency arises during your stay in Berlin, consult "Fast Facts," in Chapter 3 for emergency telephone numbers.

You may also want to take extra precautions with your possessions. Is your camera or video equipment insured anywhere in the world through your home insurance? Is your home insured against theft or loss if you're gone longer than a month (some insurance companies will not cover loss for homes unoccupied longer than a month)? If you are not adequately covered, you may wish to purchase an extra policy to cover losses.

INSURANCE FOR BRITISH TRAVELERS Most big travel agents offer their own insurance, and will probably try to sell you their package when you book a holiday. Think before you sign. Britain's Consumers' Association recommends that you insist on seeing the policy and reading the fine print before buying travel insurance. You should also shop around for better deals. Try **Columbus Travel Insurance Ltd.** (tel. 071/375-0011) or, for students,

Campus Travel (tel. 071/730-3402). If you're unsure about who can give you the best deal, contact the **Association of British Insurers,** 51 Gresham St., London EC2V 7HQ (tel. 071/600-333).

4. WHAT TO PACK

Since Germans are known throughout the world for the quality and quantity of their goods, and since they import just about everything else, you can probably find anything you might need in Berlin during your stay. Thus, pack as lightly as possible—if you shop, you'll probably end up leaving with a lot more than you came with. I always pack a lightweight, nylon bag at the bottom of my suitcase, just in case I need an extra bag for the trip home.

Since Berlin has a moderate Continental climate (warm weather in the summer and cold in the winter), bring appropriate clothing. Be prepared for unusual temperature changes as well, since it can sometimes become quite cool on a summer's evening. Dress is fairly casual in Berlin, but if you're going to the theater or opera you'll want to pack one dressy outfit. Try to get mileage out of your wardrobe by packing clothes you can mix and match. I usually travel with three tops, one skirt, and one or two pairs of pants, regardless of whether I'm traveling two weeks or two months. Almost all hotel rooms in Berlin, including those in small, inexpensive pensions, contain their own sinks, which come in handy for washing underclothing (silk dries quickly and is comfortable throughout the year). I always pack a clothesline so that I can string wet clothing up in the shower or over the sink. Never dry clothing by draping them over a chair (it leaves a mark) or a lamp (it could catch on fire).

If you're staying in youth hostels, you'll want to bring your own towel and maybe your own sleeping bag or sheets (sheets are available at hostels for an extra charge). If you're staying in a pension with a shared bathroom down the hall, you may want to pack a light robe, nightgown, or an extra-large T-shirt (something that might also double as a coverup at the beach). At all times of year it's wise to have a folding umbrella, and be sure to bring good walking shoes (ones already broken in). I also never travel without my Swiss army knife—and in some cases have had to check it in as an assurance that I don't hijack the plane. You can avoid that possibility by packing

IMPRESSIONS

I made it clear to Mr. Khrushchev that the security of Western Europe and with it our own security is intimately interlinked with our presence in and our rights of access to Berlin, that these rights are based on legal foundation and not on sufferance and that we are determined to maintain these rights at all cost and thus to stand by our commitments to the people of West Berlin and to guarantee their right to determine their own future.
—JOHN F. KENNEDY, 1961

your knife in your check-in luggage. And last but not least, bring a travel alarm clock, so that you don't have to rely on hotel wakeup calls (in cheaper pensions, you won't even have a phone in your room).

5. TIPS FOR THE DISABLED, SENIORS, SINGLES, FAMILIES & STUDENTS

FOR THE DISABLED   Due to a skiing accident, I researched the first edition of this guide while confined to crutches. I found Berliners extremely polite and helpful, holding doors open for me and offering me their seat on buses and trains (special handicapped seats are marked on buses, subways, and trains). But probably the biggest obstacle is stairs. Some of the larger subway stations have escalators, but most do not. In addition, most inexpensive pensions are located in upper floors of multistory buildings, many without elevators or bathrooms large enough to accommodate a wheelchair. When making your hotel reservation, make sure the hotel is equipped to handle your needs.

There are many organizations in Berlin for the disabled. For more information, including where to rent wheelchairs and which hotels are best equipped for the disabled, contact **Landesamt für zentral soziale Aufgaben,** Landesversorgungsamt, Sächsische Strasse 28-30 (tel. 030/867 61 14 or 867 63 71).

FOR SENIORS   Some museums offer discounts of up to 50% to senior citizens—even though such discounts may not be posted. Men must be 65, women 60—carry your passport with you at all times as proof of your age.

If you wish, you can stay at youth hostels in Berlin—that is, if you can put up with the noise and exuberance of the youth. There's no age limit but "seniors"—defined as those 27 years and older—pay a slightly higher rate.

FOR SINGLE TRAVELERS   Although it doesn't seem fair, single travelers usually pay more than half the price of a double room. Expensive hotels may even charge the same price for single or double occupancy. If you're alone, look for hotels that offer single rates; some even have a few single rooms, usually the smallest on the premises. An alternative is to live dormitory-style at a youth hostel, where your chances are good of meeting other single travelers.

Women traveling alone to Berlin may want to contact the **Fraueninfothek Berlin,** located in eastern Berlin at Dircksenstrasse 47 (tel. 233 64 63 or 282 39 80). An organization managed by women for women, it can provide general travel information about Berlin, help find accommodations, and provide more information about women's groups and meetings.

As for establishments that cater only to women, Artemisia is a bright and cheery hotel geared towards the needs of female travelers, while Extra Dry is a women-only café selling snacks and nonalcoholic beverages. Refer to Chapter 4, "Where to Stay in Berlin," and Chapter 9, "Berlin Nights," for more information on these establishments.

FOR FAMILIES   I took my six-month-old son along to update the second edition of this book and found Berlin easily accessible by stroller. Buses have marked doors for strollers, as well as a special area near the door where strollers can be parked and secured. Children younger than six travel for free on public transportation; those younger than 14 travel at a discounted rate.

Berlin has many attractions that appeal to children, including a wonderful zoo and several museums (see Section 3, "Cool for Kids," in Chapter 6). Children usually pay half fare for attractions that charge admission; admission is usually free for children younger than 3.

FOR STUDENTS   Most museums in Berlin offer student discounts, and some theaters and opera houses (including the Deutsche Oper Berlin and the Schiller-Theater) offer unsold tickets to students for up to 50% off.

A student's key to cheaper prices is the **International Student Identity Card (ISIC),** available to all students enrolled full- or part-time in a degree program. Another benefit of the card is that it gives all holders access to a worldwide traveler's assistance hotline, a toll-free service for use in medical, financial, and legal emergencies. Valid for one year, the card is available from the **Council on International Educational Exchange (CIEE),** 205 East 42nd Street, New York, N.Y. 10017 (tel. 212/661-1414). Applications must include a $15 registration fee, one passport-size photo, and proof of current student status (an official letter from the school, school transcript, or registrar's receipt). Allow 4 weeks when applying for the card by mail.

Tips for British Students   Europe is full of InterRailing students during the summer months. **Eurotrain and Route 26** (tel. 071/834-7066) provide other options for cheap train fares for travelers under 26 to and from European destinations. **Campus Travel,** 52 Grosvenor Gardens, London SW1W 0AG (tel. 071/730-3402) provides a wealth of information and offers for the student traveler, ranging from route-planning to flight insurance, and including railcards.

The **International Student Identity Card** (ISIC) is an internationally recognized proof of student status that will entitle you to savings on flights, sightseeing, food, and accommodation. It costs only £5 and is well worth the cost. Always show your ISIC when booking a trip—you may not get a discount without it.

Youth hostels are the place to stay if you're a student. You'll need an International Youth Hostels Association card, which you can purchase from the youth hostel store at 14 Southampton Street, London (tel. 071/836-8541) or **Campus Travel** (tel. 071/730-3402). Take both your passport and some passport-sized photos of yourself, plus your membership fee. In England and Wales, this is £3 (for those under 18) or £9 (for those over 18). In Scotland, the fee is slightly less: £2.50 for those under 18, and £6 for everyone else. The IYHA puts together *The Hostelling International Budget Guide,* listing every youth hostel in 31 European countries. It costs £5.95 when purchased at the Southampton Street store in London (add 50p postage if it is being delivered within the U.K.).

If you're traveling in summer, many youth hostels will be full, so it's best to book ahead. In London, you can make advance reservations for other locations from the hostel on Oxford Street or the one at 36 Carter Lane (for a £1 fee).

6. GETTING THERE

For most readers, a trip to Berlin is likely to begin with a plane trip across the Atlantic to the European continent. Berlin itself is easily accessible by plane, train, or car. Below are some pointers.

BY PLANE Airlines that fly between North America and Germany include **Lufthansa,** the German national airline (tel. toll free 800/645-3800); **American** (tel. toll free 800/433-7300); **Continental** (tel. toll free 800/231-0856); **Delta** (tel. toll free 800/241-4141); **TWA** (tel. toll free 800/892-4141); and **USAir** (tel. toll free 800/622-1015). Contact your travel agent or specific carriers for current information.

To get a head start on your travel adventure, it seems only fitting to fly Germany's own Lufthansa, known throughout the world for its punctuality, dependability, and high-quality service. It operates the most frequent flights from the United States and Canada to Germany and also flies to the greatest number of cities in Germany. It also offers the most flights to Berlin from all major cities in Germany and elsewhere.

TRANSATLANTIC AIRFARES Researching airfares from North America to Germany can be difficult and time consuming, since the cheapest fares vary depending on the season and even the day of the week you travel. In addition, airlines sometimes lower prices at the last minute to fill empty seats; or they have special promotional fares—valid at certain times—and may include car-rental options. It pays, therefore, to invest time shopping around.

While first- and business-class fares are the same year round, inexpensive tickets vary with the season. The most expensive time to fly is during peak season, usually June through September. The lowest fares are available during the winter months, usually November through March (with the exception of December 12–24). Fares vary from high to low during the shoulder season, usually April, May, and October. In addition, during all seasons there are different rates for weekday and weekend flights.

APEX [Advance Purchase Excursion] You can cut the cost of your flight to Germany by purchasing your ticket in advance and complying with certain restrictions. Reservations, ticketing, and payment for nonrefundable special **APEX** (advance purchase excursion) fares must be completed 30 days in advance and require a minimum stay of 7 days and a maximum stay of 21 days. Rates on all APEX fares vary according to the season, with peak-season rates in effect from June through September. Round-trip weekday flights (Monday through Thursday) are approximately $60 cheaper than weekend flights (Friday through Sunday). Airlines also often offer low, short-term fares that are much cheaper than their regular economy fares and even cheaper than their regular APEX fares. In 1993, for example, Lufthansa's cheapest, nonrefundable advance-purchase fare ranged from as low as $398 for a round-trip flight from New York to Berlin on a weekday in winter, to a high of $718 for the same flight in summer. Continental also offered a $718 round-trip fare between Newark and Frankfurt on weekday flights in summer.

Economy Fares In addition to its special APEX fares, Lufthansa also offers some other options for budget travel. Lufthansa's **Holiday Fare,** for example, carries fewer restrictions but still permits no stopovers and carries a penalty for cancellation. Tickets must be purchased 21 days in advance and are valid for stays lasting from 7 to 90 days, giving travelers greater flexibility. The low-season round-trip fare from New York to Berlin is $819 on a weekday; the high-season fare for the same flight is $1,197.

If you're unable to purchase your ticket in advance or wish to stay longer than 90 days, you may wish to purchase Lufthansa's round-trip **Excursion Fare,** which has no minimum stay and is valid for stays up to 1 year. No advance purchase is necessary, and cancellations are allowed without penalty. The off-season round-trip fare from New York to Berlin is $1,123 for a weekday, while the same flight during the peak season is $1,408.

Lufthansa's **Youth Fare,** available to those aged 12 to 24, is a good value for students or pupils going to Germany for a year's study since its round-trip ticket allows for a maximum stay of one year. It has a 72-hour advance purchase requirement, allows no stopovers, and requires that the return reservation be left open but made 72 hours before flying. The one-way weekday fare from New York to Germany is $332 low-season, $464 peak season.

In contrast, if you purchase Lufthansa's regular economy ticket, which carries no restrictions and allows one free stopover en route, the round-trip fare from New York to Berlin is $2,434 year-round.

First- and Business-Class Fares If you wish to fly in style, you'll want to take advantage of luxuries provided to first- and business-class passengers. Lufthansa, for example, offers wider seats, travel kits, and deluxe meals. Its fares are the same all year and allow an unlimited number of stopovers. The one-way business-class fare from New York to Berlin is $1,426, while first-class is $2,539. Remember, however, that fares are subject to change without notice. Be sure to contact your travel agent or the airlines for current information.

Other Options Certainly the best strategy for securing the lowest airfare is to shop around. Consult the travel section of major newspapers, since they often carry advertisements for cheap fares. You may, for example, find advertisements offered by so-called "bucket shops" that sell discounted tickets at reductions of about 20% to 30%. Tickets are usually restrictive, valid only for a particular date or flight, nontransferable, and nonrefundable.

Another option is a charter flight, which may offer a combination package that includes land transportation such as rental car and hotel accommodation. One reputable charter company is Condor, a Lufthansa subsidiary, which is located in Chicago (tel. 312/686-8440) and sells tickets to tour operators throughout the country.

AIRFARES FROM THE U.K. There are no hard and fast rules about where to get the best deals for European flights, but do bear the following points in mind:

1. Daily papers often carry advertisements for companies offering cheap flights. London's *Evening Standard* has a daily travel

FROMMER'S SMART TRAVELER: AIRFARES

1. Shop all the airlines that fly to your destination.
2. Keep calling the airlines, since the availability of cheap fares changes daily. As the departure date nears, you might obtain a seat at a great discount, as airlines would rather sell a seat than have it empty.
3. Read the advertisements of newspaper travel sections— they often offer special deals and packages.
4. You can also save money by buying your ticket as early as possible, since the cheapest fares such as APEX (Advance Purchase Excursion) usually require 30 days' advance purchase.
5. Ask whether there's a difference in price if you fly on a weekday—weekday flights are often $60 cheaper than weekend flights.
6. Travel off-season if you're trying to save money, since APEX and economy tickets often cost less if it's the off-season.

section, and the Sunday editions of almost any newspaper will run many ads. Highly recommended companies include **Trailfinders** (tel. 071/938-3366) and **Platinum Travel** (tel. 071/937-5122).
2. In London, there are many "bucket shops" around Victoria and Earls Court that offer cheap fares. Make sure that the company you deal with is a member of the IATA, ABTA, or ATOL. These umbrella organizations will help you out if anything goes wrong.
3. **CEEFAX,** a British television information service included on many home and hotel TVs, runs details of package holidays and flights to Europe and beyond. Just switch to your CEEFAX channel and you'll find a menu of listings that includes travel information.

FARES FROM FRANKFURT TO BERLIN Although it's cheaper to purchase a ticket that will take you from North America all the way to Berlin, you may find yourself in Frankfurt. At press time, the one-way fare from Frankfurt to Berlin was 318 DM ($199); business class was 418 DM ($261).

BY TRAIN It's easy to get to Berlin by rail, with good connections from Frankfurt, Hamburg, and other major European cities. The trip from Frankfurt to Berlin takes about 7 hours and, at press time, costs 126 DM ($78.75) one way for second class. From Munich, a one-way second-class ticket costs 127 DM ($79.25). Travelers under age 26 are entitled to reduced train fares: the following are round-trip fares costing about 150 DM ($93.75) from Frankfurt, 186 DM ($116.25) from Munich, and from Hamburg 82 DM ($51.25). Youth tickets are available at travel agencies, especially those that cater to students.

RAIL PASSES If you plan on visiting other cities in Germany or are traveling to Berlin from, say, Munich, you may be able to save on train fare by purchasing a **GermanRailpass.** A particularly good deal is the **Flexipass,** available for any 5, 10, or 15 days of travel within a 1-month period. At press time, a 5-day Flexipass cost $170 for second-class travel and only $130 for travelers under age 26. That's about the same price as a regular round-trip ticket between Munich and Berlin. What's more, with a rail pass you don't have to stand in line each time to buy a ticket. Other GermanRail options include passes valid for 4, 9, or 16 days of consecutive travel.

GermanRailpasses, which must be purchased before leaving the United States, are available at travel agencies or from GermanRail offices. For more information, call GermanRail in Rosemont, Ill., at 708/692-6300.

If you plan to travel extensively outside Germany, you may want to take advantage of a **Eurailpass**—which must also be purchased before entering Europe and is good for travel through 17 European countries. A number of options are available, including passes good for unlimited travel from 15 days to 3 months, as well as Flexipasses good for any 5, 10, or 15 days of travel within 2 months. Eurail Youthpasses are available to travelers under age 26. At press time, a 15-day Eurailpass valid for 15 days of consecutive travel cost $460; a Eurail Flexipass good for 5 days of travel within 15 days cost $298; and a 1-month Eurail Youthpass cost $508. For information on these and other fares, contact a travel agent.

Rail Passes for U.K. Residents   Many different rail passes are available in the U.K. for travel in Britain and Europe. Stop in at the **International Rail Centre,** Victoria Station, London SW1V 1JY (tel. 071/834-2345) or **Wasteels,** 121 Wilton Rd., London SW1V 1JZ (tel. 071/834-7066). They can help you find the best option for the trip you're planning.

The most popular rail ticket for U.K. residents is the **InterRail card,** available for travelers under 26 years of age. It costs £240, is valid for one month, and entitles you to unlimited second-class travel in 26 European countries. It also gives you a 34% discount on rail travel in Britain and Northern Ireland, and a 50% discount on the rail portion of travel from London to various continental ports. You'll also get a reduction (between 30% and 50%) on most sailings to Europe, and a variety of other ferry services around the Mediterranean and Scandinavia. Recently, an InterRail card for those over 26 was introduced, costing £260 for a month, or £180 for 15 days. According to BritRail, there is some doubt about its availability for 1994, but check with the International Rail Centre or Wasteels for updated information.

If you're not a resident of the U.K., you can buy an InterRail card if you've been in Britain for six months.

Eurotrain tickets are another good option for travelers under 26. Valid for two months, they allow you to choose your own route to a final destination and stop off as many times as you like along the way. Eurotrain "Explorer" tickets are slightly more expensive, but allow you to cover more ground, traveling to your final destination along one route and back on another. Eurotrain travels to over 2,000 destinations in Europe and North Africa, and the price includes roundtrip ferry crossing as well as roundtrip rail travel from London to the port. **Campus Travel,** 52 Grosvenor Gardens, London SW1W 0AG (tel. 071/730-3402) can give you prices and help you book tickets.

Route 26 (tel. 071/834-7066) provides cheap train fares for students (or those under 26) to and from European destinations.

Rail cards, covering 3, 5, or 10 days of first- or second-class travel, are also available for individual European countries (but not for Turkey). Investigate the available options at the Rail Centre in Victoria Station in London or at Wasteels.

BY BUS Daily bus service is available between Berlin and a number of German cities, including Bremen, Frankfurt, Hamburg, Munich, and Nürnberg. Buses are modern coaches, equipped with Pullman seats and toilets. Tickets—cheaper than train fares—can be purchased at all DER travel agencies. A one-way trip from Frankfurt to Berlin costs 99 DM ($61.85) and takes slightly less than 11 hours. The 9-hour trip from Munich to Berlin costs 123 DM ($76.85). Prices are even cheaper if you're younger than 27. The price of a one-way youth fare from Munich to Berlin, for example, is only 66 DM ($41.25).

By Coach & Ferry from the U.K. If you want to take your time, coach travel is a relaxing way to see Europe. Many package trips around Europe and for individual countries are available. **Cosmos Tourama** (tel. 081/464-3477) provides a wide range of trips all over Europe, from 3 to 22 nights. **Eurolines,** 52 Grosvenor Gardens, London SW1W 0AU (tel. 071/730-0202) has a range of budget coach trips around Europe, all of which include the cost of the ferry.

The U.K. ferry company **Sally Line** (tel. 081/858-1127) runs a cheap coach/ferry service from Liverpool Street to Copenhagen between April and November.

If you're looking for a cheap camping/coach tour, try **Contiki Concept** (tel. 081/290-6422). Tours range from 7 to 33 days and allow you to see much of Europe with a minimum of effort.

BY CAR Traffic can be the main obstacle to car travel. Germans are keen on exploring new territories in their unified country, and congestion in former East Germany is compounded by lagging road building and maintenance (look out for those ruts and potholes). Since Autobahns are often clogged with day-trippers and vacationers, especially on weekends, avoid driving on Saturday or during exceptionally fine weather, or else travel in the early morning or late at night. Be sure to observe all speed limits: Although there is no speed limit on Autobahns in former West Germany, eastern Germany still imposes a 100-kph (62-mph) speed limit and enforces it with radar. Keep alcoholic beverages in the trunk; in former East Germany, drivers aren't allowed even one drink if they're going to drive.

How long it takes you to drive to Berlin will depend on the roads you take and how fast you drive. Since most stretches of the Autobahn in western Germany do not have speed limits, how fast you drive is limited only by the capability of your car and your nerve. For distances between Berlin and major German cities, refer to the mileage chart in Section D, "Conversion Charts," in the Appendix of this book.

By Car and Ferry to Europe from the U.K. Ferry/drive reservations can be made with any good travel agent. There are many different options, so as always, it's advisable to shop around for the best deals.

Brittany Ferries is the U.K.'s largest ferry/drive company, sailing from the south coast of England to five destinations in France and Spain. Sailings depart from Portsmouth to St. Malo and Caen (tel. 0705/827-701); from Poole to Cherbourg (tel. 0202/666-466); and from Plymouth to Roscoff and Santander, Spain (tel. 0752/221-321). Brittany also runs ferries from Cork in Northern Ireland to Roscoff and St. Malo (tel. 0752/269-926 for a brochure). Tickets range from £133 for an open-ended return ticket from Portsmouth to Cherbourg for a family of four. Ask about standard tickets, which allow you to take "as many people as you can get into your car," according to Brittany Ferries. In some cases, these prices will be lower.

Stena Sealink Lines (tel. 0233/647-047) runs ferries from Dover to Calais; Southampton to Cherbourg; Newhaven to Dieppe; Harwich to the Hook of Holland; and from the west coast of England to Ireland.

P&O Ferries (tel. 081/575-8555) sails from Portsmouth to Cherbourg and Le Havre in France and to Bilbao, Spain; from Dover to Calais, France and Ostend, Belgium; and from Felixstowe to Zeebrugge, Belgium. Their fares are excellent, starting from £75 for a return ticket to Ostend for five people and a car.

Scandinavian Sea Ways allows you to travel farther afield— to Germany, Sweden, Finland, Denmark, and Norway. Ask about Flag Days, when fares are reduced, and about discounts for students who show valid identification.

With any ferry trip you can buy "open jaw" tickets, which allow you to depart from and return to different ports in the U.K., so long as you travel both ways with the same ferry company.

TO EUROPE FROM THE U.K. VIA THE CHANNEL TUNNEL The tunnel is set to open between December 1993 and January 1994. Running between Folkestone and Calais, in France, the Channel Tunnel will reduce the travel time to France to 30 minutes.

You can travel via the tunnel on a train from London's Waterloo station, so you don't need a car to take advantage of the service. If you do take a car, it will be stowed away on the shuttle trains, for you to drive off at the destination. No prices are yet fixed as we go to press, but you can get up-to-the-minute information by calling 0302/270-111.

7. ENJOYING BERLIN ON A BUDGET

Getting the most out of your money—that's the key to enjoying Berlin on a budget. Berlin on $50 a day means spending $50 per person per day on accommodations and meals only—expect to spend more than half this amount on accommodations (unless you stay in a youth hostel). On a recent trip to Berlin, my husband and I spent approximately $110 to $120 each day: this allowed us to stay in a clean, comfortable room in the heart of the city, dine on German and international cuisine, and spend the day sightseeing. Not bad for one of Europe's major cities.

SAVING MONEY ON ACCOMMODATIONS The cheapest place to stay in Berlin is at a youth hostel. There's no age limit (though people older than 26 pay a few marks more), but you have to have a youth hostel card. They're available from the youth hostels themselves for 30 DM ($18.75). Most rooms are dormitory style, with four to eight beds per room, and shared bathroom facilities down the hall.

If you prefer more privacy, there are a number of inexpensive pensions and hotels from which to choose. (Although the difference between the two is often negligible, a pension is generally less expensive and has fewer rooms than a hotel.) The cheapest pensions are usually very small establishments, often with fewer than 20 rooms and located on the upper floors of large apartment buildings. Many of these pensions—former mansions built at the turn of the century—have character, with large airy rooms, and a shared bathroom down the hall. You may, however, have to climb quite a few stairs to get to them. Generally speaking, if there's no elevator, rooms on the upper floors will be cheaper.

In any case, you'll save money if you take a room without a private shower or toilet. Unlike many other European cities, you usually do not have to pay extra in Berlin to take a shower. Another thing to keep in mind is whether breakfast is included in the price. Many visitors say they eat so much for breakfast that it tides them over until an early dinner, skipping lunch. If you thrive on breakfast, it makes sense to pay slightly more for a room that includes breakfast. Some establishments offer a buffet breakfast, allowing you to eat as much as you want.

With the exception of Berlin's expensive and deluxe hotels, most hotels and pensions charge the same rates year round. However, it never hurts to ask for a discount during winter or if you plan on staying for a week or longer. Since there are rooms available varying in size, location, and facilities, ask whether there's a cheaper room than the one quoted.

SAVING MONEY ON MEALS The cheapest place to grab a meal is at an *Imbiss,* a stand-up eatery where everything from sausages to pizza to fish sandwiches are offered. You can even enjoy a cup of coffee at a stand-up coffee shop for almost a third what you'd pay at a café. If the weather is fine, you might wish to head for the nearest park or bench, and watch the parade of people walk by. You can also save money by shopping in the food section of larger department stores, where you can purchase fruit, bread, cheese, desserts, wine, beer, and such take-out foods as grilled chicken or salads.

For sit-down dining, you can often eat more economically if you eat your big meal at lunch, when restaurants offer lunch specials. They're generally available from 11am to 2pm. You can even splurge and enjoy the atmosphere of Berlin's finer restaurants if you limit yourself to the less expensive items on the menu and cut out drinks, appetizers, and desserts. Just because you're on a budget doesn't mean that the more pricey places are beyond your means.

Finally, ask local people for recommendations of places they like. They may know of a place just around the corner that offers hearty portions at very reasonable prices.

SAVING MONEY ON SIGHTSEEING & ENTERTAIN-MENT There are a lot of enjoyable things to do in Berlin that don't cost money. What, for example, could beat a stroll along the Ku'damm or Unter den Linden (see Chapter 7, "Strolling Around Berlin," for walking tours), or browsing at Berlin's many markets?

If you love museums, keep in mind that most museums in Berlin offer free admission on Sundays and public holidays, including the cluster of famous museums in Dahlem and on Museum Island (note, however, that these free days are also the most crowded). Another thing to keep in mind is that museums located close together geographically usually offer a so-called combination ticket (*Sammelkarte*), which allows entry to several museums at a cheaper price than if you were to purchase individual tickets at each museum. Museums in the Tiergarten, Museum Island, and Charlottenburg each offer such combination tickets.

Another bargain in Berlin is its theaters, operas, and concerts, particularly those in former East Berlin. Opera tickets start at less than $3.75, while tickets to the Schiller-Theater begin at $5.60. As most theaters are small, the cheaper tickets are perfectly acceptable. You can avoid paying a commission by buying your ticket directly from the theater or concert hall rather than through ticket agencies. In addition, several theaters offer discounts to students.

CHAPTER 3

GETTING TO KNOW BERLIN

This chapter will answer any questions you might have upon arrival in Berlin and during your stay, from how to get to your hotel from the airport to numbers to call during an emergency. Note, however, that information about Berlin may change.

1. ORIENTATION

ARRIVING

BY PLANE AT TEGEL AIRPORT

Tegel Airport (tel. 030/41 01-1) is located in northwest Berlin only 5 miles from the main train station and the city center. It serves as the major airport for flights from Western Europe and North America. It's rather small as airports go, consisting of one main hall and a circular-shaped passenger terminal. Stop by the Berlin information counter, located in the main terminal, and pick up a free map of the city and sightseeing brochures. If you don't yet have a hotel reservation, the tourist office here will book one for you for a 5-DM ($3.10) fee. It's open from 8am to 11pm daily.

Other facilities at the airport include banks for money exchange, luggage storage, a post office from which you can make international calls, a first-aid station, a police station, car-rental firms, a restaurant, and shops selling film, newspapers, souvenirs, and travel necessities.

GETTING TO AND FROM TEGEL AIRPORT   By Bus   The best and least expensive way to get into town is on city bus no. 109, which departs about every 10 to 15 minutes from just outside the

IMPRESSIONS

Berlin is not a city at all. Berlin simply provides the arena for a number of people of intellect to gather, to whom the place is no matter. These people create the spirit of Berlin.
—HEINRICH HEINE, 1828

arrival hall. Fare is 3.20 DM ($2) one way, collected by the bus driver when you board the bus. The trip to the city center takes approximately a half hour. The bus travels to Stuttgarter Platz and along the Kurfürstendamm, where most of Berlin's hotels are concentrated, all the way to Bahnhof Zoologischer Garten (Berlin's main train station) and Budapester Strasse. At the airport tourist information counter, ask which stop is most convenient to your hotel. Once inside the bus, look for a panel at the front of the bus, which clearly displays the name of each upcoming stop.

By Taxi   The easiest and quickest way to get into town, of course, is by taxi, which is not as prohibitively expensive as in many other major cities. It costs approximately 25–30 DM ($15.60–$18.75) one way to the city center, and there are always plenty of taxis waiting to take you to your destination.

BY PLANE AT SCHÖNEFELD AIRPORT

Schönefeld Airport (tel. 030/67 87-0), formerly East Berlin's major airport, serves intercontinental flights from Asia and Latin America as well as those from Eastern Europe and the Soviet Union. It's situated less than 3 miles south of Berlin.

GETTING TO AND FROM SCHÖNEFELD AIRPORT   By S-Bahn and Subway   Berlin-Schönefeld S-Bahn station is about a 5-minute walk from the airport. From there, S-Bahn 9 (usually abbreviated to S-9) travels through Alexanderplatz to Bahnhof Zoo, Savignyplatz, and Charlottenburg stations. If you don't want to walk the 5 minutes to the S-Bahn station, an alternative is to board Bus no. 171 from Schönefeld Airport for the short ride to Rudow, where you can then board U-Bahn 7 for a ride into the city. Regardless of the transportation method you choose, both routes cost 3.20 DM ($2) one way.

BY PLANE AT BERLIN-TEMPELHOF AIRPORT

Tempelhof Airport (tel. 030/69 09-1), western Berlin's oldest airport, was resurrected for commercial use after the Wall fell and Berlin found itself unable to handle increased flights to the new capital. Serving flights from both European and German cities, it is located just a few miles south of the city center.

GETTING TO AND FROM TEMPELHOF AIRPORT   By Subway   The U-Bahn 6 subway line connects the airport's station, Platz der Luftbrücke, with Friedrichstrasse station. If your destination is Bahnhof Zoo, take U-6 two stops to Hallesches Tor, transferring there to U-1 going in the direction of Ruhleben. The fare is 3.20 DM ($2).

By Bus   Bus 119 travels directly from the airport to the Kurfürstendamm, where most of Berlin's hotels are located. The fare is 3.20 DM ($2).

BY TRAIN

BAHNHOF ZOOLOGISCHER GARTEN   If you're arriving by train from Western Europe, you'll probably end up at Bahnhof Zoologischer Garten, Berlin's main train station and popularly called Bahnhof Zoo. It's located in the center of town, not far from the

Kurfürstendamm with its hotels and nightlife. An underground, S-Bahn, and bus system connects the train station to the rest of the city. Bus no. 109, for example, travels along Kurfürstendamm and continues to Tegel Airport; bus no. 100 travels to Alexanderplatz.

Your first stop at Bahnhof Zoo, however, should be at the tourist information counter, open daily from 8am to 11pm. In addition to picking up maps and brochures on Berlin, you can also have your hotel reservation made here for a 5-DM ($3.10) fee. Both a post office and money-exchange office are also located in the train station. For information on train schedules, call 194 19 or stop by the information office in the station.

BERLIN HAUPTBAHNHOF & BERLIN-LICHTENBERG

Formerly eastern Berlin's main train stations, the **Berlin Hauptbahnhof** (once called Ostbahnhof) and **Berlin-Lichtenberg** stations now serve trains from both Eastern and Western Europe. Some trains stop at Bahnhof Zoologischer Garten in addition to both these train stations, so decide beforehand where you want to get off (Bahnhof Zoo is most convenient in most instances, since the majority of the city's hotels are located here). Both the Hauptbahnhof and Berlin-Lichtenberg stations are connected to the S-Bahn 5, with direct service to Bahnhof Zoo.

BY CAR

If you're driving to Berlin, you may want a hotel that offers parking space. Otherwise, there are many parking garages in the inner city open day and night. These include Parkhaus am Zoo, Budapester Strasse 38; Parkhaus Europa-Center, Nürnberger Strasse 5-7; Parkhaus Los-Angeles-Platz, Augsburger Strasse 30; and Parkhaus Metropol, Joachimstaler Strasse 14-19. All four are located within a few minutes' walk of the Ku'damm, the Gedächtniskirche, the Europa-Center, and Bahnhof Zoo.

BY BUS

As Berlin is easily accessible from most European cities by rail and plane, it's unlikely you'll arrive by bus. However, there are omnibus lines that connect Berlin with some of Germany's major cities, including Frankfurt, Hamburg, and Munich. In any case, if you travel by bus, you'll arrive at the Omnibusbahnhof am Funkturm (Central Bus Station), located near the Radio Tower at Messedamm. From there you can board a taxi or another bus for your hotel; the nearest subway station is Kaiserdamm U-Bahn station. If you need omnibus information, dial 301 80 28.

TOURIST INFORMATION

There are several branches of the **Verkehrsamt Berlin,** Berlin's tourist information office, ready to serve you. The main office is conveniently located in the Europa-Center, with its entrance on Budapester Strasse (tel. 030/262 60 31), just a couple minutes' walk from Bahnhof Zoo and the Ku'damm. In addition to stocking maps and brochures about the city, the tourist office will also book a hotel room for you for a 5-DM ($3.10) fee. It's open Monday to Saturday from 8am to 10:30pm and Sunday from 9am to 9pm.

Other tourist offices are located at Tegel Airport (tel. 030/41

01-31 45) and Bahnhof Zoo train station (tel. 030/313 90 63). Both are open daily from 8am to 11pm, and both will also book your hotel room. In addition, a new tourist office is expected to open at Brandenburg Gate by the time this book is published, with probable open hours from about 8am to 8pm daily.

For information in English on the latest cultural events in Berlin, your best bet is *checkpoint Berlin,* a monthly entertainment magazine available at selected newsstands for 3 DM ($1.85). In addition to telling what's being performed when and where, it carries articles of interest to visitors, including restaurant reviews, information on art exhibitions, shopping, and news items.

Although not as detailed, another source of information in English is a pamphlet called *Berlin Turns On,* available at the tourist office. It gives a six-month overview of what's happening in Berlin in the way of concerts, opera and theater, sports, and festivals and special events. Specifics—such as times, venues, and prices—are not given, but at least you can get an idea of what's going on before looking or inquiring elsewhere. Also available at the tourist office and at magazine kiosks is an excellent publication called *Berlin Programm,* published only in German but valuable for its listings of plays, operas, concerts, and other happenings. Costing 2.80 DM ($1.75) and issued monthly, it also lists museums and their hours. Even if you can't read German, you may be able to decipher what's being performed where.

If you do read German, you'll want to pick up a copy of either *tip* and/or *zitty,* two German city magazines published on alternate weeks with information on alternative theater, film, rock, and folk. *zitty* costs 3.30 DM ($2.05); *tip* costs 3.70 DM ($2.30).

CITY LAYOUT

With no more Wall slicing the city in half, Berlin of today is markedly different from what it was. Although there are no physical barriers between East and West, there is still a psychological one, and for most Berliners there is still an East and a West Berlin. In a rudimentary sketch of the city, West Berlin fanned westward from Brandenburger Tor; East Berlin was everything east of Brandenburger Tor.

IMPRESSIONS

This place recalls to the beholder at every step, the image, genius, and the actions of the reigning Sovereign. . . . If however, Berlin strikes by its regularity and the magnificence of its public buildings, it impresses not less forcibly with a sentiment of melancholy. It is neither enriched by commerce, enlivened by the general residence of the Sovereign, nor animated by industry, business and freedom. An air of silence and dejection reigns in the streets, where at noon-day scarcely any passengers are seen except soldiers. The population, much as it has augmented during the present reign, is still very unequal to the extent and magnitude of the city. . . . The splendid fronts of the finest houses, frequently conceal poverty and wretchedness. . . . We are at first disappointed, and then disgusted with this deception.
—SIR N.W. WRAXALL, 1779

Greater Berlin is composed of 23 precincts, each with its own town hall, market squares, and shopping streets. Of these, Charlottenburg and Berlin-Mitte, in former West and East Berlin, respectively, are notable. Charlottenburg contains the famous Kurfürstendamm Boulevard, most of the city's hotels, the main train station, the Europa-Center shopping and restaurant complex, many museums, and Schloss Charlottenburg (Charlottenburg Palace). Berlin-Mitte, so named because it was once the middle of Berlin, was where the city was founded more than 800 years ago. It contains Museumsinsel (Museum Island) with its outstanding museums; a famous boulevard called Unter den Linden; a replica of old Berlin called the Nikolaiviertel; and Alexanderplatz, once the heart of Communist East Berlin. If you want, you can walk from Charlottenburg to Berlin-Mitte in less than 2 hours, a pretty stroll that takes you through the Tiergarten, the largest park in the city.

Cutting a diagonal path through the city is the Spree River. From the Grosser Müggelsee at the southeast end of Berlin, the Spree runs through Köpenick, where it picks up the Dahme River; through eastern Berlin, where it's joined by the Panke River; past the Reichstag building and the Tiergarten; and on to Spandau, where it empties into the Havel River. It was on the banks of the Spree River—halfway between Köpenick and Spandau—that two villages called Berlin and Cölln sprang up centuries ago, growing and merging and eventually becoming the city we know today.

MAIN STREETS & SQUARES

The most famous street in western Berlin is the **Kurfürstendamm,** affectionately called the **Ku'damm.** About 2½ miles long, it begins at the Kaiser-Wilhelm Gedächtniskirche (Memorial Church), a ruined church left standing as a permanent reminder of the horrors of war. This is the eastern end of the boulevard, where nearby you'll find Bahnhof Zoo (western Berlin's main train station); a large park called the Tiergarten; and the Europa-Center, a 22-story building with shops and the Verkehrsamt (tourist information office). From the Europa-Center, **Tauentzienstrasse** leads straight to **Wittenbergplatz,** the location of the KaDeWe, the largest department store on the Continent.

From the Gedächtniskirche, the Ku'damm stretches toward the west and is lined with many of the city's smartest boutiques, as well as many of its hotels. Just a 5-minute walk north of the Ku'damm, off Knesebeckstrasse, is a square called **Savignyplatz,** noted for its bars and restaurants.

Wilmersdorfer Strasse, located west of Savignyplatz and north of the Ku'damm, is a pedestrian street lined with department stores, boutiques, and restaurants. This is where the natives come to shop—located at the Wilmersdorfer Strasse U-Bahn station.

Berlin's other famous boulevard—and historically much more significant—is **Unter den Linden** in eastside Berlin. This was the heart of pre–World War II Berlin, its most fashionable and liveliest street. Its most readily recognized landmark is the Brandenburger Tor (Brandenburg Gate), and buildings along the tree-lined street have been painstakingly restored. Unter den Linden leads to Museumsinel (Museum Island), which boasts the outstanding Pergamon Museum among its number of great museums. Only a 5-minute walk away is the modern center of eastern Berlin, **Alexanderplatz** with its tall television tower. Southwest of Alexanderplatz and only a few minutes' walk away is the Nikolaiviertel (Nikolai Quarter), a reconstructed neighborhood of shops, bars, and restaurants resembling old Berlin.

FINDING AN ADDRESS

Although some of Berlin's streets are numbered with the evens on one side and the odds on the other, many others are numbered consecutively up one side of the street and continuing back down the other. The numbering system of the Ku'damm, for example begins at the Gedächtniskirche and increases on the same side of the street all the way to end of the boulevard, and then jumps to the other side of the street and continues all the way back: Thus, Ku'damm 11, site of the American Express, is across the street from Ku'damm 231, location of the Wertheim department store. It's a bit complicated at first, but numbers for each block are posted on street signs.

In German, *Strasse* means "street" and *Platz* means "square." Generally speaking, streets south of the Ku'damm are named after important towns and regions—such as Augsburger Strasse, Nürnberger Strasse, and Pariser Strasse. Streets north of the Ku'damm are more likely to be named after famous Germans—such as Kantstrasse, Goethestrasse, and Schillerstrasse.

Keep in mind, too, that the ground floor of a building is called *Erdgeschoss* in German and marked *E* on elevators. The next floor up is therefore the first floor (which would be the American second floor) and so on.

In searching for an address, it helps to know that new zip codes for all of Germany were introduced in 1993 to unify the country under one postal system. Similar to the United States, Berlin now has five-digit zip codes, which vary according to the precinct and appear before the city's name.

Be aware, too, that some streets and stations in eastern Berlin have been renamed, particularly those named after former Communist party leaders who have fallen out of favor. Some have reverted back to their original names before Berlin was divided following the war. Most notably, these include Marx-Engels-Platz station (now Hackescher Markt), Platz der Akademie (now Gendarmenmarkt), and Marx-Engels-Forum (now Rathausstrasse), all in Berlin-Mitte.

MAPS

Unless the situation changes, the free map issued by the Berlin tourist office is not adequate for an in-depth study of the city. Luckily, many hotels have free maps that help supplement the tourist-office map. In addition, both *checkpoint Berlin* and *Berlin Programm,* two monthly publications, contain maps of Berlin's city center.

If you're planning to spend more than several days in Berlin or simply want a more detailed map of the city, there are many maps of greater Berlin for sale at bookstores. Both Falk and Euro City put out folding maps of the city, complete with an index of street names. Less unwieldy is Rand McNally's "City Flash," which is smaller, waterproof, and shows only central Berlin (Dahlem and Spandau, for example, are not on the map). Good places to look for maps are the

Europa Presse Center, a magazine and newspaper store in the Europa-Center, and Kiepert, a bookstore located at the corner of Knesebeckstrasse and Hardenbergstrasse less than a 10-minute walk from Bahnhof Zoo.

For a map of Berlin's transportation system, stop by the BVG kiosk in front of Bahnhof Zoo, where you can purchase a detailed map showing all bus, tram, and S- and U-Bahn lines for 3 DM ($1.85). More information on BVG is given below in "Getting Around."

NEIGHBORHOODS IN BRIEF

Charlottenburg   This is western Berlin's most important precinct, stretching from the Tiergarten all the way to the Havel River in the west and including the Ku'damm within its boundaries. This is where the majority of Berlin's hotels are, along with Bahnhof Zoo (the main train station), the Europa-Center, and such well-known theaters as the Deutsche Oper, Schiller-Theater, and Theater des Westens. The precinct takes its name from Sophie Charlotte, wife of Prussian King Friedrich I. Schloss Charlottenburg (Charlottenburg Palace), built for Sophie Charlotte, is here with a cluster of fine museums nearby—including the Ägyptisches Museum (Egyptian Museum), with its famous bust of Nefertiti, and the Bröhan Museum, with its art nouveau collection.

Savignyplatz   Actually a part of Charlottenburg and just a 5-minute walk north of the Ku'damm, Savignyplatz is a pleasant square lined with restaurants and bars, many with outdoor seating. It's a great place to relax over a beer. Radiating out from Savignyplatz, only a few minutes' walk away, are a number of other streets important for all you nightlife bloodhounds, including Kantstrasse, Schlüterstrasse, and Bleibtreustrasse.

Berlin-Mitte (eastern Berlin)   The cultural and political heart of pre–World War II Berlin, Berlin-Mitte fell on the eastern side of the wall after the city's division. It was here that Berlin began in the 13th century, when two settlements called Berlin and Cölln sprang up on opposite banks of the river. Included in this district—known as the First Precinct—is Museumsinsel (Museum Island) with its famous museums, the restored Nikolaiviertel (Nikolai Quarter), and the boulevard Unter den Linden. Unfortunately, both the war and

---

IMPRESSIONS

The two principles of Berlin architecture appear to me to be these. On the house-tops, wherever there is a convenient place, put up the figure of a man; he is best placed standing on one leg. Wherever there is room on the ground, put either a circular group of busts on pedestals . . . or else the colossal figure of a man killing, about to kill, or having killed a beast . . . a dragon is the correct thing, but if that is beyond the artist, he may content himself with a lion or a pig.
—LEWIS CARROLL, 1867

postwar years took their toll on this historic area: What wasn't bombed during the war was largely destroyed later under Communist rule, including Berlin's former royal palace, which had been the home of the Prussian monarchy for centuries; the ancient buildings on Fischerinsel, which were replaced by high-rises; and the old Academy of Architecture designed by Schinkel. Fortunately, those edifices along Unter den Linden have been painstakingly restored and Berlin-Mitte remains Berlin's most historically significant precinct.

Tiergarten Tiergarten, which literally means "animal garden," refers to both Tiergarten park and the precinct of the same name. Sandwiched in between Charlottenburg and Berlin-Mitte, it encompasses a residential district called Hansaviertel (Hansa Quarter), the Zoologischer Garten (Berlin Zoo), the Reichstag (Parliament), Bauhaus-Archiv, the Philharmonie (home to the Berlin Philharmonic Orchestra), and a cluster of museums such as the Neue Nationalgalerie (New National Gallery), the Kunstgewerbe Museum (Museum of Applied Arts), and the Musikinstrumenten Museum (Museum of Musical Instruments). By the end of the century, several museums now in Dahlem will move to new homes in this district, making it the center for European art in western Berlin.

Hansaviertel Stretching along the northern edge of Tiergarten park, the Hansaviertel (Hansa Quarter) is a residential district of housing projects—from one-family dwellings to apartment buildings. Each building was designed by a different architect as the result of an international gathering in 1957 by 48 leading architects from 13 countries, including Alvar Aalto, Walter Gropius, and Le Corbusier.

Dahlem Once its own village and now a part of Zehlendorf precinct, Dahlem is home of western Berlin's Free University (formed after World War II, when the division of Berlin gave the city's only university to the eastern sector), the Max-Planck Institute, and, most important for visitors, a number of fine museums. These include the world-renowned Gemäldegalerie (Picture Gallery), with its European masterpieces from the 13th to 18th centuries, the Skulpturengalerie (Sculpture Gallery), the Museum für Volkerkunde (Ethnological Museum), Museum für Deutsche Volkskunde (Museum of German Ethnology), the Museum für Indische Kunst (Museum of Indian Art), and the Museum für Ostasiatische Kunst (Museum of Far Eastern Art). After the Gemäldegalerie and the Skulpturengalerie move to new homes in Tiergarten by the end of this decade, Dahlem will showcase Berlin's collection of non-European art.

Spandau Located on the western edge of the city at the juncture of the Spree and Havel rivers, Spandau is older than Berlin itself, but only by five years. An independent city until engulfed by Greater Berlin in 1920, Spandau retains its own flavor and character, including an Altstadt (Old Town) and an Italian-style citadel dating from the 16th century. Notable for its Christmas market in December, shops in the Altstadt, and its woods and water recreation, Spandau is a popular destination for both Berliners and visitors alike.

Kreuzberg Once a poor neighborhood with a high concentration of immigrants and students drawn by the low rents, Kreuzberg has since become rather hip and is the scene of much of Berlin's counterculture. The most densely populated precinct of western Berlin, one-third of its inhabitants stem from Turkey, Greece, and former Yugoslavia. About 65% of its apartments were built around the turn of the century. It's fun to visit the Turkish Market, held here every Tuesday and Friday afternoon. Also in Kreuzberg is the Berlin Museum, depicting the city's history; the Martin-Gropius-Bau with its gallery of modern art; and the Museum Haus am Checkpoint Charlie, which documents the history of the Wall and nonviolent revolutions around the world.

Museumsinsel   Located in the middle of the Spree River, this island is the home of Berlin's oldest museum complex. Begun in the 1820s and under East German jurisdiction after the war, this amazing collection of museums includes the outstanding Pergamon Museum with its architectural treasures.

Alexanderplatz   Originally serving as a market for oxen, Alexanderplatz became the heart of the East German capital during Communist rule. A large, rather sterile square, Alexanderplatz is dominated by a soaring TV tower. There's also a large S-Bahn and U-Bahn station here. One of the few old buildings remaining from prewar Berlin is the Rathaus on the square's south side, built in 1930 and now serving as the home for Berlin's central government.

Nikolaiviertel   Located just southwest of Alexanderplatz and bordered by the Spree River, Nikolaiviertel has been re-created to show what Berlin might have looked like centuries ago. It's named after the Nikolaikirche (St. Nicholas's Church), Berlin's oldest church, which rises from the middle of the quarter. Grouped around the church are about 30 town houses with 788 apartments (some with ceilings as high as 12 feet), as well as a number of restaurants, pubs, and shops—all faithfully reconstructed down to the minutest historical details.

Köpenick   Located in eastern Berlin at the southeast end of the city, Köpenick dates back to the 9th century and still has a rather provincial atmosphere. An important industrial area, it is home primarily to the working class. The 17th-century Köpenick Palace now houses the Kunstgewerbe Museum (Museum of Applied Arts). With its wealth of woods and lakes (including the Müggelsee, one of Berlin's largest lakes), it's a pleasant place for a stroll.

2. GETTING AROUND

Berlin has an excellent public transportation network, including buses, the U-Bahn (underground), and the S-Bahn (overhead inner-city railway). All are run by Berlin's **BVG** (tel. 752 70 20 or 256 24 62), the largest public transportation department in Germany. You can ride farther for less money in Berlin than anywhere else in Germany. In fact, even a trip to Potsdam is included in Berlin's transportation network, costing only 3 DM ($1.85) one way, the normal price of a ticket. If you have any questions regarding public transportation throughout Berlin, drop by the BVG information booth located in front of Bahnhof Zoo on Hardenbergerplatz. It's open daily from 8am to 8pm and in addition to giving information on how to get where, it also sells the various tickets described below, including the 24-hour ticket and the Sammelkarte. It also has a free map of Berlin's S- and U-Bahn system.

BY PUBLIC TRANSPORTATION   One of the best things about Berlin's public transportation system is that the same ticket can be used throughout Greater Berlin for every branch of it, including the S-Bahn, U-Bahn, and buses. Furthermore, you can use the same ticket to transfer from one line to another, anywhere in Greater Berlin. But even better is the fact that your ticket is good for up to 2 hours, allowing transfers, round trips, or even interruptions of your trip (you could, for example, go to Spandau for an hour or so and then return with the same ticket, as long as your entire trip is completed in two hours).

An important thing to remember is that prices are expected to rise during the lifetime of this book. If you have any questions, contact the BVG.

At press time, a single ticket costs 3.20 DM ($2); children between 6 and 14 pay 2.10 DM ($1.30). If you're traveling only a short distance (only six stops by bus or three stops by subway), you can purchase a **Kurzstreckenkarte** for 2.10 DM ($1.30) for adults and 1.60 ($1) for children. In addition, there's also a special **Ku'damm Ticket** costing only 1.50 DM (95¢), valid for travel on all buses that traverse the Ku'damm between Wittenbergplatz and Rathenauplatz.

If you plan on traveling frequently by bus or subway, you're much better off buying a **Sammelkarte,** a card with four tickets at discounted rates. A normal Sammelkarte costs 11 DM ($6.85); a Sammelkarte with short-distance tickets costs 6.70 DM ($4.20). You can also buy a 24-hour ticket, which costs 12 DM ($7.50) for adults and 6 DM ($3.75) for children. It's good for trips throughout Greater Berlin, including trips to Potsdam. And if you're going to be in Berlin for 6 days from Monday through Saturday, you might wish to purchase a 6-day ticket for 30 DM ($18.75).

You can purchase tickets from automatic machines at all S- and U-Bahn stations, from bus drivers, and even at some machines located at bus stops. Some of the larger stations, such as Zoologischer Garten at Bahnhof Zoo, have ticket windows staffed with personnel. You can also purchase tickets from the BVG kiosk in front of Bahnhof Zoo. Since the automatic machines are in German only and can be quite confusing, you may be best off heading for the BVG kiosk or a ticket window to purchase one or more Sammelkarte.

By U-Bahn & S-Bahn   The fastest and easiest way to get around Berlin, especially during rush hour, is by underground (U-Bahn) and the inner-city rail system (S-Bahn). Trains run from about 4am until midnight or 1am, except on Saturday night, when they run about an hour later. Two subway lines, the U-1 (the major east-west axis) and the U-9 (the north-south axis) run all night on Friday and Saturday nights, with departures from Bahnhof Zoologischer Garten approximately every half hour. Some stations have ticket windows where you can purchase a single ticket or Sammelkarte; most, however, have only automatic vending machines for tickets. In any case, you must validate your ticket yourself at one

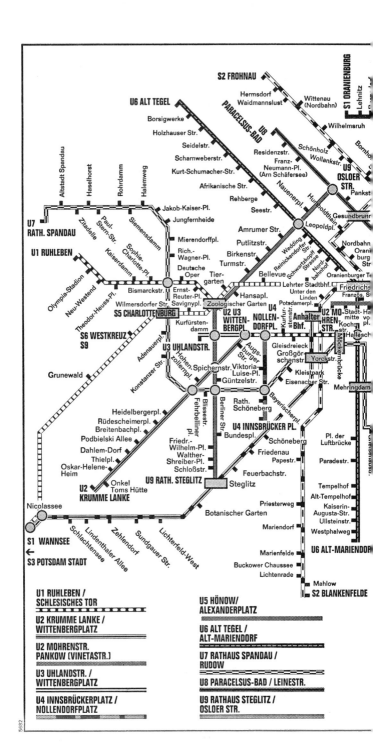

U-BAHN & S-BAHN

S7 AHRENSFELDE

S8 BERNAU
Zepernick
Röntgental

S85 S86 BUCH
Karow

S86 BLANKENBURG

Hohen Neuendorf
Bergfelde
Schönfließ
Mühlenbeck-Mönchmühle

Pankow-Heinersdorf

nkow

U2 PANKOW (VINETASTR.)
Schönhauser Allee
Hohenschönhausen

S75 WARTENBURG
Geherenseestr.

Raoul-Wallenberg-Str.
Mehrower Allee

U5 HÜNOW
Louis-Lewin-Str.
Marzahn
Poelchaustr.
Hellersdorf
Cottbusser Pl.
Gottkauer Str.
Kaulsdorf Nord

S5 STRAUS-BERG NORD

Strausberg Stadt
Hegermühle

Itastr.
Bernauer Str.
Rosenthalerpl.

Eberswalder Str.
Senefelderpl.
Rosa-Luxemborg-Pl.
Ernst-Thälmann-Park
Prenzlauer Allee
Landsberger Allee
Schillingstr.
Strausbergerpl.
Weberwiese
Rathaus Friedrichshain
Samariterstr.
Magdalenenstr.
Storkower Str.
Springpfuhl
Friedrichsfelde Ost.
Friedrichsfelde
Wuhletal
Biesdorf
Biesdorf Nord

Strausberg
Petershagen Nord
Fredersdorf
Neuenhagen
Hoppegarten
Mahlsdorf
Kaulsdorf

S7, S75, U5 ALEXANDERPL.
Jannowitzbr.

Frankfurter Allee
OSTKREUZ
S2 LICHTENBERG
Tierpark
Rummelsburg

Eisterwerdaer Pl.
Biesdorf-Süd

inster-str.
Hacke sche
Klosterstr.
Märkisches Museum

Heinrich-Heine-Moritzpl.
Str.

U1 SCHLESISCHES TOR
Hauptbahnhof
Warschauer S.
Betriebsbahnhof Rummelsburg
Karlshorst
Wuhlheide
Köpenick
Hirschgarten

Kottbusser Tor
Görlitzer Bhf.

Baumschulenweg
Treptower Park Plänterwald
Oberspree

Köpenick
Hirschgarten
Friedrichshagen

Kottbusser Damm

Schöneweide
Adlershof
S85 SPINDLERS-FELD

S9 S10 FLUGHAFEN BERLIN-SCHÖNEFELD

Altglienicke
Grunberg Allee
Grünberg Allee

S8 GRÜNAU
Eichwalde
Zeuthen
Wildau

S6 KÖNIGS WUSTERHAUSEN

Rahnsdorf
Wilhelmshagen
S3 ERKNER

idstern

Hermannpl.
Rath. Neukölln
Karl-Marx-Str.
Neukölln

ddinstr.

Grenz Allee
Blaschko Allee
Parchimer Allee

U8 LEINESTR.

Britz-Süd
Johannisthaler Ch.
Lipschitz Allee
Wutzky Allee
Zwickauer Damm
RUDOW U7

S5 – CHARLOTTENBURG/STRAUSBERG NORD

S6 – WESTKREUZ/KÖNIGS WUSTERHAUSEN

S7 – ALEXANDERPLATZ/AHRENSFELDE

S75 – ALEXANDERPLATZ/WARTENBURG

S8 – BERNAU/GRÜNAU

S86 – BUCH & BLANKENBURG/SPINDELERSFELD

S9 – FLUGHAFEN BERLIN-SCHÖNEFELD/WESTKREUZ

S10 – FLUGHAFEN BERLIN-SCHÖNEFELD/BIRKENWERDER

S1 WANNSEE / ORIENIENBURG

S2 SCHÖNHOLZ/BLANKENFELDE

S3 POTSDAM STADT/ERKNER

of the little red boxes before boarding the train. This is the honor system—and if you're caught without a ticket you'll be charged a 60-DM ($37.50) fine.

To board the right U- or S-Bahn line for your destination, you have to know that line's final stop. If, for example, you're in Bahnhof Zoologischer Garten and you wish to board the U-1 to Nollendorfplatz, you have to know that Nollendorfplatz is in the direction of Schlesisches Tor because you won't find Nollendorfplatz mentioned on any signs. If you board U-1 headed toward Ruhleben, you'll end up going the wrong direction. Refer to the subway map in this book or the subway map in all stations to determine the direction you need to go. It's not complicated, but Berlin has yet to figure out that everything would be a lot easier if directional signs included a list of stations along the way in addition to the final stop.

By Bus With more than 170 routes, buses are the most widely used mode of transportation in Berlin. They are easy to use, and many are double-deckers, affording great views of the city. Some of the newer buses even have lighted panels at the front of the bus, clearly displaying the next stop. In any case, a list of all stops is posted in each bus as well as at bus stops. One of my favorite buses is no. 100, which travels around the clock from Bahnhof Zoo to Alexanderplatz, passing the Reichstag building and Brandenburger Tor and traveling the length of Unter den Linden along the way. It's a great way to travel to eastern Berlin's most important sites since you can see much more on a bus than via S-Bahn. You may also wish to take advantage of the buses that run along the Ku'damm (nos. 109, 119, and 129), which cost only 1 DM (60¢) for short distances between Wittenbergplatz and Adenauerplatz. If you have any questions regarding which bus to take or where a bus stop is located, drop by the BVG booth at Bahnhof Zoo.

You can purchase only a single ticket from the bus driver, or use your Sammelkarte (described above). If you're transferring, simply show the bus driver your ticket. Apart from the normal day services, there are also 34 Nachtbusse (night buses, marked with an "N" before their number) that run all night, most from Bahnhof Zoo. You can pick up a brochure of their routes and schedules from the BVG booth at Bahnhof Zoo. In summer, there are special excursion buses marked with a triangle that make express trips from Theodor-Heuss Platz to recreation areas at Grunewald, from Wannsee station to Pfaueninsel, and from Nikolassee station to Wannsee Beach.

BY TAXI If you need a taxi, you can find one at the many taxi stands in the city, or you can telephone one of several taxi companies: 6902, 26 10 26, 69 10 01, 21 01 01, or 21 02 02. The meter starts at 3.60 DM ($2.25), plus 1.79 DM ($1.10) per kilometer. There's an extra 20 Pfennig (12¢) per kilometer surcharge on fares from 11pm to 6am, Sunday and holidays. Luggage costs 1 DM (60¢) extra.

BY CAR You don't need a car for trips within Berlin: Public transportation is excellent, traffic jams are horrendous, and being burdened with a car means having to find a parking space (for a list of parking garages in the city center near the Ku'damm, consult Section 1, "Orientation: Arriving," above). However, you may wish to rent a car for forays to the outskirts of town or destinations such as Potsdam.

You'll find driving in the outskirts of Berlin no more complicated than elsewhere in Germany. Driving is on the right side of the street, and standard international road signs are used. Be sure to obey the speed limit, which is 100 kilometers per hour (60 m.p.h.) on the expressways surrounding Berlin.

If you wish to rent a car, you'll need a valid driver's license (your U.S. license is fine) or an international driving license. Third-party insurance is compulsory in Germany. Foreign visitors, with the exception of most European drivers, must either present their international insurance certificate (Green Card) or take out third-party insurance.

There are several well-known car-rental agencies in Berlin. **Avis** has a counter at Tegel Airport (tel. 030/410 13 148), as well as an office near Bahnhof Zoo at Budapester Strasse 43 (tel. 030/261 18 81). The latter office is open Monday to Friday from 7am to 6pm and Saturday from 8am to 1pm. Prices here start at 165 DM ($103) for one day in an Opel Corsa Swing, including 15% sales tax and unlimited mileage.

Hertz, another big name, also has a counter at Tegel Airport (tel. 030/410 13 315) and at Budapester Strasse 39 (tel. 030/261 10 53). The downtown office is open Monday to Friday from 7am to 6:30pm, Saturday from 8am to 4pm, and Sunday from 9am to 2pm. Its rates for a Ford Fiesta or Opel Corsa start at 165 DM ($103.10) for one day, including 15% sales tax and unlimited mileage.

Keep in mind, however, that there are often special promotions with cheaper prices than those given above, including weekend rates. It pays to shop around.

BY BICYCLE You'll probably want to forgo the experience of riding a bicycle in the heart of Berlin with its traffic-clogged streets, but it is a fast and pleasant way to see other parts of the city. It's important to know that you're allowed to take bicycles onto certain compartments of both the U- and S-Bahn for an extra 2 DM ($1.25). Thus, you may wish to rent a cycle, take the subway to the outskirts, and then begin your ride from there. Note that you cannot take your bike on the S- or U-Bahn during rush hour, which is Monday to Friday before 9am and again in the afternoon between 2 and 5:30pm.

Berlin by Bike, Möckernstrasse 92 (tel. 216 91 77), is located in Kreuzberg near the Yorckstrasse and Möckernbrücke U-Bahn stations (from the Ku'damm, you can also reach the shop by taking bus no. 119). Rental prices for bikes begin at 20 DM ($12.50) for one day, 50 DM ($31.25) for three days, and 85 DM ($53.10) for one week. Students receive a 15% discount. Mountain bikes, racers, and tandems are also available. The staff gives advice on sightseeing and dispenses a free map with recommended routes. It's open Monday to Saturday from 10am to 2pm.

 BERLIN

This section is designed to make your stay in Berlin as problem free as possible. However, keep in mind that the information below may have changed by the time you arrive. The concierge at your hotel may be able to help you if problems arise; another invaluable source is the Berlin tourist information office in the **Europa-Center** (tel. 262 60 31).

Airports   Berlin has three major airports. If you're arriving from North America or Western Europe, you'll probably arrive at Tegel Airport in western Berlin. If you're arriving from the Soviet Union or Eastern Europe, you're likely to land at Schönefeld Airport. Berlin-Tempelhof serves flights from Europe and Germany. For more information, refer to the beginning of this chapter under "Orientation."

American Express   The office is located in the center of town, across the plaza from the Gedächtniskirche at Kurfürstendamm 11 (tel. 882 75 75). Located on the first floor (the entrance is not directly on the Ku'damm but around the corner on Breitscheidplatz), it's open Mon–Fri 9am–5:30pm, and on Sat 9am–noon.

Area Code   The telephone area code for Berlin is 030 if you're calling from within Germany, 30 if you're calling from outside Germany.

Bookstores   Kiepert is a well-known bookstore within a 10-minute walk from Bahnhof Zoo, near the Technical University at the corner of Knesebeckstrasse and Hardenbergstrasse (tel. 311 00 9). It has maps and travel books and is open Mon–Fri 9am–6:30pm and Sat 9am–2pm. The nearest U-Bahn station is Ernst-Reuter-Platz.

Even more extensive is the selection offered by the British Book Shop, Mauerstrasse 83–84 (tel. 238 46 80), located just a couple minutes' walk from Museum Haus am Checkpoint Charlie near the Kochstrasse or Stadtmitte U-Bahn stations. It stocks English-language books on all subjects, including fiction, travel, and books on Berlin. It's open Mon–Fri 9am–6:30pm and Sat 9am–2pm (to 4pm the first Sat of the month).

Business Hours   Downtown businesses and shops are open Mon–Fri 9 or 10am–6 or 6:30pm and Sat 9am–1 or 2pm. On the first Sat of the month (called *langer Samstag*), shops remain open until 4 or 6pm. In addition, some shops remain open later on Thursdays till 8:30pm.

Banks are open Mon–Fri 9am–1 or 3pm, with slightly later hours one or two days of the week depending on the bank.

Most bars stay open until 2am; some remain open until 6am. Refer to Chapter 9, "Berlin Nights," for more information.

Car Rentals   See Section 2, "Getting Around: By Car," above.

Climate   Refer to Section 2, "When to Go," in Chapter 2 for information on Berlin's climate and how to pack accordingly.

Currency   For a brief description of Germany's currency, the Deutsche Mark (DM), see Section 1, "Information, Entry Requirements, and Money," in Chapter 2.

Currency Exchange   You can exchange money at any bank or at the American Express office (see listing above). There's an exchange counter at Tegel Airport open daily 8am–10pm. You can also exchange money at the Wertheim and KaDeWe department stores, and at major hotels, but the best exchange rate is offered at banks.

Since banks are open only Mon–Fri 9am–1 or 3pm—with slightly later hours one or two days of the week depending on the bank—your best bet if you need to exchange money outside these hours is at the **Deutsche Verkehrs-Kredit-Bank** (tel. 881 71 17), an exchange office at Bahnhof Zoo. It's open Mon–Sat 7:30am–10pm and Sun and holidays 8am–7pm.

The Deutsche Verkehrs-Kredit-Bank will also accept major credit cards for cash, including DC, MC, VISA (for American Express, see listing above); bring your passport. International credit cards will also be accepted at various cash machines throughout Berlin.

Dentists and Doctors The Berlin tourist office in the Europa-Center has a list of English-speaking doctors and dentists in Berlin. Your embassy can also supply you with information regarding medical care in Berlin. If you need a doctor in the middle of the night or in an emergency, call 31 00 31, in western Berlin, 280 91 28 in eastern Berlin.

Documents Required The only document needed for travel to Berlin is a valid passport. No visas are necessary for travel to Berlin. For more information, refer to Section 1, "Information, Entry Requirements, and Money," in Chapter 2.

Driving Rules See Section 2, "Getting Around: By Car," earlier in this chapter for information on driving in Berlin.

Drugstores Called *Apotheken* in Germany, drugstores have normal business hours just like any shop. However, there are a few that stay open all night and on the weekends and holidays. All drugstores post the addresses of those that are open. Otherwise, to find out which pharmacies are open, call **11 41.**

Electricity Berlin's electrical current is 220 volts AC, 50 cycles, which is different from the American current of 110 volts, 60 cycles. In addition, plugs are different from those in the United States, so you'll need an adapter if you're bringing a hair dryer, electric razor, or other electrical appliance.

Embassies and Consulates The **U.S. Consulate** is in Dahlem at Clayallee 170 (tel. 832 40 87). It's open Mon–Fri 8:30am–noon for Americans who have lost their passports, while its visa section is open Mon–Fri 8:30–10:30am.

The **British Consulate,** located just north of the Ku'damm at Uhlandstrasse 7-8 (tel. 309 52 93 or 309 52 92), is open Mon–Fri 9am–noon and 2–4pm (visa section, only in the morning).

The **Canadian Consulate,** located at Friedrichstrasse 95 in Berlin-Mitte (tel. 261 11 61), is open Mon–Fri 1:30–3pm, with extra morning hours for visa matters. Call first to make sure the department you need is open.

The **Australian Consulate** is at Markgrafenstrasse 46 in Berlin-Mitte (tel. 392 21 09 or 392 15 58), open Mon–Fri 9am–noon and 2–4pm.

Emergencies Throughout Berlin, the emergency number for police is **110;** for fires it's **112.** If you need an ambulance, call **112** in western Berlin, **115** in eastern Berlin. For an emergency doctor, dial **31 00 31** in western Berlin, 280 91 28 in eastern Berlin. To find out which pharmacies are open nights, call **11 41.**

Eyeglasses If you need a pair of eyeglasses, visit the opticians in the area of the Ku'damm and Tauentzienstrasse. Apollo Optik, at Kurfürstendamm 40-41 (tel. 882 52 58), is open Mon–Friday 9:30am–6:30pm, and Sat 9am–2pm (to 4pm first Sat of the month). It's best to carry your prescription with you from home.

Hairdressers and Barbers Many first-class hotels have beauty salons and barbershops, which may be your best bet for an English-speaking specialist.

Holidays For a list of Germany's holidays, see Section 2, "Where to Go," in Chapter 2.

Hospitals If you need to go to a hospital, the ambulance service will deliver you to the one best suited to your case. In western Berlin, summon an ambulance by dialing **112;** in eastern Berlin, dial **115.** Otherwise, if you wish to check into a hospital and it's not an emergency, contact your embassy for recommendations.

Information Locations of the Verkehrsamt Berlin (tourist office) branches are given in Section 1, "Orientation," above. For the addresses and telephone numbers of the German National Tourist Organization in the United States and other countries, see Section 1, "Information, Entry Requirements, and Money," in Chapter 2.

Language See the Appendix for useful phrases. See Section 2, "Food and Drink," in Chapter 1 for a description of German cuisine. If you wish to learn German in more depth, *German for Travellers* published by Berlitz is quite useful.

Laundry and Dry Cleaning Some hotels and pensions provide laundry and/or dry-cleaning service. If not, ask the staff where there is a convenient laundry. There's a Wasch Center near the center of town at Leibnizstrasse 72 (on the corner of Kantstrasse), and another at Uhlandstrasse 53 (between Pariser Strasse and Düsseldorfer Strasse). Hours for both locations are 6am–10:30pm. A wash cycle with detergent is 6 DM ($3.70), 1 DM (60¢) for a spin, and 1 DM for a dryer.

Libraries The Amerika-Gedenkbibliothek, Blücherplatz 1 in Kreuzberg (tel. 6905-0), was founded to commemorate the blockade and Berlin airlift in 1948. Located near the Hallesches Tor U-Bahn station, it's open Tues–Sat 11am–7pm and Mon 4–7pm. In addition, the Amerika-Haus, located at Hardenbergstrasse 20 (tel. 31 10 99 10) next to Bahnhof Zoo, houses a small library and is open Mon, Wed, and Fri 11:30am–5:30pm and Tues and Thurs 11:30am–8pm. In both cases, out-of-town visitors may read books only inside the library.

Liquor Laws Compared to U.S. liquor laws, Germany's seem rather liberal. As in many countries in Europe, drinking beer or wine with a meal is a part of the culture—even teenagers receive a glass at home. The minimum drinking age is 16 if accompanied by parents; 18 if alone. However, laws against drunk driving in Germany are strictly enforced and respected. In western Berlin, don't drink more than two beers if you intend to drive; on the eastside, the allowed alcohol limit amounts to less than one beer.

Lost Property Berlin's general-property office is at Platz der Luftbrücke 6 (tel. 699 364 44). For property lost on public transportation services, check the BVG lost-and-found at Lorenzweg 5, Tempelhof (tel. 751 80 21).

Luggage Storage There's luggage storage at both Tegel Airport and at the main train station, Bahnhof Zoologischer Garten, where you'll find lockers.

Mail Mailboxes are yellow in Germany. Airmail letters to North America cost 1.65 DM ($1.05) for the first 5 grams, while postcards cost 1.05 DM (65¢). On the average it takes anywhere from 5 to 7 days for an airmail letter to reach North America. For nonlocal mail, including air mail, be sure to use the *Andere Richtungen* slot of the mailbox. Letters up to 20 grams sent anywhere in Germany and much of Europe cost 1 DM (60¢); postcards require a 60-Pfennig (35¢) stamp.

The **post office** in Bahnhof Zoo is open 24 hours a day for mail, telephone calls, and telegrams. You can have your mail sent here in care of Hauptpostlagernd, Postamt 120 Bahnhof Zoo, 10623 Berlin 12 (tel. 313 97 99 for inquiries). You can also have your mail sent to you via the American Express office at Kurfürstendamm 11 (tel. 882 75 75), a service that is free if you have American Express traveler's checks or an American Express card. Otherwise, the service costs a steep 2 DM ($1.25) *per inquiry*.

If you want to mail a package, you'll have to go to one of the city's larger post offices: There's one at Goethestrasse 2-3, and another at Marburger Strasse 12-13, which is near the Europa-Center. Both are open Mon–Fri 8am–6pm and Sat 8am–1pm. Both sell cardboard boxes—complete with string and tape—which come in five sizes ranging in price from 1.10 DM (70¢) to 3.60 DM ($2.25).

In the eastern part of Berlin, there's a post office open 24 hours at the Hauptbahnhof, Strasse der Pariser Kommune 8-10.

Maps   Refer to Section 1, "Orientation: Maps," above.

Money   For a brief description of Germany's currency, the Deutsche Mark (DM), see Section 1, "Information, Entry Requirements, and Money," in Chapter 2.

Newspapers and Magazines   *checkpoint Berlin,* an English-language city magazine, is published monthly with listings of current concerts, exhibits, restaurant reviews, news items, and other information of interest to visitors to Berlin. There are no English-language newspapers published in Berlin, but the *International Herald Tribune* and *USA Today,* as well as news magazines *Time* and *Newsweek,* are available at newsstands such as Europa Presse Center, located on the ground floor of the Europa-Center (tel. 216 30 03) and open daily 9am–11pm.

If you read German, Berlin dailies are the *Berliner Morgenpost, Berliner Zeitung,* and *BZ.* National dailies include *Frankfurter Allgemeine Zeitung, Süddeutsche Zeitung,* and *Die Welt. Der Spiegel* and *Stern* are weekly news magazines.

Photographic Needs   Film, batteries, and other photographic necessities are available at Wertheim and KaDeWe department stores, described in Chapter 8, "Berlin Shopping." In addition, Photo Huber is conveniently located in the Europa-Center (tel. 262 46 66) and provides color print development in 1 hour. It's open Mon–Fri 10am–6:30pm (to 8:30pm on Thurs), and Sat 10am–2pm (to 4pm on the first Sat of the month).

Police   The emergency number for police throughout Berlin is **110.**

Post Office   See "Mail," above.

Radio and TV   For radio programs in English, tune into 90.2 FM (87.6 on cable) for the BBC; 87.9 AM (94 on cable) for the American Forces Network; and 98.8 FM (102.85 on cable) for the British Forces Broadcasting Services.

As for television, some hotels offer cable TV with CNN news broadcasts from the United States, a sports channel in English, Super Channel with programs from the United Kingdom, and MTV, a music channel.

Restrooms   If you ask for the "bathroom" in Germany, your host is going to think it strange that you wish to take a bath in his home or restaurant. A restroom in Germany is called a *Toilette* and is often labeled *WC* (which stands for water closet) in public places. Women's toilets are often marked with an *F* for *Frauen* or *D* for

Damen, while men's are identified with an *H* for *Herren* or *M* for *Männer.*

In the center of Berlin, there are public facilities at Wittenbergplatz and near the Europa-Center on Tauentzienstrasse. Other places to look for facilities include fast-food outlets, department stores, hotels, restaurants, and pubs. If there's an attendant, it's customary to tip 30–50 Pfennig (20¢–30¢).

Safety   Berlin is a safe city, particularly in places frequented by tourists such as the Ku'damm. However, as in any unfamiliar city, it's wise to stay alert and be aware of your immediate surroundings, as every society has its criminals. Avoid parks after dark. Wear a money belt and keep a close eye on your possessions. Be particularly careful with cameras, purses, and wallets, all favorite targets of thieves and pickpockets. This will minimize the possibility of becoming the victim of a crime. Keep your valuables in a safe-deposit box at your hotel.

Germany has recently seen a number of violent acts committed against minorities by right-wing extremists. Although Berlin has remained relatively untouched by these crimes, it would be wise to avoid the outskirts of former East Berlin (an area of little touristic interest) if this is of concern to you.

Shoe Repairs   For quick service on shoe repairs, head for the Wertheim department store, 231 Kurfürstendamm, or either Karstadt or Hertie department stores, both on Wilmersdorfer Strasse, where you'll find a Mister Minit counter specializing in repairs.

Taxes   Germany's 15% governmental tax is included in the price of restaurants, hotels, and goods in Germany. On many goods, however, tourists can obtain a refund of the Value-Added Tax (see Chapter 8, "Berlin Shopping," for information on how to obtain a refund). There is no airport departure tax.

Taxis   Refer to Section 2, "Getting Around," above for information on taxis and telephone numbers.

Telephone   Berlin's telephone system is not much different from that in the United States when it comes to a dial tone and busy tone, but it does differ in the amount of telephone digits. Some telephone numbers have four digits, others may have seven or eight. Area codes in Germany are often enclosed by parentheses—such as (030) for Berlin—and the rest of the digits are simply grouped into twos or threes. Thus, a seven-digit number in Berlin would be written (030) 881 47 68. If you come across a number with a dash, the number following the dash is the extension number, which you can reach directly simply by dialing the entire number.

Local telephone calls cost 30 Pfennig (20¢) for the first 3 minutes and allow you to telephone throughout Berlin. To make sure you don't get cut off in the middle of a conversation, insert more coins—unused coins will be returned to you at the end of the call. If you want to make an international call, look for phone booths with the green "International" sign, and make sure you have a handful of change. Otherwise, you can purchase a telephone card, available at post offices. They come in values of 12 DM ($7.50) and 50 DM ($31.25). Simply insert them into the telephone slot. Telephone cards are becoming so popular in Germany, that many public telephones no longer accept coins. The 12-DM card gives you approximately 40 minutes of local telephone calls; the 50-DM card is useful for long-distance calls.

It's much easier to make long-distance calls from a post office, where you can also send telegrams. The main post office at Bahnhof Zoo (West Berlin's main train station) is open 24 hours. It costs 12.60 DM ($7.85) to make a 3-minute long-distance phone call to the United States. Try to avoid making telephone calls from your hotel room—a surcharge added to the bill may double or even triple the rate.

Time Berlin is 6 hours ahead of Eastern standard time in New York, 7 hours ahead of Chicago, and 9 hours ahead of Los Angeles. Berlin operates on Central European time—except that it's officially 6 minutes and 22 seconds behind Central European time. Germany goes on and off daylight saving time at slightly different dates than the United States, with the result that Berlin is 7 hours ahead of New York for short periods in spring and fall. As this can affect rail schedules, if you're traveling during spring or fall, make sure you double-check times.

Tipping Since a service charge is usually included in hotel and restaurant bills, you are not obliged to tip. However, it is customary to round up restaurant bills to the nearest mark; the check is handed directly to the waiter or waitress rather than left on the table. If your bill is 14 DM, tell the waitress "15 DM"; and if you hand her a 20-DM note, you'll receive 5 DM in change. If your meal costs more than 20 DM ($12.50), most Germans will add a 10% tip. For taxi drivers, it's customary to tip a mark. Tip hairdressers or barbers 10%. Porters receive 2 DM ($1.25) per bag.

Water Although the water is technically safe to drink in Berlin, take your cue from the Germans, who almost never drink their tap water. Instead, they ask for bottled water, either carbonated or noncarbonated.

Weather For a recorded message on Berlin's weather and temperature (in German only), dial **1164.**

3. NETWORKS & RESOURCES

If you need additional information, contact the Berlin tourist information office or telephone one of the organizations below.

FOR STUDENTS Berlin's oldest university, now called Humboldt University, was founded in 1810. Unfortunately, after World War II, most departments and institutes of Humboldt fell within the Soviet Sector; and when some students were suspended for political reasons in 1948, teachers and students founded the Free University in West Berlin. Also in western Berlin is the University of Technology, located near Bahnhof Zoo.

Today, with a population of well over 100,000 students, Berlin is Germany's largest "university city." Berlin has student cafeterias with budget-priced meals (see Chapter 5, "Where to Eat in Berlin"); most museums offer student discounts. In addition, some theaters (such as the renowned Schiller-Theater) offer half-price discounts on unsold tickets to students on the night of the performance.

For student discounts, you'll need an International Student Identity Card. It's easiest to apply for the card before leaving home (refer to Section 5, "Tips for the Disabled, Seniors, Singles, Families, and Students," in Chapter 2), but if you've arrived in Berlin without one and can show proof of current student status, you can obtain one at **ARTU,** a travel agency located at Hardenbergstrasse 9 (tel. 31 04 66)—not far from Bahnhof Zoo. ARTU also offers discount plane fares around the world, as well as cheap train tickets to people under 26 years old; it's open Monday to Friday from 10am to 6pm (on Wednesday from 11am to 6pm), and on Saturday from 10am to 1pm.

FOR GAY MEN & WOMEN   Berlin has a very active alternative scene, with many different organizations for gay men and women. Kommunikations- und Beratungszentrum für Homosexuelle Männer und Frauen is a support group and counseling center for both gay men and women and is located at Kulmerstrasse 20 in Schöneberg. Call 215 90 90 for the Schwulenberatung (counseling for gay men) and 215 20 00 for Lesbenberatung (counseling for lesbians); hours are Monday, Tuesday, and Thursday from 4 to 8pm and Wednesday from 10am to 2pm.

FOR WOMEN   **Fraueninfothek Berlin,** Dircksenstrasse 47, Berlin-Mitte (tel. 030/233 64 63 or 282 39 80), is a women's information center run by and for women. The center, located near Alexanderplatz, provides sightseeing information, makes hotel reservations, recommends counseling centers sensitive to women's issues, and even gives advice on transportation routes and tips about restaurants and bars. If you need help or advice and don't know where to turn, this is the best place to start. It's open Tuesday through Saturday from 10am to 8pm.

Artemisia, Brandenburgische Strasse 18 (tel. 87 89 05), is a bright and cheery hotel open only to women and has a well-informed staff that can steer guests to organizations and events of interest to women. Extra Dry, Mommsenstrasse 34 (tel. 324 60 38), is a women-only café selling snacks and nonalcoholic beverages in a comfortable, friendly, and pleasant atmosphere. Refer to the accommodations (Chapter 4) and nightlife (Chapter 9) chapters for more information on these establishments.

IMPRESSIONS

It is distressing to see the multitude of soldiers here—to think of the nation's vitality going to feed 300,000 puppets in uniform. In the streets one's legs are in constant danger from officers' swords.
—GEORGE ELIOT, 1854

WHERE TO STAY IN BERLIN

Not surprisingly, your biggest daily expense will be for accommodations. Ever since Germany became reunified, the demand for rooms in Berlin has increased dramatically and some hotels responded by doubling their rates. Escalating real-estate prices have also affected hotel rates. Although Berlin is no longer the bargain it was, it still offers a wide range of accommodations for the budget traveler. What's more, most of its cheapest accommodations are in the heart of the city, conveniently located near subway stations, restaurants, and the city's many bars. The majority of hotels and pensions are clustered along and around the Ku'damm. Even those a bit farther from the Ku'damm are never more than a short bus or subway ride from Bahnhof Zoo.

Many of Berlin's cheaper hotels and pensions are small establishments, in what were once grand apartments. Many haven't changed over the decades. You'll find them on the upper floors of older buildings usually with no elevator. Generally speaking, the higher up your room, the cheaper it is, especially if it's a walk-up.

Your private room in Berlin is likely to contain a sink, as well as the usual bed, table, and chairs. Your room will be heated in winter, but you won't find any air conditioning: except for an occasional 2 weeks in August, it rarely gets hot enough to warrant it. Rooms are generally sparsely decorated, and rarely do they include such luxuries as telephones or televisions. If your room does have a telephone or television, you can bet you're paying extra for it. You will also pay more if you stay in a room with its own private shower and toilet (a WC or water closet). Bathtubs are generally even more expensive, simply because they are rare and are considered a luxury. If you're on a budget, therefore, request a room without private facilities. Unlike many European cities, in Berlin you do not have to pay extra to use the shower down the hall.

The hotels and pensions below are divided according to price, with the cheapest presented first, and listed by location. Most convenient is the area around the Ku'damm, which is close to Bahnhof Zoo, the Europa-Center, and Savignyplatz with its many restaurants and bars.

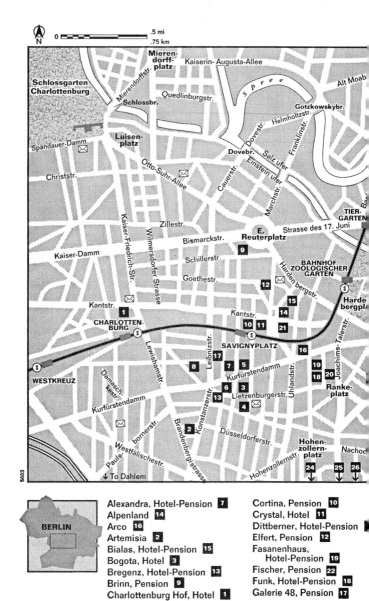

Alexandra, Hotel-Pension **7**	Cortina, Pension **10**
Alpenland **14**	Crystal, Hotel **11**
Arco **16**	Dittberner, Hotel-Pension **▶**
Artemisia **2**	Elfert, Pension **12**
Bialas, Hotel-Pension **15**	Fasanenhaus,
Bogota, Hotel **3**	Hotel-Pension **19**
Bregenz, Hotel-Pension **13**	Fischer, Pension **22**
Brinn, Pension **9**	Funk, Hotel-Pension **18**
Charlottenburg Hof, Hotel **1**	Galerie 48, Pension **17**

Note that in Germany, floors are counted beginning with the ground floor (which would be the American first floor) and go up to the first floor (the American second floor) and beyond. Directions from Tegel Airport or Bahnhof Zoo to each establishment are listed below, as well as from the nearest U-Bahn or S-Bahn station when applicable.

All rates given below include the 15% government tax and the service charge. Many hotels and pensions also include breakfast in their rates. This is usually a continental breakfast consisting of coffee

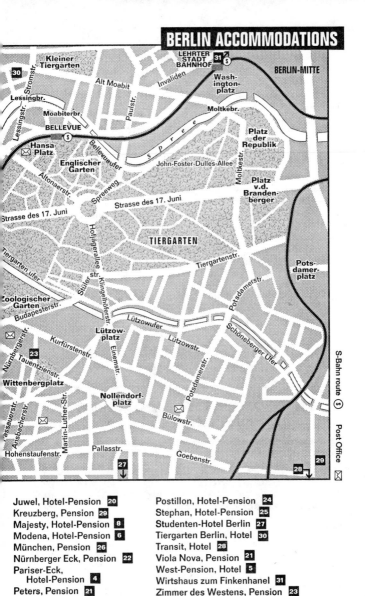

BERLIN ACCOMMODATIONS

BERLIN-MITTE

Juwel, Hotel-Pension **20**
Kreuzberg, Pension **29**
Majesty, Hotel-Pension **8**
Modena, Hotel-Pension **6**
München, Pension **26**
Nürnberger Eck, Pension **22**
Pariser-Eck,
  Hotel-Pension **4**
Peters, Pension **21**
Postillon, Hotel-Pension **24**
Stephan, Hotel-Pension **25**
Studenten-Hotel Berlin **27**
Tiergarten Berlin, Hotel **30**
Transit, Hotel **28**
Viola Nova, Pension **21**
West-Pension, Hotel **5**
Wirtshaus zum Finkenhanel **31**
Zimmer des Westens, Pension **23**

and rolls; a few of the more expensive accommodations offer all-you-can-eat breakfast buffets. Many visitors report that they eat so much for breakfast that it tides them over until an early dinner, saving on lunch. If you like a big breakfast, it makes sense to pay slightly more for a room that includes breakfast in its rates. On the other hand, if all you want is a quick cup of coffee at a coffee shop down the street, you may opt for one of the cheaper accommodations where breakfast is either optional or not offered at all.

Keep in mind that although every effort was made to be as

accurate as possible, the rates below may change during the lifetime of this book—that means they may go up. Prices quoted here should be taken as an approximation. Be sure to ask the current rate when making your reservation. It's best to first telephone and make your reservation, and follow up with a letter reconfirming your date of arrival, departure, and the price of your room.

In any case, it's always a good idea to reserve a room in advance. Rooms become scarce during the International Film Festival (end of February) and the Berlin Festival (running from the end of August to October), as well as during international conferences, fairs, and conventions—all frequently held in Berlin. And because Berlin is now one of the hottest new places to visit in Europe, even winters—once a slow period—are lively.

Remember, if the accommodations below are full, the tourist office (tel. 262 60 31) will find you a room for a 5-DM ($3.10) fee. If you wish to strike out on your own, you'll find many inexpensive hotels and pensions along the side streets radiating from the Ku'damm, especially at its eastern end near the Kaiser-Wilhelm Gedächtniskirche (Memorial Church). Other places to look include Savignyplatz and Bahnhof Charlottenburg. Unfortunately, eastside Berlin does not yet have an adequate number of inexpensive accommodations. Hopefully that will change in the near future.

1. DOUBLES FOR LESS THAN 96 DM ($60)

ON OR NEAR THE KU'DAMM & BAHNHOF ZOO

These hotels and pensions are within a 10-minute walk from the Ku'damm Bahnhof Zoo.

BIALAS, HOTEL-PENSION, Carmerstrasse 16, 10623 Berlin. Tel. 030/312 50 25 or 312 50 26. Telex 186506. 40 rms (2 with WC only, 10 with shower and WC). **S-Bahn:** Savignyplatz. **Directions:** A 6-minute walk from Bahnhof Zoo.
$ Rates (including continental breakfast): 65–70 DM ($40.60–$43.75) single without shower or WC, 75–80 DM ($46.85–$50) single with WC, 85–90 DM ($53.10–$56.25) single with shower and WC; 75–110 DM ($46.85–$68.75) double without shower or WC, 140–150 DM ($87.50–$93.75) double with shower and WC. Extra bed 35 DM ($21.85) in room without shower or WC, 50 DM ($31.25) in room with shower and WC. No credit cards.

There's a fine distinction between a hotel and pension, the Bialas calls itself both. It's located on a quiet, tree-lined street between Savignyplatz and Steinplatz. Reception is on the first floor. Rooms are simply furnished, but most are large, with prices varying according to floor. The cheapest are those on the fifth floor, quite a climb since there is no elevator.

CORTINA, PENSION, 140 Kantstrasse, 10623. Tel. 030/ 313 90 59. 21 rms (5 with shower). TEL **Bus:** 109 from Tegel Airport to Schlüterstrasse, then a 6-minute walk. **S-Bahn:** Savignyplatz, a 2-minute walk.

$ Rates (including continental breakfast): 60–65 DM ($37.50–$40.60) single without shower; 90–100 DM ($56.25–$62.50) double without shower, 110–120 DM ($68.75–$75) double with shower; 120–130 DM ($75–$81.25) triple without shower, 160–175 DM ($100–$109.35) triple with shower. No credit cards.

A native Berliner and her Italian husband have managed this small pension for more than 25 years. Located just west of Savignyplatz, it occupies part of the first floor of a century-old building and features mostly large rooms, no two alike; two family-size rooms can sleep up to six people. There are telephones in some rooms. The breakfast room, pleasantly remodeled, is a good place to start the day. Reception is up on the first floor.

FISCHER, PENSION, Nürnberger Strasse 24a, 10789 Berlin. Tel. 030/218 68 08. Fax 030/213 42 25. 10 rms (8 with shower). **Directions:** An 8-minute walk from Bahnhof Zoo. **Bus:** 109 from Tegel Airport to Joachimstaler Strasse, then a 5-minute walk. **U-Bahn:** Augsburger Strasse, less than a 1-minute walk.

$ Rates: 45–50 DM ($28.10–$31.25) single without shower, 60–65 DM ($37.50–$40.60) single with shower; 80–90 DM ($50–$56.25) double without shower, 100–110 DM ($62.50–$68.75) double with shower; 120–130 DM ($75–$81.25) triple with shower. Breakfast 8 DM ($5) extra. No credit cards.

⑤ There's no better location than this, especially at these prices. You'll find this pension on the second floor of a simple building (there is no elevator). Clean and pleasant, the rooms have high ceilings and large windows letting in plenty of sunshine. Each room has an old-fashioned tiled heater, the kind that once heated all German homes. If you like quiet, ask for a room on the courtyard. The breakfast room is cozy with plants and flowers and has a TV. There's a coffee machine and refrigerator for guest use.

NÜRNBERGER ECK, PENSION, Nürnberger Strasse 24a, 10789 Berlin. Tel. 030/218 53 71. Fax 030/214 15 40. 8 rms (none with bath). **Directions:** An 8-minute walk from Bahnhof Zoo. **Bus:** 109 from Tegel Airport to Joachimstaler Strasse, then a 5-minute walk. **U-Bahn:** Augsburger Strasse, a 1-minute walk.

$ Rates: 60–65 DM ($37.50–$40.60) single; 95–110 DM ($59.35–$68.75) double; 140–150 DM ($87.50–$93.75) triple. Breakfast 10 DM ($6.25) extra. No credit cards.

⑤ Tucked on a side street not far from the Europa-Center and located in the same building as Pension Fischer, above, this is a prewar style pension with comfortable Biedermeier-reproduction furniture and massive doors to each guest room. It could have been used as a set for *Cabaret*. Good atmosphere and location.

PARISER-ECK, HOTEL-PENSION, Pariser Strasse 19, 10707 Berlin. Tel. 030/881 21 45. Fax 030/883 63 35. 14 rms (6 with shower only). **Bus:** 109 from Tegel Airport to Bleibtreustrasse, then a 5-minute walk. **U-Bahn:** Spichernstrasse, Uhlandstrasse, or Adenauerplatz, all within a 10-minute walk.

$ Rates (including continental breakfast): 59–80 DM ($36.85–$50) single without shower, 90 DM ($56.25) single with shower;

90–120 DM ($56.25–$75) double without shower, 105–135 DM ($65.60–$84.35) double with shower. Extra bed 40 DM ($25). No credit cards.

This simple first-floor pension, located south of the Ku'damm near Olivaer Platz, is not as convenient but is worth a try if the others in this category are full. Overall this establishment could use some sprucing up. Rooms have high ceilings, the best are numbers 5 and 7—bright and sunny but without showers—and Room 5 even has a balcony. There are also family-size rooms.

ZIMMER DES WESTENS, PENSION, Tauentzienstrasse 5, 10789 Berlin. Tel. 030/214 11 30. 8 rms (2 with shower and WC). **Directions:** About a 7-minute walk from Bahnhof Zoo, past Europa-Center. **U-Bahn:** Wittenbergplatz, a 1-minute walk.
$ Rates (including continental breakfast): 85–90 DM ($53.10–$56.25) single with shower and WC; 95–105 DM ($59.35–$65.60) double without shower or WC, 100–110 DM ($62.50–$68.75) double with shower and WC. Extra bed 40 DM ($25). No credit cards.

Tauentzienstrasse, a busy thoroughfare, seems like an unlikely address for this modestly priced pension. You'll find it tucked away in an inner courtyard, up three flights of rickety stairs. But the pension itself is pleasant, clean, and quiet. Since rooms with showers are slightly smaller, they're almost the same price as those without. All in all, a good value and a great location, between the Europa-Center and KaDeWe department store.

NEAR WILMERSDORFER STRASSE & BAHNHOF CHARLOTTENBURG

CHARLOTTENBURG HOF, HOTEL, Stuttgarter Platz 14, 10627 Berlin. Tel. 030/324 48 19. Fax 030/323 37 23. 45 rms (38 with shower and WC). TV **Bus:** 109 from Tegel Airport or Bahnhof Zoo to Bahnhof Charlottenburg, then a 1-minute walk. **S-Bahn:** Charlottenburg, a 1-minute walk.
$ Rates: 75–80 DM ($46.85–$50) single without shower or WC, 90–120 DM ($56.25–$75) single with shower and WC, 90–120 DM ($56.25–$75) double without shower or WC, 110–150 DM ($68.75–$93.75) double with shower and WC. Extra bed from 45–50 DM ($28.10–$31.25). Discounts in winter or for longer stays. No credit cards.

One of Berlin's finest budget hotels, it's great in terms of price, facilities, and location—only two S-Bahn stops from Bahnhof Zoo. Rooms are bright and modern and have cable TV; the staff is young and friendly. Rooms with shower and WC have telephones. Breakfast is not included in its rates, but go to the adjoining Café Voltaire, open 24 hours, for a continental breakfast, costing 5 to 8 DM ($3.10–$5) for hotel guests. The triples and quads are of particularly good value.

NEAR RATHAUS SCHÖNEBERG

STUDENTEN-HOTEL BERLIN, Meininger Strasse 10, 10823 Berlin. Tel. 030/784 67 20 or 784 67 30. Telex 0181287. 50 rms (none with bath). **Bus:** 149 from Bahnhof Zoo to JFK Platz, then a 4-minute walk. **U-Bahn:** Rathaus Schöneberg.

IMPRESSIONS

I love Germany so much I am glad there are two of them.
—FRANÇOIS MAURIAC, quoted by ROGER BERTHOUD, 1978

$ Rates (including continental breakfast): 80–85 DM ($50–$53.10) double; 35 DM ($21.85) per person for bed in multibed dormitory room. No credit cards.

Although it calls itself a student hotel and occupies a former dormitory, this simple establishment also welcomes nonstudents and guests of any age. The dormitory-style rooms have four to five beds each, and there are 20 double rooms. There's a game room. It's located near Rathaus Schöneberg and John-F.-Kennedy Platz.

SOUTH OF CITY CENTER

These two smaller pensions are located two subway stops south of the Ku'damm. If you like walking, you can stroll to the Ku'damm in less than half an hour.

MÜNCHEN, PENSION, Güntzelstrasse 62, 10717 Berlin. Tel. 030/854 22 26. Fax 030/853 27 14. 8 rms (3 with shower and WC). **U-Bahn:** U-9 from Bahnhof Zoo to Güntzelstrasse station (three stops), then a 3-minute walk.

$ Rates: 58–60 DM ($36.25–$37.50) single without shower and WC; 85–95 DM ($53.10–$59.35) double without shower and WC, 130–140 DM ($81.25–$87.50) double with shower and WC. Breakfast 9 DM ($5.60) extra. No credit cards. **Parking:** 12 DM ($7.50).

You can tell upon entering this third-floor, spotless pension that it belongs to an artist. Frau Renate Prasse, the charming proprietress, is a sculptress and has updated this older pension without losing its original character. The building, serviced by an elevator, is only two subway stops south of the Ku'damm.

STEPHAN, HOTEL-PENSION, Güntzelstrasse 54, 10717 Berlin. Tel. 030/87 41 21. 6 rms (3 with shower only). **U-Bahn:** U-9 from Bahnhof Zoo to Güntzelstrasse stop, then a 3-minute walk.

$ Rates (including continental breakfast): 55–60 DM ($34.35–$37.50) single without shower; 95–105 DM ($59.35–$65.60) double without shower, 100–110 DM ($62.50–$68.75) double with shower; 150 DM ($93.75) triple without shower, 160 DM ($100) triple with shower. No credit cards.

Housed in an older building with super-tall ceilings, it offers clean and comfortable rooms—a few are wonderfully decorated with old-fashioned furniture. Some of the rooms are small, so if you're claustrophic ask for a large room. Breakfast is served in a cozy living room with lots of plants and a color TV.

IN KREUZBERG

KREUZBERG, PENSION, Grossbeerenstrasse 64, 10963 Berlin. Tel. 030/251 13 62. 13 rms (none with bath). **Bus:** 119 from the Ku'damm to Grossbeerenstrasse stop; from Tegel

Airport, bus 109 to Adenauerplatz, then bus 119 to Grossbeeren-strasse. **U-Bahn:** Möckernbrücke, about a 6-minute walk.

$ Rates: 55–60 DM ($34.35–$37.50) single; 80–90 DM ($50–$56.25) double; 105 DM ($65.60) triple; 150 DM ($93.75) quad. Breakfast 7 DM ($4.35) extra. No credit cards.

A pension for more than 50 years and located on the second floor of an older building that still shows traces of grander days (there is no elevator), the Kreuzberg was recently renovated and has a bright and airy breakfast room complete with plants and artwork. The tall-ceilinged guest rooms are comfortably furnished and each has a wardrobe, table, and chairs. It caters largely to young backpackers.

TRANSIT, HOTEL, Hagelberger Strasse 53–54, 10965 Berlin. Tel. 030/785 50 51. 39 rms (all with shower only). **U-Bahn:** U-1 from Bahnhof Zoo to Möckernbrücke, then U-7 to Mehringdamm. **Bus:** 119 from Ku'damm to Mehringdamm stop; from Tegel Airport, bus 109 to Adenauerplatz, then bus 119 to Mehringdamm.

$ Rates (including buffet breakfast): 70–75 DM ($43.75–$46.85) single; 95–105 DM ($59.35–$65.60) double; 130 DM ($81.25) triple; 150–165 DM ($93.75–$103.10) quad; 30 DM ($18.75) in dormitory-style room. AE, MC, V.

Hotel Transit opened in 1987 in what was a tobacco factory; ever since it's been a hit with young international travelers, who exchange travel advice and tips. The buffet breakfast offers unlimited coffee and tea. Although the single and double rooms are a bit pricey, there are also triples, quads, and dormitory-style rooms sleeping six that are very economical. Great for the price.

ON THE OUTSKIRTS

WIRTSHAUS ZUM FINKENHANEL, Steinkirchener Strasse 17, 13435 Berlin. Tel. 030/415 49 53. 2 rms (none with bath). **S-Bahn:** Wittenau Nord, then a 5-minute walk.

$ Rates (including continental breakfast): 45 DM ($28.10) single; 80 DM ($50) double; 110 DM ($68.75) triple. No credit cards.

The two rooms here, located on the third floor above a restaurant in a residential area, are way out there—at least 30 minutes by S-Bahn from Bahnhof Zoo. Another drawback is that no one speaks English. However, you might try here if other accommodations are full. Rooms are comfortable, sharing a bathroom and a living room outfitted with a TV and fridge. Note that prices are slightly higher than those given above if you plan on staying only one night.

2. DOUBLES FOR LESS THAN 135 DM ($84.35)

ON OR NEAR THE KU'DAMM & BAHNHOF ZOO

ALEXANDRA, HOTEL-PENSION, Wielandstrasse 32, 10629 Berlin. Tel. 030/881 21 07. Fax 881 88 94. 8 rms (4

**FROMMER'S SMART TRAVELER:
HOTELS**

VALUE-CONSCIOUS TRAVELERS SHOULD TAKE
ADVANTAGE OF THE FOLLOWING:

1. Inexpensive lodging in the heart of town, near the Ku'damm, the Europa-Center, shops, restaurants, and bars.
2. Rooms without private showers or toilets.
3. Rooms on upper floors of pensions without elevators.
4. Accommodations that offer breakfast in the price.
5. Youth hotels and hostels, open throughout the year.

QUESTIONS TO ASK IF YOU'RE ON A BUDGET

1. Is breakfast included in the price? Is it buffet style, allowing you to eat as much as you wish?
2. Is there a cheaper room available, such as one that is smaller, on an upper floor, or farther from the shared bathroom?
3. What is the surcharge on local and long-distance telephone calls from the room? It's usually cheaper to call from a public telephone.
4. Is there parking space at the hotel, and if so, what is the charge per day? Some hotels outside the city center offer free parking.

with shower only, 4 with shower and WC). TEL TV **Bus:** 109 from Tegel Airport or Bahnhof Zoo to Olivaer Platz, then a 2-minute walk. **S-Bahn:** Savignyplatz, a 5-minute walk. **U-Bahn:** Adenauer-platz, a 5-minute walk.

$ Rates (including breakfast buffet): 95–140 DM ($59.35–$87.50) single with shower and WC; 110–145 DM ($68.75–$90.60) double with shower, 150–180 DM ($93.75–$112.50) double with shower and WC. Extra bed 45–60 DM ($28.10–$37.50). No credit cards.

Located near the western end of the Ku'damm, this simple pension offers clean rooms equipped with cable TVs and radio. Reception is on the second floor, while rooms are on the third. Guests receive a key to operate the elevator. The wide range of prices above reflect the seasons. If you stay here in summer, you're going to spend a lot more than our budget allows; but it's a bargain in winter.

ALPENLAND, Carmerstrasse 8, 10623 Berlin. Tel. 030/ 312 39 70 or 312 48 98. Fax 030/313 84 44. 43 rms (25 with shower and WC). TEL **Directions:** A 10-minute walk from Bahnhof Zoo. **Bus:** 109 from Tegel Airport to Uhlandstrasse, then a 6-minute walk. **S-Bahn:** Savignyplatz, a 3-minute walk.

$ Rates (including continental breakfast): 85–90 DM ($53.10–$56.25) single without shower or WC, 130 DM ($81.25) single with shower and WC; 120 DM ($75) double without shower or WC, 160–180 DM ($100–$112.50) double with shower and WC. Extra bed 65 DM ($40.60). No credit cards.

Appropriately called Alpenland, this hotel is decorated in Tyrolean kitsch, with lots of wood, antiques, and mounted antlers. Although the building itself is a bit run down, the pension itself is clean and caters mostly to group travelers. Its rooms (with safes) are on four floors and there is no elevator. Quiet rooms are in the back; those with view, in front. All rooms have telephones and TVs are available on request. Located just off Savignyplatz.

ARCO, Kurfürstendamm 30, 10719 Berlin. Tel. 030/882 63 88. Fax 881 99 02. 20 rms (10 with shower only, 6 with shower and WC). TEL **Bus:** 109 from Tegel Airport to Uhland-strasse, then a 1-minute walk. **U-Bahn:** Uhlandstrasse, a 1-minute walk.

$ Rates (including continental breakfast): 120 DM ($75) single with shower; 120 DM ($75) double without shower or WC, 140 DM ($87.50) double with shower, 180 DM ($112.50) double with shower and WC. AE, DC, MC, V.

A delightful third-floor pension with no elevator. Rooms are spacious and tastefully decorated, and the reception and breakfast room serve as an art gallery. Four of the seven rooms that overlook the Ku'damm have balconies, but those facing the back courtyard are much quieter. If you like being in the center of things, this is a good choice.

BOGOTA, HOTEL, Schlüterstrasse 45, 10707 Berlin. Tel. 030/881 50 01. Fax 030/883 58 87. Telex 0184946. 130 rms (12 with shower, 65 with shower and WC). TEL **Bus:** 109 from Tegel Airport or Bahnhof Zoo to Bleibtreustrasse stop, then a 1-minute walk. **U-Bahn:** Adenauerplatz, a 6-minute walk.

$ Rates (including continental breakfast): 75–80 DM ($46.85–$50) single without shower, 105 DM ($65.60) single with shower, 125–130 DM ($78.10–$81.25) single with shower and WC; 120–130 DM ($75–$81.25) double without shower or WC, 155 DM ($96.85) double with shower, 185 DM ($115.60) double with shower and WC; 160–170 DM ($100–$106.25) triple without shower or WC, 195 DM ($121.85) triple with shower, 220–240 DM ($137.50–$150) triple with shower and WC. AE, DC, MC, V.

The Bogota is an older hotel with character, and such architectural quirks as a stairway that wraps itself around an ancient elevator. Each floor with its own lobby is slightly different; the rooms vary greatly in size and style. The quiet ones face an inner courtyard. There's a cozy TV room where you can spend a relaxing evening, and the English-speaking staff is friendly and accommodating. If you like old-fashioned, well-maintained hotels, you'll like this place. Conveniently located near Olivaer Platz.

BREGENZ, HOTEL-PENSION, Bregenzer Strasse 5, 10707 Berlin. Tel. 030/881 43 07. Fax 030/882 40 09. 22 rms (5 with shower, 10 with shower and WC). TEL TV MINIBAR **Bus:** 109 from Tegel Airport or Bahnhof Zoo to Leibnizstrasse, then a 3-minute walk. **U-Bahn:** Adenauerplatz, a 5-minute walk.

$ Rates (including continental breakfast): 75–80 DM ($46.85–$50) single without shower or WC, 120–130 DM ($75–$81.25) single with shower and WC; 110–120 DM ($68.75–$75) double without shower or WC, 140–150 DM ($87.50–$93.75) double with shower, 170–185 DM ($106.25–$115.60) double with shower and WC; 160 DM ($100) quad with shower, 200 DM ($125) quad with shower and WC. Crib available. MC.

The rooms in this family-run pension, located on a quiet residential street, are clean and spacious and have cable TV. They have double doors, which helps cut down on noise. The friendly staff will make bookings for the theater and sightseeing tours, and families are welcome. The only disadvantage to staying here is that it's a bit far from Bahnhof Zoo and the east end of the Ku'damm.

BRINN, PENSION, Schillerstrasse 10, 10625 Berlin. Tel. 312 16 05. Fax 030/313 95 07. 6 rms (1 with shower and WC). TEL TV **U-Bahn:** Ernst-Reuter-Strasse, a 2-minute walk.

$ Rates (including continental breakfast): 90 DM ($56.25) single without shower or WC; 130 DM ($81.25) double without shower or WC, 150 DM ($93.75) double with shower and WC. Extra person 40 DM ($25). Winter discounts available. No credit cards.

Located about a 10-minute walk north of the Ku'damm near the Schiller-Theater and Deutsche Oper, this small and intimate pension is bright and cheerful, with period furniture giving it an Old World atmosphere. The ornate building dates from the turn of the century; the pension itself has been around for almost 50 years. There is only one single room, three double rooms, and two large rooms perfect for families.

CRYSTAL, HOTEL, Kantstrasse 144, 10623 Berlin. Tel. 030/312 90 47 or 312 90 48. Fax 030/312 64 65. 33 rms (7 with shower, 21 with tub or shower and WC). TEL **Bus:** 109 from Tegel Airport to Bleibtreustrasse stop; or bus 149 from Bahnhof Zoo to Savignyplatz (two stops). **S-Bahn:** Savignyplatz, a 2-minute walk.

$ Rates (including continental breakfast): 70 DM ($43.75) single without bathroom, 80 DM ($50) single with shower, 80–120 DM ($50–$75) single with bathroom; 90 DM ($56.25) double without bathroom, 110–120 DM ($68.75–$75) double with shower, 130–150 DM ($81.25–$93.75) double with bathroom; 170–190 DM ($106.25–$118.75) triple with bathroom. Crib available. AE, MC, V. **Parking:** Free.

This older hotel has a good location just west of Savignyplatz and has recently been updated with a new lobby and renovated facade. There's a small bar with TV for hotel guests just off the lobby; televisions are also available for guest rooms. Rooms are plain but comfortable, and spotless beyond reproof. The owners, John and Dorothee Schwarzrock (John is an American), are outgoing and entertaining, and the entire staff speaks English.

DITTBERNER, HOTEL-PENSION, Wielandstrasse 26, 10707 Berlin. Tel. 030/881 64 85 or 882 39 63. 22 rms (13 with shower only, 7 with tub or shower and WC). TEL **Bus:** 109 from Tegel Airport or Bahnhof Zoo to Leibnizstrasse stop, then a 1-minute walk. **U-Bahn:** Adenauerplatz, a 6-minute walk.

$ Rates (including continental breakfast): 90–100 DM ($56.25–$62.50) single with shower, 125–140 DM ($78.10–$87.50) single with bathroom; 130–140 DM ($81.25–$87.50) double with shower, 150–200 DM ($93.75–$125) double with bathroom. No credit cards.

⭐ This is a lovely pension, beautifully decorated with antiques and artwork. The small lobby is flanked by a Japanese screen with chandeliers above; the corridor is lined with woodblock prints and posters. The breakfast room is comfortable yet elegant. Located in an older building (guests receive a special key for the elevator) above an exclusive gallery, the best room overlooks a small courtyard with the gallery's sculpture garden. Little wonder that guests return again and again, including a number of artists. It's located just off the Ku'damm, near Olivaer Platz. TVs are available on request.

ELFERT, PENSION, Knesebeckstrasse 13/14, 10623 Berlin. Tel. 030/312 12 36. 13 rms (6 with shower). **Bus:** 109 from Tegel Airport to Bahnhof Zoo, then a 7-minute walk. **S-Bahn:** Savignyplatz, a 3-minute walk.

$ Rates (including continental breakfast): 130 DM ($81.25) single with shower, 85–90 DM ($53.10–$56.25) single without shower; 130 DM ($81.25) double without shower, 160 DM ($100) double with shower. No credit cards.

This simple pension offers clean, large rooms. There's no elevator to its first-floor reception, but the entryway is so ornate and the carved staircase so unusual that the mostly middle-aged clientele don't mind. Close to the restaurants and nightlife on Savignyplatz.

FUNK, HOTEL-PENSION, Fasanenstrasse 69, 10719 Berlin. Tel. 030/882 71 93. Fax 030/882 71 93. 15 rms (11 with shower only, 1 with shower and WC). TEL **Directions:** A 10-minute walk from Bahnhof Zoo. **Bus:** 109 from Tegel Airport to Uhlandstrasse stop, then a 2-minute walk. **U-Bahn:** Uhlandstrasse, a 1-minute walk.

$ Rates (including continental breakfast): 65–70 DM ($40.60–$43.75) single without shower or WC, 80 DM ($50) single with shower; 110 DM ($68.75) double without shower or WC, 120–130 DM ($75–$81.25) double with shower only or shower and WC; 165 DM ($103.10) triple with shower; 200 DM ($125) quad with shower. No credit cards.

Fasanenstrasse is one of my favorite streets because of its elegant, turn-of-the-century houses and the Käthe-Kollwitz Museum. This pension, on the first floor, is decorated with French provincial reproduction furniture and flowered wallpaper; the staff speaks English. Within a 15-minute walk to Bahnhof Zoo.

GALERIE 48, PENSION, Leibnizstrasse 48, 10629 Berlin. Tel. 030/324 26 58 or 323 23 51. Fax 030/892 38 57. 8 rms (3 with shower). **Bus:** 109 to Olivaer Platz. **U-Bahn:** Adenauerplatz, a 5-minute walk.

$ Rates (including continental breakfast): 85 DM ($53.10) single without shower; 120 DM ($75) double without shower, 130 DM ($81.25) double with shower. No credit cards.

This small and personable pension offers clean and cheerful rooms, all on the first floor. The breakfast room is especially nice, with a long wooden bar that serves as the reception desk. Paintings line the corridor, giving it the feel of an art gallery. A good location, north of the Ku'damm.

JUWEL, HOTEL-PENSION, Meinekestrasse 26, 10719 Berlin. Tel. 030/882 71 41. 22 rms (15 with shower only, 3 with shower and WC). TEL **Directions:** A 10-minute walk south of Bahnhof Zoo. **Bus:** 109 from Tegel Airport to Uhlandstrasse, then a 2-minute walk. **U-Bahn:** Uhlandstrasse or Kurfürstendamm, each a 2-minute walk.

$ Rates (including continental breakfast): 85 DM ($53.10) single without shower or WC, 95 DM ($59.35) single with shower, 130 DM ($81.25) single with shower and WC; 130 DM ($81.25) double without shower or WC, 160–170 DM ($100–$106.25) double with shower, 199–220 DM ($124.35–$137.50) double with shower and WC. Crib available. No credit cards.

You'll like the convenience of this small and unpretentious first-floor pension on a quiet side street off the Ku'damm. Since all but two rooms face a back street, noise is not a problem. Some of the singles, however, are quite small. The breakfast room is pleasant, equipped with a TV and decorated with proprietor Roswitha Schreiterer's patchwork quilts.

MAJESTY, HOTEL-PENSION, Mommsenstrasse 55, 10629 Berlin. Tel. 030/323 20 61. Fax 030/323 20 62. 24 rms (13 with shower only). TEL **Bus:** 109 from Tegel Airport to Olivaer Platz. **U-Bahn:** Adenauerplatz, a 5-minute walk.

$ Rates: 70–85 DM ($43.75–$53) single without shower; 105–130 DM ($65.60–$81.25) double without shower, 110–150 DM ($68.75–$93.75) double with shower. Breakfast 9 DM ($5.60) extra. No credit cards.

This older, second-floor pension has a nice breakfast room. Rooms are well maintained. Some are large enough to dance in; four have balconies. A vending machine dispenses drinks, and guests receive a key to operate the elevator. Near Ku'damm.

MODENA, HOTEL-PENSION, Wielandstrasse 26, 10707 Berlin. Tel. 030/881 52 94, 88 57 01-0, or 883 54 04. Fax 030/881 52 94. 21 rms (9 with shower only, 5 with shower and WC). TEL **Bus:** 109 from Tegel Airport or Bahnhof Zoo to Leibnizstrasse, then a 1-minute walk. **U-Bahn:** Adenauerplatz, a 6-minute walk.

$ Rates (including continental breakfast): 65–70 DM ($40.60–$43.75) single without shower or WC, 80–90 DM ($50–$56.25) single with shower, 110 DM ($68.75) single with shower and WC, 110–120 DM ($68.75–$75) double without shower or WC, 130–140 DM ($81.25–$87.50) double with shower, 150–160 DM ($93.75–$100) double with shower and WC; 160 DM ($100) triple with shower, 175–190 DM ($109.35–$118.75) triple with shower and WC. No credit cards.

This pension is on the second floor of a lovely building dating from the turn of the century; it's managed by Frau Kreutz, who keeps rooms spotless. Upon check in, she'll give you a key to operate the elevator, an ancient-looking box: You may prefer the stairs. Good price and location, near Olivaer Platz.

PETERS, PENSION, Kantstrasse 146, 10623 Berlin. Tel. 030/312 22 78. Fax 030/664 41 61. 8 rms (none with bath). **S-Bahn:** Savignyplatz, a 2-minute walk. **Bus:** 109 from Tegel Airport to Bleibtreustrasse, or 149 from Bahnhof Zoo to Savignyplatz (second stop).

$ Rates: 75–80 DM ($46.85–$50) single; 120–150 DM ($75–$93.75) double; 160 DM ($100) triple; 200 DM ($125) quad. Breakfast 9 DM ($5.60) extra. No credit cards.

Located just east of Savignyplatz and within a 10-minute walk of Bahnhof Zoo, this small pension occupies the second floor (no elevator) of a building dating from 1890, complete with stucco ceilings and double-paned windows. It offers four single rooms, as well as four doubles which can sleep up to four persons, making them perfect for families or small groups. One room has a television.

VIOLA NOVA, PENSION, Kantstrasse 146, 10623 Berlin. Tel. 030/31 64 57. Fax 030/312 33 14. 9 rms (none with bath). TEL **S-Bahn:** Savignyplatz, a 2-minute walk. **Bus:** 109 from Tegel Airport to Bleibtreustrasse, or 149 from Bahnhof Zoo to Savignyplatz (second stop).

$ Rates (including continental breakfast): 90 DM ($56.25) single; 130 DM ($81.25) double; 180 DM ($112.50) triple. No credit cards.

Located in the same building as Pension Peters (see above) but this time up on the first floor, this pension offers bright and cheerful rooms, with tall ceilings, telephone, and either antique or modern furniture. Televisions are available for rent. The proprietor, who speaks English, hopes to add another six rooms (all with private bathroom) by the time you read this. If available, ask for room 5, a double corner room, bright with antique furnishings.

WEST-PENSION, HOTEL, Kurfürstendamm 48–49, 10707 Berlin. Tel. 030/881 80 57 or 881 80 58. Fax 030/881 38 92. 33 rms (8 with shower, 15 with shower and WC). TEL **Bus:** 109 from Tegel Airport or Bahnhof Zoo to Bleibtreustrasse. **U-Bahn:** Uhlandstrasse, a 3-minute walk.

$ Rates: 75–80 DM ($46.85–$50) single without shower or WC, 85–90 DM ($53.10–$56.25) single with shower, 105 DM ($65.60) single with shower and WC; 120 DM ($75) double without shower or WC, 135 DM ($84.35) double with shower, 160–200 DM ($100–$125) double with shower and WC. Extra bed 30 DM ($18.75). Buffet breakfast 11 DM ($6.85) extra. MC, V.

With a great location right on the Ku'damm, this pension occupies the second floor of a beautiful turn-of-the-century building complete with elevator and has an Old-World feel to it. In addition to its pleasant breakfast room with its high stucco ceiling, it also has a comfortable bar for hotel guests. Some rooms have antique furnishings; others have modern. Some of the double rooms with shower and toilet face the Ku'damm; the rest face toward the back. Since a variety of rooms are available, specify what you want when making your reservation.

POSTILLON, HOTEL-PENSION, Gasteiner Strasse 8, 10717 Berlin. Tel. 030/87 52 32. Fax 030/87 38 59. Telex 182 946. 24 rms (5 with shower, 4 with shower and WC). TEL **U-Bahn:** U-9 from Bahnhof Zoo to Berliner Strasse, then U-7 to Blissestrasse. **Bus:** 109 from Tegel Airport to Jakob-Kaiser-Platz (first stop), then U-7 to Blissestrasse.

$ Rates (including buffet breakfast): 70–75 DM ($43.75–$46.85) single without shower or WC, 80–85 DM ($50–$53.10) single with shower, 90–100 DM ($56.25–$62.50) single with shower and WC; 110–120 DM ($68.75–$75) double without shower or

WC, 130–140 DM ($81.25–$87.50) double with shower, 160 DM ($100) double with shower and WC. Extra bed 40–45 DM ($25–$28.10). No credit cards.

This hotel-pension is less conveniently located than the others above (about a 20-minute walk from the Ku'damm), but is worth a try if other establishments are full. It's owned by English-speaking Herr Bernd Lucht, who offers simple but large rooms in this older building. Those that face the front have balconies.

3. YOUTH HOSTELS & YOUTH HOTELS

YOUTH HOSTELS

Youth-hostel cards are required for stays at Berlin's youth hostels; these cards are available at hostels for 30 DM ($18.75). There's no age limit, but "seniors" (27 years and older) pay slightly higher rates. Berlin youth hostels have a midnight curfew, which can be painfully early in the city that never sleeps.

JUGENDHERBERGE ERNST REUTER, Hermsdorfer Damm 48–50, 13467 Berlin. Tel. 030/404 16 10. 110 beds. **Directions:** From Tegel Airport, bus 128 to Kurt Schumacher Platz, then U-6 to Tegel stop, then bus 125 to Jugendherberge stop; from Bahnhof Zoo, U-9 to Leopoldplatz, then U-6 to Tegel station, then bus 125 to Jugendherberge stop.
$ Rates (including breakfast and sheets): 22 DM ($13.75) per person for ages 26 and younger; 27 DM ($16.85) per person for ages 27 and older. Dinner 8.50 DM ($5.30) extra. No credit cards.

Although this is Berlin's cheapest, it's at least 35 minutes from the city center (longer if connections are bad and you have to wait for the bus). However, it's surrounded by woods in a peaceful part of town and offers table tennis and a TV lounge. All rooms have eight beds.

FROMMER'S COOL FOR KIDS: HOTELS

Artemisia *(see p. 82)* This women-only hotel allows children under 8 to stay free with their mother, while children up to 12 pay half price.

Hotel-Pension Bregenz *(see p. 74)* Families are welcome at this centrally located establishment, and cribs are available.

Pension Cortina *(see p. 68)* This pension offers a large family room that sleeps six persons.

JUGENDGÄSTEHAUS BERLIN, Kluckstrasse 3, 10785 Berlin. Tel. 030/261 10 97. 364 beds. **Bus:** 129 from Bahnhof Zoo to Kluckstrasse, then a 1-minute walk. **U-Bahn:** Kurfürstenstrasse, a 12-minute walk.

$ Rates (including breakfast and sheets): 27 DM ($16.85) per person for ages 26 and younger; 33 DM ($20.60) per person for ages 27 and older. Dinner 9.50 DM ($5.95). No credit cards.

This is the most popular youth hostel, because of its convenient location—just three subway stops from the Ku'damm. Write at least 1 month in advance to reserve a room. All rooms are dormitory style, with four to six beds, and everyone gets a locker with key.

JUGENDGÄSTEHAUS AM WANNSEE, Badeweg 1, 14129 Berlin. Tel. 030/803 20 34. Telex 186606. 264 beds. **S-Bahn:** S-3 to Nikolassee, then a 7-minute walk.

$ Rates (including breakfast and sheets): 27 DM ($16.85) per person for ages 26 and younger; 33 DM ($20.60) per person for ages 27 and older. Dinner 9.50 DM ($5.95) extra. No credit cards.

This is Berlin's newest and most modern youth hostel, a handsome brick building with red trim. It's close to Wannsee, a lake popular for swimming and boating in summer, with bathing facilities nearby. Rooms have four beds each, with showers per every two rooms. A relaxing place in summer.

YOUTH HOTELS

JUGENDGÄSTEHAUS AM ZOO, Hardenbergstrasse 9a, 10623 Berlin. Tel. 030/312 94 10. 58 beds. **Directions:** A 10-minute walk from Bahnhof Zoo.

$ Rates: 50–55 DM ($31.25–$34.35) single; 95–100 DM ($59.35–$62.50) double; 35 DM ($21.85) per bed in dormitory room. No credit cards.

It's easy to overlook this place as there's no sign outside the run-down building. But take the elevator up to the fourth floor (if it's working) and you'll find a no-frills establishment that appeals to backpackers and youth groups. Although there's an age limit of 27, any age is welcome if there's room. No reservations are accepted for single or double rooms, so you have to inquire when you arrive in town. There are also larger, dormitory-style rooms that sleep four to eight persons. This hostel with the best location even has a bar that's open from 9:30pm to an astonishing 6am. It's across the street from Technical University with its Mensa student cafeteria, one of the cheapest places to eat in town.

JUGENDGÄSTEHAUS CENTRAL, Nikolsburger Strasse 2-4, 10717 Berlin. Tel. 030/87 01 88. 456 beds. **U-Bahn:** Güntzelstrasse, Spichernstrasse, or Hohenzollernplatz, all a 5-minute walk.

$ Rates (including breakfast): 31 DM ($19.35) per person. Sheets 7 DM ($4.35) extra for stays of 1 or 2 nights, free for stays of 3 nights or longer. Lunch and dinner 5 DM ($3.10) extra. No credit cards.

This large, dormitory-style accommodation caters to school groups but will accept single travelers if there's room. It's open only to those under 25 or bona-fide students, and there's a 1am curfew. There are a few double rooms available (used mostly by teachers and group leaders), but most rooms are equipped with bunk beds sleeping 8 to 12 people per room. You'll need your own towel here. For only 5 DM ($3.10), you can have both lunch and dinner (lunch boxes are provided for those gone all day). Two subway stops south of the Ku'damm, or a 20-minute walk.

JUGENDGÄSTEHAUS FEURIGSTRASSE, Feurigstrasse 63, 10827 Berlin. Tel. 030/781 52 11. 200 beds. **Bus:** 146 from Bahnhof Zoo to Dominicusstrasse. **U-Bahn:** Kleistpark, about a 5-minute walk.
$ Rates (including buffet breakfast and sheets): 40–45 DM ($25–$28.10). No credit cards.

This youth hotel, located in Schöneberg, caters primarily to school groups, but will take individual travelers if there's room, giving preference to younger people. There's no curfew here, and the bunk beds are a bit sturdier than elsewhere. Two-, four-, and six-bed rooms are available.

4. CAMPING

If you're between 14 and 26 years of age and you don't mind roughing it, you might try the **Internationales Jugendcamp,** Ziekowstrasse 161, 13509 Berlin (tel. 030/433 86 40). Take U-Bahn 6 to Tegel, and continue by bus 125 to the third stop, Titusweg stop. This camp has a large tent, with mattresses and sheets provided. Showers are free. Open only from mid-June to the end of August, it costs 8 DM ($5) per person per night. Guests must leave the premises during the day, from 9am to 5pm. No written reservations are accepted, so call when you get to Berlin.

There are three campgrounds in the vicinity of Berlin, but they fill up fast in summer. They are equipped with modern sanitary facilities and stores. All charge the same rates: 7 DM ($4.35) per adult; 2.50 DM ($1.55) per child; 6 DM ($3.75) for the camping site. **Dreilinden** (in Wannsee), Albrechts-Teerofen, 14109 Berlin (tel. 030/805 12 01), has 100 tent sites, is open from the beginning of April to October, and is reached by bus 118, followed by a 20-minute walk. **Haselhorst** (in Spandau), Pulvermühlenweg, 13599 Berlin (tel. 334 59 55), is open year round and has about 80 sites for both tents and camper vehicles (U-Bahn: Haselhorst). **Kladow** (in Spandau), Krampnitzer Weg 111-117, 14089 Berlin (tel. 365 27 97), is the largest, with 300 tent and camper-vehicle sites available year round (Bus: 149 and 135).

5. WORTH THE EXTRA BUCKS

Although these hotels and pensions are beyond a budget of $50 a day, you may find yourself ready for a splurge. These establishments offer more luxurious surroundings and more personal service than those listed above.

ON OR NEAR THE KU'DAMM & BAHNHOF ZOO

ARTEMISIA, Brandenburgischestrasse 18, 10707 Berlin. Tel. 030/87 89 05. Fax 030/861 86 53. 8 rms (all with shower and WC). TEL **Bus:** 109 from Tegel Airport or Bahnhof Zoo to Adenauerplatz, then a 5-minute walk. **U-Bahn:** Konstanzer, a 1-minute walk.

$ Rates (including buffet breakfast): 169–260 DM ($105.60–$162.50) single; 179–270 DM ($111.85–$168.75) double. Children under 8 stay free, children 8 to 12 pay half price. AE, MC, V.

This wonderful pension. named after Italian artist Artemisia Gentileschi, is *for women only*. It was opened in 1989 by a team of four women, who bought and renovated a run-down pension and turned it into this modern, spotless, and thoughtfully planned establishment. Reception is up on the fourth floor, with elevator. There's a sunny breakfast room, a rooftop terrace and winter garden, a small library, and a hotel bar with a fireplace. The hallways provide gallery space for artists.

Rooms are decorated with antiques and modern furniture. Each room is dedicated to a famous "forgotten" woman, such as the composer/pianist Fanny Mendelssohn-Hensel, who lived in her brother's shadow and whose room contains a few items in memory of her. Boys up to 14 years of age can stay here with their mothers. Highly recommended, especially for single women travelers.

FASANENHAUS, HOTEL-PENSION, Fasanenstrasse 73 10719 Berlin. Tel. 030/881 67 13. Fax 030/882 39 47. 25 rms (15 with shower only, 10 with shower and WC). **Directions:** A 10-minute walk from Bahnhof Zoo. **Bus:** 109 from Tegel Airport to Uhlandstrasse, then a 2-minute walk. **U-Bahn:** Uhlandstrasse, a 1-minute walk.

$ Rates (including continental breakfast): 100–110 DM ($62.50–$68.75) single with shower only, 130–140 DM ($81.25–$87.50) single with shower and WC; 155–170 DM ($96.85–$106.25) double with shower only, 200–220 DM ($125–$137.50) double with shower and WC; 190–210 DM ($118.75–$131.25) triple with shower only, 240–260 DM ($150–$162.50) triple with shower and WC. Crib available. No credit cards.

On the fashionable Fasanenstrasse just a minute's walk from the Ku'damm, this delightful establishment is reached by a grandly ornate stairway. It has a very pleasant breakfast room with exposed ceiling beams and a living room with a TV and French doors that

---

IMPRESSIONS

The Wall is a kind of masterpiece of the squalid, the cruel and the hideous, the most naked assertion one could find anywhere that life was not intended to be anything but nasty, brutish, and short.
—GORONWY REES, *DIARY FROM BERLIN TO MUNICH*, 1964

open onto a balcony. Rooms are large; all have showers and many have toilets as well—which is reflected in its higher prices.

NORTH OF TIERGARTEN PARK

This establishment is centrally located just north of the Tiergarten and the Hansaviertel (Hansa Quarter), just two stops from Bahnhof Zoo on the U-Bahn.

TIERGARTEN BERLIN, HOTEL, Alt-Moabit 89, 10559 Berlin. Tel. 030/391 30 04 or 391 41 79. Fax 030/393 86 92. Telex 186812 tgt d. 38 rms (5 with shower only, 33 with shower and WC). TEL TV MINIBAR **U-Bahn:** U-9 to Turmstrasse, then a 3-minute walk.

$ Rates (including buffet breakfast): 140–150 DM ($87.50–$93.75) single with shower, 170–180 DM ($106.25–$112.50) single with shower and WC; 165–180 DM ($103.10–$112.50) double with shower, 210–230 DM ($131.25–$143.75) double with shower and WC. AE, DC, MC, V.

This small, intimate hotel has all the makings of a first-rate establishment: polite and efficient staff, turn-of-the-century charm and elegance, and light and airy rooms sporting high stucco ceilings and outfitted with cable TV, minibar, radio, and alarm clock. Bathrooms are modern and spotless, complete with magnifying glass for shaving or applying makeup. There are four no-smoking rooms. The breakfast room is a cheerful place to start the day. In short, this is the kind of place that appeals to both business and pleasure travelers, the kind you'd come back to again and again. It's certainly one of my favorites in Berlin. You'll find the reception up on the first floor; there's an elevator.

CHAPTER 5

WHERE TO EAT IN BERLIN

1. **MEALS FOR LESS THAN 12 DM ($7.50)**
2. **MEALS FOR LESS THAN 25 DM ($15.60)**
- **FROMMER'S SMART TRAVELER: RESTAURANTS**
3. **SPECIALTY DINING**
- **FROMMER'S COOL FOR KIDS: RESTAURANTS**
4. **WORTH THE EXTRA BUCKS**

To me travel and dining are synonymous: The atmosphere of a restaurant and the celebration of a meal can make it as culturally enriching as a visit to a museum—and in Berlin it doesn't have to cost much. Crowded and lively neighborhood pubs (or *Gaststätten*) offer generous platters of German cuisine and the opportunity to strike up conversations with fellow diners. Outdoor cafés are perfect for drinks, dessert, and lighter meals, to be enjoyed while watching the endless parade of people. Even a simple picnic of bread, cheese, and wine in the middle of the Tiergarten park can be a unique Berlin experience.

The choices for dining in Berlin seem endless—even for the budget traveler—with more than 6,000 pubs and restaurants. As one would expect of a city with a large international population and many foreign visitors, there is an astounding diversity of ethnic restaurants. Only half the Germans recently surveyed said they preferred their own heavier native cuisine over international fare.

The vast majority of Berlin's restaurants are found on and around the Ku'damm, as well as Savignyplatz, Wilmersdorfer Strasse, and the Europa-Center. In addition to the many take-out establishments here, there are also a number of *Imbisse* (food stands) serving everything from sausages to french fries.

The restaurants that follow are listed according to cost: meals less than 12 DM ($7.50), meals less than 25 DM ($15.60), and those "Worth the Extra Bucks."

Unless otherwise stated, prices given for each restaurant are for main courses, which for German cuisine almost always include one or more side dishes and are often complete meals in themselves. Thus, don't assume a restaurant is beyond your budget just because it's listed in a more expensive price category. If you opt for the less expensive items on the menu and cut out alcohol, appetizers, and desserts, you can enjoy a fine restaurant. Keep in mind that many restaurants offer daily specials, usually complete meals that include a soup or appetizer, main dish, and sometimes coffee and dessert. Some of the more expensive restaurants also offer a cheaper menu during lunch hours, usually available until 3pm.

Each price category is further divided according to geographical location. After all, if you're visiting the museums in Dahlem or are shopping on Wilmersdorfer Strasse, you're probably much more interested in knowing what's readily available in the immediate area.

And if you're craving a certain cuisine, refer to "Restaurants by Cuisine" in the Index. An explanation of German cuisine is given in Chapter 1; a translation of menu items appears in the Appendix.

Keep in mind that most Germans eat their big meal of the day at lunch, which is served in most restaurants from about 11:30am to 2 or 3pm and may include lunch specials at reduced prices. The most popular dinner hours are from 7 or 8pm to 10pm. Since the vast majority of restaurants are open throughout the day, try to eat in the off-hours to avoid having to wait for a table. This is especially prudent in eastside Berlin, since there are still too few restaurants to meet the demand.

Although tax and service charge are included in all restaurant bills, you should still leave a small tip for your server. For meals costing less than 20 DM ($12.50), simply round off to the nearest mark or add a mark tip. For meals costing more than 20 DM, most Germans will add a 10% tip. Unlike in the United States where tips are left on the table, in Germany tips are indicated to the server before change is given back. Thus, if your bill is 14 DM and you want to give your waiter a 1-DM tip, say "15 DM" when you hand over your 20-DM bill. If she doesn't understand English (or your high-school German), simply hand back the 1-DM.

Though increasingly rare, some of the larger, tourist-oriented restaurants in Berlin charge extra for use of their public facilities—usually 30 Pfennig (18¢). In eastern Berlin, it is sometimes expected to give your coat or jacket to the coat clerk at the *Garderobe*, for which the clerk expects a small tip of a mark or so (60¢).

In addition to the restaurants listed in this chapter, check Chapter 9 "Berlin Nights," for pubs and locales that serve food in addition to wine and beer.

1. MEALS FOR LESS THAN 12 DM ($7.50)

Many restaurants in this category serve ethnic food, including Turkish, Italian, and Chinese. For German fare, your best bet are the food counters and cafeterias in Berlin's larger department stores, as well as the Würste sold at Berlin's many stands. Be sure to also check the listings under "Meals for Less than 25 DM ($15.60)," since some of these offer some main courses or stews for less than 12 DM. Also, many of the bars described in Chapter 9, "Berlin Nights," offer German meals and snacks as well.

ON OR NEAR THE KU'DAMM

ASHOKA, Grolmanstrasse 51. Tel. 313 20 66.
Cuisine: INDIAN. **S-Bahn:** Savignyplatz, less than a 4-minute walk.
$ Prices: 5–14 DM ($3.10–$8.75). No credit cards.
Open: Daily 10am–midnight.

Located just north of Savignyplatz, this minuscule Indian establishment with outdoor seating has an open kitchen that takes up half the restaurant. It's popular with students living in the area, who come for its vegetarian or meat dishes. For an appetizer, try the *pakoras,* a kind

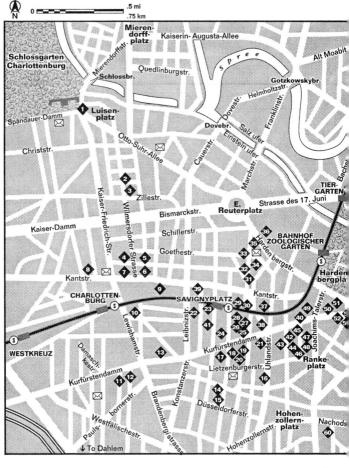

Angora	Café Kranzler	Dorfgasthaus	Istanbul
Ano Kato	Café Möhring	Eierschale	Italia Snack
Ashoka	Café Sidney	Einhorn	Jahrmarkt
Asia-Quick	Café-Restaurant	Einstein	Jimmy's Diner
Athener Grill	China Imbiss Dali	Fofi's Estiatorio	Joseph Langer
Avanti	Chung	Grossbeerenkeller	KaDeWe
Berliner Stube	Ciao Ciao	Grung Thai	Kalkutta
Café Bleibtreu	Ciao Italia	Hardtke	Karavan
Café Hardenberg	Club Culinare	Ihre Frisch-	Le Buffet
Café Im Literaturhaus	Die Buffeteria	Backstübe	Lekkerbek

of biscuit with cauliflower and other vegetables, with a dash of chutney. Also recommended is the vegetable curry served with either rice or Indian bread and its lamb biryani.

ASIA-QUICK, Lietzenburger Strasse 96. Tel. 882 15 33.
   Cuisine: CHINESE. **U-Bahn:** Uhlandstrasse, about a 6-minute walk.
$ Prices: 9–15 DM ($5.60–$9.35). No credit cards.
   Open: Mon–Fri noon–11:30pm, Sat 4pm–midnight.

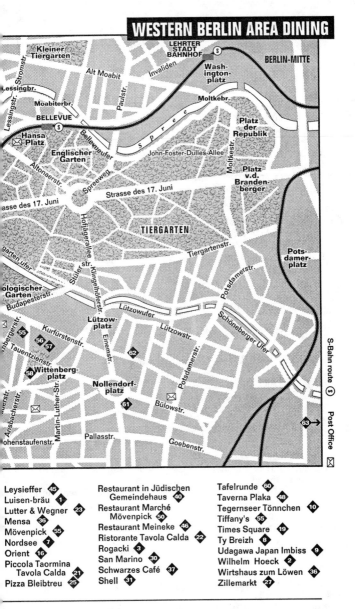

WESTERN BERLIN AREA DINING

Leysieffer **45**
Luisen-bräu **1**
Lutter & Wegner **23**
Mensa **36**
Mövenpick **55**
Nordsee **7**
Orient **16**
Piccola Taormina Tavola Calda **21**
Pizza Bleibtreu **25**

Restaurant in Jüdischen Gemeindehaus **40**
Restaurant Marché Mövenpick **50**
Restaurant Meineke **46**
Ristorante Tavola Calda **22**
Rogacki **3**
San Marino **30**
Schwarzes Café **37**
Shell **31**

Tafelrunde **60**
Taverna Plaka **48**
Tegernseer Tönnchen **10**
Tiffany's **55**
Times Square **19**
Ty Breizh **8**
Udagawa Japan Imbiss **9**
Wilhelm Hoeck **2**
Wirtshaus zum Löwen **36**
Zillemarkt **27**

Located south of the Ku'damm near Bleibtreustrasse, this clean, fast-food establishment (aptly named) has a TV in the corner just like in Asia. It offers soups and appetizers for less than 6 DM ($3.75), while most of its main dishes are less than 12 DM ($7.50). Fish, pork, beef, and chicken dishes come in three styles: chop suey (with soy sauce), sweet-and-sour, and Szechuan (spicy). There are also rice, noodle, and vegetarian dishes. For dining in or take-out.

ATHENER GRILL, Kurfürstendamm 156. Tel. 892 10 39.

Cuisine: GREEK/ITALIAN. **U-Bahn:** Adenauerplatz, a 1-minute walk.
$ Prices: 4–15 DM ($2.50–$9.35). AE, DC, MC, V.
Open: Sun–Thurs 11am–4am, Fri–Sat 11am–5am.

Located on the western end of the Ku'damm past Adenauerplatz. A cafeteria with various counters offering different cuisines, it occupies a modern brick building with an imaginative interior—it's not garishly bright like most fast-food joints. Its menu is on a wall near the front door and includes pizza, spaghetti, moussaka, souvlaki, gyros, ice cream, and salads, to name only a few. After deciding what you want, pay the cashier and then hand your ticket to the cook at the appropriate counter. Greek wines are available starting at 2.50 DM ($1.55).

AVANTI, Rankestrasse 2. Tel. 883 52 40.

Cuisine: ITALIAN. **U-Bahn:** Kurfürstendamm, a 2-minute walk.
$ Prices: 6–16 DM ($3.75–$10). No credit cards.
Open: Daily 11am–2am.

Italian fast-food restaurants are so popular that they seem to occupy every corner. This one has a great location just off the Ku'damm, near the Gedächtniskirche and Wertheim department store. It's clean and modern, with contemporary artwork on the walls and an ice-cream/cocktail bar (a rather strange combination). Pizzas and pastas are all priced under 10 DM ($6.25), and there's a salad bar where you can help yourself for 5 DM ($3.10) for a small plate. There are also daily specials.

CAFE HARDENBERG, Hardenbergstrasse 10. Tel. 312 33 30.

Cuisine: GERMAN/INTERNATIONAL. **U-Bahn:** Ernst-Reuter-Platz, less than a 3-minute walk.
$ Prices: 8–14 DM ($5–$8.75). No credit cards.
Open: Daily 9am–midnight.

Located across from the Technical University less than a 6-minute walk from Bahnhof Zoo, this popular café is always packed with students and people who work nearby. Decorated with museum posters, plants, and ceiling fans, it serves as a coffeehouse, restaurant, and as a bar in the evening. In summer there are tables and chairs outside. Classical music is played through the sound system until 4pm, after which it's music of the 20th century. It's a good place for a meal, since portions are hearty and the menu has an interesting range of dishes that change daily—which can include spaghetti, Schnitzel, Greek salads, omelets, dolmades, pork chops, and chili con carne. Breakfast is served to a late 5pm, with prices starting at around 5 DM ($3.10).

CHINA IMBISS DALI, Savignyplatz S-Bahn-Bogen 604. Tel. 312 64 23.

Cuisine: CHINESE. **S-Bahn:** Savignyplatz, less than a minute's walk.
$ Prices: Soups and appetizers 3–6.50 DM ($1.85–$4.05); entrées 9–15 DM ($5.60–$9.35). No credit cards.
Open: Daily noon–midnight.

Savignyplatz Bogen is a string of establishments located under the S-Bahn tracks between Savignyplatz and Bleibtreustrasse. China Imbiss Dali, just off Bleibtreustrasse, is a simply decorated Chinese restaurant offering rice and noodle dishes, as well as hearty pork, duck, beef, chicken, fish, and vegetable dishes. There's an English menu, and candles on each table make for slightly more intimate dining than what is usually offered at fast-food Chinese restaurants.

CIAO ITALIA, Goethestrasse 84. Tel. 313 76 67.

Cuisine: ITALIAN. **U-Bahn:** Ernst-Reuter-Platz, a 5-minute walk.
S-Bahn: Savignyplatz, a 4-minute walk.
$ Prices: 8–14 DM ($5–$8.75). No credit cards.
Open: Mon–Sat 9am–midnight.

It's easy to walk right by this Italian grocery store without realizing that it serves some of the best and cheapest pasta in Berlin. During lunch, a self-service counter offers tortellini, ravioli, rigatoni, and lasagne with choice of sauce: tomato, mushroom, Gorgonzola, or meat. Ciao Italia also serves dinner, but it's cheaper to come for lunch. At any rate, this place is as casual as it gets, since the only decorations are a few tables and shelves lined with goods. You'll find it at the corner of Goethe and Knesebeck streets, about a 5-minute walk north of Savignyplatz or a 10-minute walk north of the Ku'damm.

CLUB CULINARE, basement of Wertheim department store, Kurfürstendamm 231. Tel. 88 20 61.

Cuisine: GERMAN/INTERNATIONAL. **U-Bahn:** Kurfürsten-damm, a 1-minute walk.
$ Prices: 6–25 DM ($3.75–$15.60). No credit cards.
Open: Mon–Wed and Fri 11am–6pm, Thurs 11am–8pm, Sat 11am–1:30pm (to 5:30pm first Sat of the month).

Like many department stores, Wertheim has a grocery store in its basement; but what's unique here is that there are several sit-down counters—each one with a different cuisine. Simply walk around until you find what's most tempting to you. Among the choices are scrambled eggs, salads (several dozen kinds), stews, pasta, potato pancakes, grilled chicken, daily specials, desserts, and wines. Wertheim is conveniently located on the Ku'damm, across the street from the Kaiser-Wilhelm Gedächtniskirche.

EINHORN, Wittenbergplatz 5-6. Tel. 218 63 47.

Cuisine: VEGETARIAN. **U-Bahn:** Wittenbergplatz, a 1-minute walk.
$ Prices: 7–11 DM ($4.35–$6.85). No credit cards.
Open: Mon–Fri 9am–6pm, Sat 10am–1:30pm.

This natural-foods shop, on the north end of Wittenbergplatz, has vegetarian daily specials, such as curry risotto with vegetables, spinach cannelloni, vegetarian lasagne, stews, salads, spinach casserole, and vegetarian moussaka. There is also a tempting variety of fruit juices; if you've been dying for some wholesome cereal or snacks, this is your best bet. There are stand-up counters inside; but if the weather is fine, you'll want to find a seat on one of the benches lining the square.

There's another location at Mommsenstrasse 2 (tel. 881 42.41), a minute's walk north of the Ku'damm near Knesebeckstrasse, with the same hours.

IHRE FRISCH-BACKSTÜBE, Knesebeckstrasse 12. Tel. 31 06 00.

Cuisine: GERMAN/SANDWICHES. **S-Bahn:** Savignyplatz, a 4-minute walk. **U-Bahn:** Ernst-Reuter-Platz, about a 5-minute walk.

$ Prices: 4–10 DM ($2.50–$6.25). No credit cards.
   Open: Mon–Sat 6:30am–6:30pm, Sun 1–5pm.

Located on the corner of Knesebeckstrasse and Goethestrasse north of Savignyplatz, this neighborhood bakery has a self-service counter with a variety of take-out or eat-in food, as well as cheerful dining area. In addition to the breads and cakes, it also offers pizza by the slice, sandwiches, and a changing menu of warm dishes—from smoked pork chops to Leberkäs and Sauerkraut. With its competitive prices and well-prepared food, this place is a good alternative to the usual fast-food joint. It's a 10-minute walk north of the Ku'damm.

It has several branches throughout the city, including a convenient corner *Imbiss* at Wilmersdorfer Strasse and Pestalozzistrasse (tel. 310 600), open Monday to Friday from 6am to 6:30pm (to 8:30pm on Thursday), and Saturday from 6am to 2pm (to 4pm first Saturday of the month). Much smaller than the above store, it sells take-out sandwiches, cakes, desserts, and breads.

ITALIA SNACK, Kurfürstendamm 63. Tel. 881 18 42.

   Cuisine: ITALIAN. **U-Bahn:** Adenauerplatz, about a 3-minute walk.
$ Prices: 9–18 DM ($5.60–$11.25). No credit cards.
   Open: Daily 11am–1am.

With a great location on the Ku'damm, this self-service restaurant has soups, omelets, pasta, salads, seafood, pizza, and beef dishes, as well as a daily set menu for 13 DM ($8.10). All the pizzas and pastas are under 12 DM ($7.50).

JIMMY'S DINER, Pariser Strasse 41. Tel. 882 31 41.

   Cuisine: AMERICAN/MEXICAN. **Directions:** A 5-minute walk south of the Ku'damm, on the corner of Sächsischer and Pariser streets.
$ Prices: 8–15 DM ($5–$9.35). No credit cards.
   Open: Sun–Thurs noon–4am, Fri–Sat noon–6am.

If you're dying for a hamburger or Mexican tacos—especially in the middle of the night—this '50s-style American diner with bright-red plastic furniture and lots of chrome is just the place. Drive-in speakers dangle above the windows. It has an eclectic menu, from corn on the cob to Aunt Mary's chicken to "quarter pownders"—as well as sandwiches, spareribs, spaghetti, tacos, enchiladas, and chili con carne. The burgers are gigantic. There's even Mexican beer and Mexican and country music.

KADEWE, Wittenbergplatz. Tel. 212 10.

   Cuisine: INTERNATIONAL. **U-Bahn:** Wittenbergplatz, less than a 1-minute walk.
$ Prices: 4–20 DM ($2.50–$12.50). No credit cards.
   Open: Mon–Fri 9am–6pm (to 8pm on Thurs), Sat 9am–1pm (to 5:30pm first Sat of the month).

Every visitor to Berlin should visit KaDeWe, simply for the experience. KaDeWe is the popular name for Kaufhaus des Westens, the largest department store on the European continent. And its top attraction is its food emporium on the sixth floor. It's massive, with row after row of gourmet foods, including exotic teas and coffees, spices, jams, sweets, vegetables, fruits, and an amazing array of sausages and cuts of pork. Spread throughout are more than a dozen sit-down counters, each specializing in a different type of food—such as pasta, Asian cuisine, grilled chicken, salads, sandwiches, oysters, and more. One counter is devoted to the potato—you can order it baked or fried in a number of styles. There's also a wine bar and a coffee bar. It's easy to get lost in this huge place, and you'll find the abundance of food either wonderful or decadent.

KARAVAN, Kurfürstendamm 11. Tel. 881 50 05.
   Cuisine: TURKISH. **U-Bahn:** Kurfürstendamm or Bahnhof Zoo, each less than a 2-minute walk.
$ Prices: 4–9 DM ($2.50–$5.60). No credit cards.
   Open: Daily 9am–midnight.

A good place to sample Turkish cuisine—at very inexpensive prices—faces the Kaiser-Wilhelm Gedächtniskirche. It's tiny and informal, consisting of a glass counter displaying the various dishes available. There are stools along the wall where you can eat your meal, or better yet, order take-out and sit at the restaurant's outdoor tables or public benches on the plaza, a great spot for people-watching. Try the Turkish pizza, which has a thick, soft crust with a thin spread of minced meat and spices, or the *kofti* burger, a Turkish-style burger. There's also a changing daily special, such as meat-filled eggplant, as well as Turkish sandwiches and salads.

There's another branch nearby called Meister Snack, located under the eaves of the Bilka department store on the corner of Joachimstaler Strasse and Kantstrasse, not far from Bahnhof Zoo. It offers the same Turkish food.

LEKKERBEK, Ansbacherstrasse 11. Tel. 211 90 34.
   Cuisine: PASTA/PIZZA/SANDWICHES. **U-Bahn:** Wittenberg-platz, about a 3-minute walk.
$ Prices: 4–10 DM ($2.50–$6.25). No credit cards.
   Open: Mon–Fri 7:30am–8pm, Sat 9am–8pm.

I wish there were more places like this: inexpensive food, an imaginative dining area, centrally located, and even a no-smoking section. Lekkerbek is a cafeteria specializing in sandwiches, with a dozen or so fillings prepared fresh each day such as egg, salami, ham, or tuna fish. There are also pasta dishes, pizza, salads, and daily specials ranging from spaghetti to moussaka to rice pilaf with chicken. Its walls are hand-painted in fanciful murals.

MENSA, Technische Universität, Hardenbergstrasse 34. Tel. 3140.
   Cuisine: GERMAN. **U-Bahn:** Ernst-Reuter-Platz, a few minutes' walk.
$ Prices: 3–5 DM ($1.85–$3.10). No credit cards.
   Open: Year round Mon–Fri 11:30am–2:30pm.

Every German university has a Mensa, a student cafeteria offering inexpensive meals for its enrolled students. Berlin's Technical University has this, as well as a self-serve restaurant on its top floor that is open to everyone, students and nonstudents alike. It's one of the cheapest places in Berlin for a meal and only a 6- to 10-minute walk from Bahnhof Zoo. Simply walk through the Mensa and follow the signs for *Restaurant,* up the stairs to the top floor. Pick up a tray and choose from one of the daily changing menus, complete meals that may range from *Gulasch* (beef stew) to curried rice, liver, or a vegetarian ragoût.

ORIENT, Lietzenburgerstrasse 77. Tel. 881 24 60.

Cuisine: MIDDLE EASTERN. **U-Bahn:** Uhlandstrasse, about a 3-minute walk.
$ Prices: 8–20 DM ($5–$12.50). No credit cards.
Open: Daily noon–3am.

Located south of the Ku'damm, the Orient specializes in Middle Eastern and Mediterranean dishes. Although it does a brisk business in take-out orders, there's a dining area—nothing fancy but pleasant. There are only a dozen items on the menu, but many are priced under 12 DM ($7.50). There's felafel, kebab, *maali* (a vegetarian dish of cauliflower, potatoes, and eggplant), gyros, and *muhamara* (puréed red paprika with walnuts). Daily specials are displayed behind the take-out counter.

PICCOLA TAORMINA TAVOLA CALDA, Uhlandstrasse 29. Tel. 881 47 10.

Cuisine: ITALIAN. **U-Bahn:** Uhlandstrasse, a 2-minute walk.
$ Prices: 6–15 DM ($3.75–$9.35). No credit cards.
Open: Daily 10:30am–2am.

Located just south of Ku'damm, it's especially popular for its pizza by the slice for 2.50 DM ($1.55), attracting hungry customers around the clock. A menu on the wall lists more than 25 different personal-size pizzas (big enough for two), omelets, risotto, beefsteak, and pasta. The cooks, all Italian, will have your order ready in no time. Wine and beer are also available, and there's plenty of dining space in the back or you can order take-out. Cheap.

PIZZA BLEIBTREU, Bleibtreustrasse 41. Tel. 883 47 78.

Cuisine: ITALIAN. **S-Bahn:** Savignyplatz, about a 2-minute walk.
$ Prices: 6–20 DM ($3.75–$12.50). No credit cards.
Open: Daily 11am–1am.

This tiny place—with only four stools outside and two tables inside, offers about 26 various kinds of pizza, as well as omelets, salads, pasta, meat dishes, and fish. All its pizza and pasta dishes are priced below 12 DM ($7.50), with a slice of pizza at 2 DM ($1.25).

RESTAURANT MARCHE MÖVENPICK, Kurfürstendamm 14–15. Tel. 882 75 78.

Cuisine: INTERNATIONAL. **U-Bahn:** Kurfürstendamm, a 1-minute walk.
$ Prices: 8–15 DM ($8–$9.35). V.
Open: Daily 8am–midnight.

Run by the Swiss-owned Mövenpick chain of restaurants, this cafeteria imitates the neighborhood market, with various stands of fresh meals—most prepared in front of the customers. A raw vegetable stand offers lettuce and cut carrots, while the grill stand offers a selection of meat dishes. Other stands have soups, pasta, salads, daily specials, cakes, ice cream, and desserts. You have a choice of several dining areas, including sidewalk seating. A great place for a casual meal on the Ku'damm.

BERLIN-MITTE [EASTERN BERLIN]

These budget-priced establishments are located in eastside Berlin, convenient if you're visiting Museumsinsel. In addition to the restaurants listed here, several restaurants listed under "Meals for less than 25 DM ($15.60)" offer some dishes for less than 12 DM ($7.50), such as Würste or omelets.

CASINO, in the Staatsbibliothek, Unter den Linden 8. Tel. 2037 83 10.

Cuisine: GERMAN. **Bus:** 100 or 157 to the Staatsoper stop.

$ Prices: Soup or salad 2.50–5.50 DM ($1.55–$3.45); main courses 6–10 DM ($3.75–$6.25). No credit cards.

Open: Mon–Fri 8am–6pm.

This inexpensive cafeteria, located in a public library right on Unter den Linden, offers a limited number of soups, a salad of the day, and daily specials written on a blackboard. Offerings may include Schnitzel, Rumpsteak, fish, or Boulette. Coffee is a cheap 1.30 DM (80¢) a cup. It's a small place, so you may want to avoid the lunch-hour rush. Convenient for sightseeing jaunts along Unter den Linden and to Museumsinsel with its many museums.

NORDSEE, Spandauer Strasse 4. Tel. 242 68 81.

Cuisine: SEAFOOD. **S-Bahn and U-Bahn:** Alexanderplatz, a 3-minute walk. **Bus:** 100 to Spandauer Strasse.

$ Prices: 7–12 DM ($4.35–$7.50). No credit cards.

Open: Mon–Sat 10am–9:30pm, Sun 11am–7pm.

One of the first chain restaurants to open in what was formerly East Berlin, this Nordsee just off Alexanderplatz is bigger than most, offering plenty of tables and doing a brisk business. An illustrated menu behind the self-service counter makes ordering easy. There are more than a half dozen choices available, including fish soup, paella, fried haddock, fish sticks, and salads. There are also fish sandwiches available for take-out.

SELF-SERVICE TERRACE OF OPERNPALAIS, Unter den Linden 5. Tel. 200 22 69.

Cuisine: GERMAN/SNACKS. **U-Bahn:** Französische Strasse, about a 7-minute walk.

$ Prices: 2.50–5 DM ($1.55–$3.10). No credit cards.

Open: Summer daily 8am–10pm; winter daily noon–6pm.

The Opernpalais (formerly Operncafé), is one of Berlin's best-known restaurants and coffeehouses, with prices well over 12 DM ($7.50). However, outside the café, in a pretty, tree-shaded square, is a self-service *Imbiss* selling sandwiches, croissants, Würste, and Boulettes, as well as coffee, wine, beer, and other drinks. Eat your purchase at one of the tables beside the *Imbiss*—but don't wander to the tables on the terrace, as these are reserved for coffeehouse customers with waitress service.

ZUM PADDENWIRT, Eiergasse. Tel. 2431 32 31.

Cuisine: GERMAN. **U-Bahn or S-Bahn:** Alexanderplatz or Klosterstrasse, each about a 5-minute walk.

$ Prices: 7–17 DM ($4.35–$10.60). No credit cards.

Open: Daily 11am–midnight.

Located in the Nikolaiviertel behind the Nikolaikirche (St. Nicholas's Church), this is a simple tavern that serves hearty portions of German food at inexpensive prices, including Boulette, *Sülze, Kasslerbraten,* and daily specials. Beer is 5.20 DM ($3.25) for a half of a liter.

ZUR LETZTEN INSTANZ, Waisenstrasse 14–16. Tel. 242 55 28.
Cuisine: GERMAN. **U-Bahn:** Klosterstrasse, about a 2-minute walk.
$ Prices: 6–18 DM ($3.75–$11.25). No credit cards.
Open: Mon 4pm–midnight, Tues–Sun 11am–midnight.

Open since 1621, this tiny restaurant claims to be Berlin's oldest *Gaststätte*. Its rooms have plank floors, wainscoting, and a few antiques here and there. Its menu offers Berlin specialties, including Boulette, *Gefüllte Kohlroulade* (stuffed cabbage rolls), Schnitzel, and *Berliner Eisbein*. For dessert there's *Rote Grütze* (cooked fruits with a vanilla sauce). In summer, there are a few tables tucked into a tiny garden under spreading trees. You might have trouble finding this place—it's located about a 5-minute walk behind the red-colored Rathaus (city hall).

NEAR WILMERSDORFER STRASSE & BAHNHOF CHARLOTTENBURG

All these budget-priced restaurants and stand-up eateries are located on Wilmersdorfer Strasse, Berlin's main pedestrian-only shopping lane. Several of them are located in department stores, always a good bet for budget-priced meals.

CAFE-RESTAURANT, Karstadt, Wilmersdorfer Strasse 109–111. Tel. 31 891.
Cuisine: GERMAN. **U-Bahn:** Wilmersdorfer Strasse, a 1-minute walk.
$ Prices: 7–19 DM ($4.35–$11.85). No credit cards.
Open: Mon–Fri 9:30am–6pm (Thurs to 8pm), Sat 9:30am–1:30pm (to 5:30pm first Sat of the month in winter, to 3:30pm first Sat of the month in summer).

One of several large department stores on Wilmersdorfer Strasse, Karstadt has an inexpensive restaurant with waitress service on the fourth floor. Daily specials may include Schnitzel, Rumpsteak, fish filet with rémoulade sauce, chicken fricassee, or spaghetti—most about 12 DM ($7.50) for a complete meal. There's also a salad bar, and you can order breakfast until 11:30am. In the afternoons there's a tempting array of desserts for the traditional coffee break.

DIE BUFFETERIA, Quelle, Wilmersdorfer Strasse 54. Tel. 320 05 211.
Cuisine: GERMAN. **U-Bahn:** Wilmersdorfer Strasse, a 1-minute walk.
$ Prices: 9–15 DM ($5.60–$9.35). No credit cards.
Open: Mon–Fri 9:30am–6pm (Thurs to 8pm), Sat 9:30am–1:30pm (to 3:30pm first Sat of the month in summer, to 5:30pm in winter).

Not to be outdone is Die Buffeteria, located on the second floor of Quelle department store. I consider this the most cheerful of the store restaurants, with its white, summerlike atmosphere (though I could do without the plastic plants). This cafeteria offers a wide variety of daily specials, such as fish of the day, grilled chicken, steak, a pork spaghetti, *Gulasch,* Schnitzel, curried lamb ragoût, and Sauerbraten. There's also a help-yourself salad bar, a selection of soups, and beer. Breakfast is served until 11am. There's even a no-smoking section, rare in Germany's restaurants.

(Map of the Berlin-Mitte area showing streets including Alexanderstrasse, Dircksenstrasse, Alexanderplatz, S-Bahn Alexanderplatz, Nikolaiviertel, Stralauer Strasse, Spree, Mühlendamm, Rathausstrasse, Grünerstrasse, Karl-Liebknecht-strasse, S-Bahn Hackescher Markt, Bodestrasse, Spandauer Strasse, Marx-Engels-Forum, Breite Strasse, Museumsinsel, Marx-Engels-Platz, Kurstrasse, Werder-Strasse, Graben, Am Kupfer-, Bebelplatz, Universitäts-, Strasse, Behrenstrasse, Ziegestrasse, Charlotten Strasse, S-Bahn Friedrichstrasse, Mittelstrasse, Friedrichstrasse, Französische Strasse, Neustadt Kirch-, Glinka-Strasse, Mauerstrasse, Reinhardtstrasse, Spree am Wedend, Uber am, Clara-Zetkin-, UNTER DEN LINDEN, Marienstrasse, Brandenburger Tor, Otto-, Grotewohl-Strasse, Matern-Strasse, WEST BERLIN AREA)

Casino ◆4
Dom Klause ◆6
Ermeler Haus ◆2
Nordsee ◆7

Operncafé ◆4
Opernpalais ◆5
Oren ◆3
Wienerwald ◆10

Zille Stube ◆11
Zum Paddenwirt ◆8
Zur Letzten Instanz ◆9

JOSEPH LANGER, Wilmersdorfer Strasse 118. Tel. 31 67 80.
   Cuisine: GERMAN. **U-Bahn:** Wilmersdorfer Strasse, a 1-minute walk.
$ Prices: 2–9 DM ($1.25–$5.60). No credit cards.
   Open: Mon–Fri 9am–6:30pm, Sat 8:30am–2pm (to 6pm first Sat of the month).
Joseph Langer is a butcher shop that specializes in inexpensive, simple

meat dishes. You can order take-out or eat standing up at one of its chest-high tables. There's Würste for 2 DM ($1.25); other offerings include Leberkäs, Gulasch soup, Schnitzel, Eisbein, Boulette, and potato salad.

LE BUFFET, Hertie, Wilmersdorfer Strasse 118–119. Tel. 31 10 50.

Cuisine: GERMAN. **U-Bahn:** Wilmersdorfer Strasse, a 1-minute walk.

$ Prices: 8–13 DM ($5–$8.10). No credit cards.

Open: Mon–Fri 9:30am–6pm (Thurs to 8pm), Sat 9am–1:30pm (to 5:30pm first Sat of the month in winter, 3:30pm in summer).

Le Buffet is a department store restaurant on the first floor with waitress service. Its menu lists spaghetti, scrambled eggs, chicken breast filet, and Schnitzel, and there are also changing specials for less than 11 DM ($6.85).

NORDSEE, Wilmersdorfer Strasse 58. Tel. 323 10 44.

Cuisine: SEAFOOD. **U-Bahn:** Wilmersdorfer Strasse, a 1-minute walk.

$ Prices: 6.50–11 DM ($4.05–$6.85). No credit cards.

Open: Mon–Fri 9am–7pm (Thurs to 8:30pm), Sat 9am–3pm (to 6:30pm first Sat of the month).

As the name suggests, Nordsee is a chain of fast-food fish restaurants that originated in northern Germany. Ordering is easy, since the menu is illustrated on the wall, and there's fried haddock, herring, fish sticks, and fish soup. Take-out service is offered with fish sandwiches starting at around 3 DM ($1.85).

ROGACKI, Wilmersdorfer Strasse 145–146. Tel. 341 40 91.

Cuisine: GERMAN. **U-Bahn:** Bismarckstrasse, a 1-minute walk.

$ Prices: 4–15 DM ($2.50–$9.35). No credit cards.

Open: Mon–Fri 9am–6pm, Sat 8am–2pm.

S This butcher shop—in business more than 60 years and famous throughout Berlin for its meats—is a great place if you want to dine like a king on less than 10 DM ($6.25) and don't mind standing up. This large store is devoted mostly to retail sales of Würste, fish, cheeses, and breads, but it also has a self-service counter located in the back left corner of the shop. Main courses may include pig's knuckle, fish, grilled chicken, Würste, salads, and stews. North of Bismarckstrasse; look for a picture of a blue fish on its facade.

IN DAHLEM

Since Dahlem is primarily residential, the Gaststätte below is your best bet for an inexpensive meal. For even cheaper dining, head for Inge Drei Sterne Imbiss, a thatched-roof food stall across from the Dahlem U-Bahn station on Königin-Luise-Strasse. Open daily from 6:30am to 8pm, it offers a variety of Würste, Boulette, noodle salad, potato salad, french fries, beer, and soft drinks. In addition to its stand-up tables, there are a couple park benches where you can sit down.

Right beside the U-Bahn station is another food stall, called Imbiss am U-Bahnhof Dahlem-Dorf. It also offers a variety of Würste, as well as Boulette, Hähnchen Schnitzel (chicken Schnitzel) with french fries and salad, and a gyros hamburger with kraut salad and tzatziki. Prices range from about 3 to 7 DM ($1.85–$4.35).

LUISE, Königin-Luise-Strasse 40. Tel. 832 84 87.
   Cuisine: GERMAN/INTERNATIONAL. **U-Bahn:** Dahlem-Dorf, about a 1-minute walk.
$ Prices: 8–16 DM ($5–$10). No credit cards.
   Open: Daily 10am–11pm.

To reach this extremely popular watering hole and informal dining establishment, turn right out of the Dahlem-Dorf U-Bahn station, cross the street, and almost immediately to your right you'll see a large baroque-style building, with a large beer garden. Although people living in the area come here mainly to drink and socialize, Luise also serves snacks and main courses—including onion soup, spaghetti, eggplant casserole, Schnitzel, Gulasch, and garlic chicken. Its drinking menu is substantial, including wines, grog, champagne, Schnaps, liqueur, brandy, and long drinks. I'm fond of the Weissbier, a wheat beer. And of course, the wonderful beer garden is open in fine weather. Indoor dining tends to be a bit smoky, since every other German seems to smoke.

NEAR RATHAUS SCHÖNEBERG

KASINO BEIM SENATOR FÜR WIRTSCHAFT UND VERKEHR, Martin-Luther-Strasse 105. Tel. 784 77 24.
   Cuisine: GERMAN. **U-Bahn:** Rathaus Schöneberg, about a 2-minute walk.
$ Prices: Fixed-price lunches 4.80–6.50 DM ($3–$4.05). No credit cards.
   Open: Mon–Fri 11:30am–2pm.

This simple cafeteria on the fifth floor of the administration building for trade and industry—look for the sign on the front door that says "Senatsverwaltung für Wirtschaft"—is open to the general public. Take the elevator and then follow the sign that says "Zur Kantine" (it won't look as if there's a restaurant when you step out of the elevator). Popular with young and old alike, this canteen offers two fixed-price lunches a day, as well as one stew for about 3 DM ($1.85). The menu changes daily; dishes in the past have included Schweinebraten with red cabbage and potatoes, stuffed cabbage rolls with potatoes, Gulasch with mushrooms and noodles, and grilled trout with salad and potatoes. Be sure to clear your own tray when you leave.

IN KREUZBERG

HENNE, Leuschnerdamm 25. Tel. 614 77 30.
   Cuisine: CHICKEN. **Reservations:** Imperative. **U-Bahn:** Moritzplatz, an 8-minute walk.
$ Prices: 9.50 DM ($5.95). No credit cards.
   Open: Wed–Sun 7pm–midnight.

You'll never get a table if you don't have a reservation—proof that here you'll find the best grilled chicken in town (*Henne* means hen). In fact, that's all it serves besides potato salad and kraut salad. Its chickens are milk-fed, and their skins are deliciously crispy. A half chicken costs 9.50 DM ($5.95), while potato salad or kraut salad is an extra 3 DM ($1.85). The beer's good, too, especially the dark Klosterschwarzbier, and the ambience is even better. Packed with everyone from students to professionals—the restaurant looks ancient, with brown spotted walls, a clock that runs late, antlers everywhere, an elaborate wooden bar, and small wooden barrels that used to hold grog and raspberry juice. Behind the bar hangs a photo of John F. Kennedy, who was invited to Henne during his Berlin trip: He didn't eat here, but he did send a letter of apology.

2. MEALS FOR LESS THAN 25 DM ($15.60)

You can expect to pay 15 to 25 DM ($9.35 to $15.60) for meals at places listed in this category, excluding alcoholic beverages but including an appetizer or soup and one of the more reasonably priced main courses. On the other hand, if you want to splurge, you could easily spend more than 30 DM ($18.75) by indulging in one of the more expensive dishes. Remember, main courses usually include one or two side dishes, making them complete meals in themselves.

ON OR NEAR THE KU'DAMM

ANGORA, Schlüterstrasse 29/30. Tel. 323 70 96.
Cuisine: TURKISH. **S-Bahn:** Savignyplatz, a 2-minute walk.
$ **Prices:** Appetizers 8–14 DM ($5–$8.75); main courses 18–28 DM ($11.25–$17.50). No credit cards.
Open: Sun–Thurs 5pm–2am, Fri–Sat 5pm–4am.

Named after Turkey's ancient capital, Angora is an upscale restaurant coolly decorated with stone walls upon which are carved reproductions of stone reliefs dating from 1300 B.C. Candles are on each table, the staff is courteous and efficient, and the clientele is well dressed. Its menu includes all the national favorites, including shish kebab, rack of lamb, veal, fish, and grilled dishes.

ANO KATO, Leibnizstrasse 70. Tel. 31 04 70.
Cuisine: GREEK. **S-Bahn:** Savignyplatz, a 4-minute walk. **U-Bahn:** Wilmersdorfer Strasse, a 4-minute walk.
$ **Prices:** Main courses 11–22 DM ($6.85–$13.75). No credit cards.
Open: Daily 6pm–12:30am.

This unpretentious Greek restaurant with its wooden floor, wainscoting, white tablecloths, candles, and cheerful Greek music is a popular choice for a casual meal, which can range from moussaka, souvlaki, lamb, and gyros to calamari. Most dishes average 16 DM ($10); a half liter of retsina (a resin-flavored wine) is 10 DM ($6.25).

BERLINER STUBE, Steigenberger Hotel, Los-Angeles-Platz 1. Tel. 210 80.
Cuisine: GERMAN. **U-Bahn:** Kurfürstendamm, a 2-minute walk.
$ **Prices:** Appetizers and soups 6–20 DM ($3.75–$12.50); main courses 12–35 DM ($7.50–$21.85). AE, DC, MC, V.
Open: Daily noon–3pm and 6–11:30pm.

I usually recommend eating outside of hotels, as local places better represent the city's cuisine. But this rustic-looking restaurant—designed to resemble an old-style Berliner pub—is a favorite with visiting and native businesspeople, especially for lunch. Conveniently

MEALS FOR LESS THAN 25 DM ($15.60) • 99

 FROMMER'S SMART TRAVELER: RESTAURANTS

VALUE-CONSCIOUS TRAVELERS SHOULD TAKE ADVANTAGE OF THE FOLLOWING:

1. Daily specials—usually not on the regular menu—which often include a main course and side dishes.
2. Fixed-price lunches—available from about 11am to 2pm, which include an appetizer or soup, main course, and dessert—cheaper than those on the dinner menu.
3. Less expensive main courses, such as Würste (sausages) or stews, offered by more stylish and expensive restaurants.
4. Ethnic cuisine—reasonably priced.
5. Restaurants and food counters in department stores—a good value in Berlin.
6. Restaurants in former East Berlin and Potsdam—often much cheaper than those in western Berlin.
7. Berlin's food stands called *Imbisse*—selling Würste, french fries, and other fast foods.
8. Pubs and bars open late and serving snacks or complete meals—reasonably priced.
9. Coffee-shop chains such as Tschibo, with coffee at 1.20 DM (75¢) a cup.

QUESTIONS TO ASK IF YOU'RE ON A BUDGET

1. Is there an extra charge for each piece of bread consumed? Many restaurants charge extra for each slice you take from the basket in the middle of your table.
2. Does the main course come with side dishes? If so, it may be all you want to order, unless you have a voracious appetite.
3. Is there a special of the day or a fixed-price lunch not listed on the regular menu? It's important to ask about specials if you're reading from an English menu—as these are often printed only in German.

located near the Ku'damm and the Europa-Center, it offers seasonal German specialties that include smoked eel, Swabian ravioli, lamb stew, veal roulade, fresh fish, and knuckle of pork. There are always several choices for fish, from poached halibut to roasted salmon steak. Take advantage of the changing lunch special, a complete meal usually priced between 15 and 20 DM ($9.35–$12.50). Sundays feature a buffet for 39 DM ($24.35). In summer there's outdoor seating.

CHUNG, Kurfürstendamm 190. Tel. 882 15 55.
Cuisine: CHINESE. **U-Bahn:** Uhlandstrasse or Adenauerplatz, each a 6-minute walk.
$ Prices: Appetizers 5–16 DM ($3.10–$10), main courses 15–30 DM ($9.35–$18.75), fixed lunches 11–14 DM ($6.85–$8.75). AE, MC, V.
Open: Daily 11:30am–midnight.
This ornate Chinese restaurant with hanging lanterns and a red-and-

black ceiling occupies a prime spot on the Ku'damm—its glass-enclosed front dining room extends right over the sidewalk and affords a wonderful view. The best time to come is for lunch, when fixed-price meals are available Monday to Friday (excluding holidays) from 11:30am to 3pm. These consist of a choice of soup or spring roll, along with almost two dozen choices of a main dish. The menu in English has a seemingly endless list of dishes, including roast duck and chicken Shanghai style. The Asian staff is friendly and obliging.

CIAO CIAO, Kurfürstendamm 156. Tel. 892 36 12.

Cuisine: ITALIAN. **U-Bahn:** Adenauerplatz, a 1-minute walk.

$ Prices: Appetizers and soups 7–30 DM ($4.35–$18.75), pizzas and pastas 12–24 DM ($7.50–$15). MC, V.

Open: Sun–Thurs noon–2am, Fri–Sat noon–3am.

This lively, informal Italian restaurant is a great place to dine, with an animated Italian staff and plenty to watch on the Ku'damm if you can get a seat outside in summer. In fact, it gets so crowded in summer, you should make a reservation for dinner. Since its main dishes are a bit pricey for what they offer, your best bet is to order the carpaccio and one of the dozen choices of pizza or pasta. West of Adenauerplatz, past Athener Grill.

DORFGASTHAUS, Sächsische Strasse 7. Tel. 882 60 60 or 881 92 39.

Cuisine: GERMAN. **Directions:** A 5-minute walk south of the Ku'damm, south of Bleibtreustrasse.

$ Prices: Soups and salads 6–15 DM ($3.75–$9.35), main courses 12–33 DM ($7.50–$20.60). AE, DC, MC, V.

Open: Daily 11am–midnight.

This great German restaurant, decorated in old-Berlin style, has an atmosphere that is both traditional and trendy, casual and refined. Whereas many Gaststätten appeal to an older clientele, this one draws a younger crowd, who come for the Schnitzel, steak béarnaise, Sauerbraten, and specialties of southern Germany. You might wish to start your meal with a traditional bowl of Leberknödelsuppe or Schwäbische Maultaschensuppe (Swabian soup with meat-filled ravioli). The *Filet-teller* Baden-Baden is a platter of pork médaillons with a mushroom sauce and green pepper, along with side dishes of broccoli with cheese, sauce béarnaise, and homemade *Spätzle* (noodles). You'll need to go on a diet after you've eaten this meal.

GRUNG THAI, Ku'damm Passage, Kurfürstendamm 202. Tel. 881 53 50.

Cuisine: THAI. **U-Bahn:** Uhlandstrasse, less than a 4-minute walk.

$ Prices: Appetizers and soups 6–14 DM ($3.75–$8.75), main courses 17–30 DM ($10.60–$18.75). AE, DC, MC, V.

Open: Mon–Thurs 5pm–3am, Fri–Sun noon–3am.

This Thai restaurant is located in a small mall on the corner of the Ku'damm and Knesebeckstrasse, and strives for an exotic atmosphere with elephant statues and Thai artifacts. There are more than 100 items on the menu, including my favorites: chicken soup with coconut milk and lemongrass, Thai noodles with seafood, and spicy beef salad. There are also curries, salads, and fish, pork, and beef dishes. Try Singha beer, Thailand's national drink. With live music and dancing every Friday and Saturday evening starting at 9pm. After midnight, you must enter the restaurant through the passage on Knesebeckstrasse.

HARDTKE, Meinekestrasse 27 A & B. Tel. 881 98 27.

Cuisine: GERMAN. **U-Bahn:** Uhlandstrasse, less than a 2-minute walk.

$ Prices: Appetizers and soups 6.50–17 DM ($4.05–$10.60), main courses 15–29 DM ($9.35–$18.10). No credit cards.

Open: Daily 11am–12:30am.

This is one of Berlin's best-known restaurants. Just a minute's walk south of the Ku'damm, this establishment has been serving hearty German fare for almost 40 years and is very popular with German visitors to Berlin, especially retired men and women. Packed almost every night of the week, Hardtke boasts its own butcher shop, assuring the freshest cuts, and its sausages are excellent. The dining area is divided into two separate halls (hence the two addresses A and B), both with the same menu and rustic appearance of a Gaststätte. Specialties include Berliner Eisbein with vegetables, Sauerkraut, and potatoes; Brathering with potatoes; Sauerbraten or Schweinebraten with red cabbage and potato dumplings; and Berliner Boulette with red cabbage and potatoes. You could easily spend 30 DM ($18.75) on a great meal, or dine on sausages for 10.50 DM ($6.55) if you come during the day (after 6pm, the price of sausages increases to 15 DM or $9.35). Try the fresh bloodwurst and liverwurst, gigantic Bockwurst with potato salad, Bratwurst with potatoes and Sauerkraut, or the Würste platter—all Hardtke's homemade sausages. All around, one of the best places in town for a typical German meal.

ISTANBUL, Knesebeckstrasse 77. Tel. 883 27 77 or 312 92 55.

Cuisine: TURKISH. **S-Bahn:** Savignyplatz, less than a 2-minute walk.

$ Prices: Soups and salads 8–10 DM ($5–$6.25); appetizers 10–13 DM ($6.25–$8.10), main courses 20–30 DM ($12.50–$18.75). AE, DC, MC.

Open: Daily noon–midnight.

Located between the Ku'damm and Savignyplatz, this family-run establishment remains one of the oldest and best of Berlin's Turkish restaurants. Try to get a seat in one of the back rooms, dreamily decorated like a mosque. On Friday and Saturday, a belly dancer entertains after 9:30pm. You might wish to start your meal with a Turkish aperitif called *raki,* which is sun-ripened raisins flavored with anise. For an appetizer, try the *yaprak dolmast* (grape leaves stuffed with rice, pine nuts, currants, and herbs) or *hummus* (chick peas with garlic). Main courses range from so-called Turkish pizza (flat bread with chopped meat, the cheapest entrée on the menu) to *donner Kebab* (veal grilled on a rotating spit and served with rice), shish kebab (skewered meat and vegetables), and a wide variety of lamb dishes. With menu in English.

JAHRMARKT, Bleibtreustrasse 49. Tel. 312 14 33.

Cuisine: GERMAN. **Reservations:** Imperative. **S-Bahn:** Savignyplatz, a 1-minute walk.

$ Prices: Soups and salads 6–13 DM ($3.75–$8.10); main courses 12–24 DM ($7.50–$15). DC, MC, V.

Open: Daily noon–midnight.

This wonderful restaurant is one of the best deals in town. Simply decorated with a pub-like atmosphere, it offers a changing daily menu with most main dishes for less than 20 DM ($12.50): such as Schnitzel with potatoes and Sauerkraut; cabbage with smoked sausage and potatoes; beef Gulasch with kidney beans, paprika, and onions with potatoes and mixed salad; pork chops with vegetables, french fries, and salad; and Viennese-style grilled beef with onions served with fried potatoes and mixed salad. The first Sunday of each month also features a warm and cold buffet table; in summer there's outdoor seating.

RESTAURANT IN JÜDISCHEN GEMEINDEHAUS, Fasanen-strasse 79. Tel. 884 20 339.

Cuisine: KOSHER. **U-Bahn:** Uhlandstrasse, a 2-minute walk.

$ Prices: Appetizers 9–12 DM ($5.60–$7.50); fixed-price meals 20–24 DM ($12.50–$15); Sabbath fixed-price meals 35–50 DM ($21.85–$31.25); Tues buffet 38 DM ($23.75). AE, MC, V.

Open: Sun–Fri 11:30am–3pm and 6:30–11pm; Sat 11:30am–2:30pm and 6:30–11pm.

This simple dining hall, in the Jewish Community House, is one of the few places in town for kosher foods. It offers Jewish and Israeli specialties, with about three choices of fixed-price meals that change daily and include soup and dessert. Main courses range from Gulasch to roast veal to lamb chops; appetizers may include tuna fish salad, felafel with pita, moussaka, and stuffed cabbage roll. In fact, one or two appetizers may be all you want to order. If you have a big appetite, you may wish to come for the Tuesday night buffet with warm and cold dishes, 38 DM ($23.75) per person; Sabbath fixed-price meals must be ordered at least a day in advance. It's located north of the Ku'damm, not far from the Bristol Hotel Kempinski.

KALKUTTA, Bleibtreustrasse 17. Tel. 883 62 93.

Cuisine: INDIAN. **S-Bahn:** Savignyplatz, about a 2-minute walk.

$ Prices: Main courses 13–24 DM ($8.10–$15); buffet lunches 9.50–13 DM ($5.90–$8.10). AE, DC, MC, V.

Open: Daily noon–midnight.

Located a block north of the Ku'damm, this tiny and unpretentious restaurant has been serving great curries for 25 years and claims to be Berlin's first Indian restaurant. It is also the only Indian restaurant in Berlin licensed to operate an original clay oven imported from India, which it uses for its breads and excellently prepared grilled foods and tandoori. With painted murals on the wall and Indian music, it attracts a young well-traveled clientele, many of whom have been to India. Dinner offers a wide assortment of tandoori, vegetable curries, and fish, as well as pork, chicken, beef, and veal dishes. Lunch is more economical, with an all-you-can-eat buffet offered Monday to Friday from noon to 3pm. Top off your meal with mango Schnaps or a Darjeeling tea liqueur.

RESTAURANT MEINEKE, Meinekestrasse, 10. Tel. 882 31 58.

Cuisine: GERMAN. **U-Bahn:** Uhlandstrasse or Kurfürsten-damm, each a few minutes' walk.

$ Prices: Soups and appetizers 5–16 DM ($3.10–$10); main courses 10–25 DM ($6.25–$15.60). No credit cards.

Open: Daily noon–12:30am.

Although it's only a decade old, this Gaststätte was cleverly designed to resemble an old Berliner pub, with a wooden floor, a dark-paneled wainscot, and wooden benches built into private niches in the front-room wall. Both a bar and a restaurant, it serves hearty helpings of Kasseler with bread and butter, Brathering, Berliner Boulette, *Bauernsalat* (farmer's salad), Leberkäs, Sülze, Eisbein, Schnitzel, *Forelle* (trout), and Rumpsteak.

MÖVENPICK, Europa-Center. Tel. 262 70 77.

Cuisine: INTERNATIONAL. **U-Bahn:** Kurfürstendamm or Wittenbergplatz, each about a 3-minute walk.

$ Prices: Pizzas and pastas 10.50–17 DM ($6.55–$10.60); main courses 11.50–34 DM ($7.20–$21.25). AE, DC, MC, V.

Open: Sun–Thurs 8am–midnight, Fri–Sat 8am–1am.

Mövenpick is a Swiss chain of restaurants, and this one up on the second floor of the Europa-Center is huge—divided into sections serving different kinds of food. The Backstube specializes in pizza and quiche, and offers seating on a terrace overlooking the inner atrium of the Europa-Center. Le Caveau, a wine cellar with more than 100 different kinds of wine from around the world, is more upscale and offers a changing menu that might include shrimp, roast hare, or turkey breast—with most main dishes from 18 to 34 DM ($11.25 to $21.25). The largest dining area, called Café des Artistes, offers herring, smoked salmon, pasta dishes, curries, steaks, fish, and pork cutlets, as well as a self-service salad bar. One trip through the salad bar with a small plate costs 9 DM ($5.60). In summer, there's outdoor seating with views of the Gedächtniskirche at Mövenpick's ground-floor coffeehouse, which sells snacks and desserts.

SAN MARINO, Savignyplatz 12. Tel. 313 60 86.

Cuisine: ITALIAN. **S-Bahn:** Savignyplatz, a 1-minute walk.

$ Prices: Pizza and pasta 7.50–17 DM ($4.70–$10.60), main courses 15–30 DM ($9.35–$18.75). AE, MC, V.

Open: Daily 11am–1am.

This Italian restaurant is ideally located right on Savignyplatz, just north of Ku'damm. You can dine outside on the square in the summer months, with a pleasant view of grass and trees, and afterward go for a drink in one of the many bars in the neighborhood. In winter, you dine indoors surrounded by artwork and flowers. Although there are steaks and seafood on the English menu, all you need order is a personal-size pizza or pasta dish, most priced under 12 DM ($7.50). It's hard to resist a glass or two of Lambrusco or Chianti.

SHELL, Knesebeckstrasse 22. Tel. 312 83 10.

Cuisine: INTERNATIONAL/VEGETARIAN. **S-Bahn:** Savignyplatz, less than a 2-minute walk.

$ Prices: Soups and salads 8–21 DM ($5–$13.10); main courses 17.50–30 DM ($10.95–$18.75). MC, V.

Open: Mon–Sat 9am–midnight, Sun 10am–midnight.

A corner gas station used to occupy this site, so it seemed only natural that when it changed into a restaurant, its name should be Shell. A simple and pleasant restaurant popular with the many young residents of the area, it has a curved facade of huge windows. The main menu—available throughout the day and evening—has several vegetarian choices, such as risotto with black rice and cashews; tofu with sweet chili, vegetables, sprouts, and noodles; a vegetable plate with hollandaise, potatoes, and salad. Also available are crab with vegetables, Tafelspitz, and pork chops. In addition, there's also a lunch menu until 6pm, with daily specials for less than 20 DM ($12.50). An evening menu offers daily specials for less than 30 DM ($18.75). My only complaint is that service tends to be slow—come here only if you have time or for just a cup of coffee or a beer.

TAVERNA PLAKA, Joachimstaler Strasse 14. Tel. 883 15 57.

Cuisine: GREEK. **U-Bahn:** Kurfürstendamm, less than a 2-minute walk.

$ Prices: Appetizers and salads 7–13 DM ($4.35–$8.10); main courses 16–30 DM ($10–$18.75). No credit cards.

Open: Mon–Fri 4pm–1am, Sat–Sun and holidays noon–2am.

This first-floor Greek restaurant, just south of the Ku'damm, is decorated in a cheerful Mykonos white-and-blue. The Greek waiters are friendly and the food is good no matter what you order or how much you spend. There's the usual moussaka, fish, souvlaki, and gyros on the menu; but if you're on a budget, order the Mesedes Plaka for 12 DM ($7.50). Although it's an appetizer plate, it's plentiful, with *dolmades* (stuffed grape leaves), eggplant salad, feta cheese, and a sampling of other Greek delicacies. An alternative is to order the huge Greek salad (called *choriatiki*). A fun place to dine, especially if you indulge in Greek wine.

TIFFANY'S, Europa-Center, Tauentzienstrasse and Budapester Strasse. Tel. 262 28 76.

Cuisine: INTERNATIONAL. **U-Bahn:** Kurfürstendamm or Wittenbergplatz, each about a 3-minute walk.

$ Prices: Soups and appetizers 6–15 DM ($3.75–$9.35); main courses 9.50–20 DM ($5.95–$12.50). AE, DC, MC, V.

Open: Sun–Thurs 10:30am–12:30am, Fri–Sat 10:30am–1am.

The mall-like setting of the Europa-Center may deter some people from dining here; but if it's raining or snowing, Tiffany's provides an outdoor-café atmosphere. On a stepped terrace under a large skylight and surrounded by plants, this is a good vantage point from which to people-watch. The food itself is rather standard fare, ranging from omelets, spaghetti, fish, and quiche Lorraine to sandwiches. Recommended for a drink or one of its freshly made tortes.

TIMES SQUARE, Kurfürstendamm 203–205. Tel. 881 30 91.

Cuisine: SANDWICHES/AMERICAN/MEXICAN. **U-Bahn:** Uhlandstrasse, less than a 5-minute walk.

$ Prices: 10–20 DM ($6.25–$12.50). AE, DC, MC, V.

Open: Sun–Tues 11am–midnight, Wed–Sat 11am–3am.

Back home you expect a deli to offer affordable sandwiches, but here you're paying for the "exotic" atmosphere of this American-style eatery, right up to the posters of famous New York buildings adorning the wall. However, if you're craving a burger, a corned-beef sandwich, a BLT, club sandwich, chili, a taco, burrito, or tostada, you may be willing to pay any price. More than two dozen sandwiches are available, all served with french fries, coleslaw, and a pickle. Omelets are served around the clock.

WIRTSHAUS ZUM LÖWEN, Hardenbergstrasse 29. Tel. 262 10 20.

Cuisine: GERMAN. **U-Bahn:** Bahnhof Zoo or Kurfürstendamm, each a 1-minute walk.

$ Prices: 10–20 DM ($6.25–$12.50). MC, DC, V.
Open: Sun–Thurs 10am–midnight, Fri–Sat 10am–2am.

This beer hall, tucked away in a plaza, is ingeniously constructed to resemble a tree-filled Bavarian plaza. Like the beer halls of Munich, they serve Bavarian beer, Löwenbräu. It's unabashedly tourist-oriented but is conveniently located near the Gedächtniskirche, in the direction of Bahnhof Zoo. As with most beer halls, there's live music beginning at 7pm, and hearty platters of Bratwurst, Schnitzel, and Berliner Eisbein.

BERLIN-MITTE (EASTERN BERLIN)

These restaurants are convenient if you're visiting the many museums on Museumsinsel.

DOM KLAUSE RESTAURANT/CAFÉ, Palasthotel, Karl-Liebknecht-Strasse 5. Tel. 2382 76 03.
   Cuisine: INTERNATIONAL. **S-Bahn:** Alexanderplatz and Hackescher Markt, each about a 5-minute walk. **Bus:** 100 to Spandauer Strasse.
$ Prices: Soups 6 DM ($3.75); main courses 13–28 DM ($8.10–$17.50). AE, DC, MC, V.
   Open: Daily 11:30am–midnight.

The closest restaurant to Museumsinsel, this eating establishment offers the extra attraction of outdoor dining in summer, with tables set up beside the Spree river affording a view of the Berliner Dom. There are two dining rooms, both with the same menu but with different atmospheres. The Dom Klause is formal, while the Bistro boasts a modern and more casual decor. The menu changes often, offering seasonal and regional specialties that may range from California-style pizza to curries, fish, and rack of lamb. Sundays feature a brunch complete with Dixieland jazz music for 40 DM ($25) per person.

ERMELER HAUS, Märkisches Ufer 10. Tel. 279 36 17.
   Cuisine: GERMAN. **U-Bahn:** Märkisches Museum.
$ Prices: Main courses 10–24 DM ($6.25–$15). AE, MC, V.
   Open: Mon–Fri 11am–midnight.

This ornate, rococo-style mansion, built in the 17th century and once the private residence of a tobacco merchant, has been one of Berlin's best-known restaurants for more than two decades. Facing a canal and located about a 15-minute walk southwest of Alexanderplatz, it's actually two restaurants in one. Up on the first floor is the elegant Weinrestaurant, with entrées averaging about 40 DM ($25). For more affordable dining, head for the basement where you'll find the Raabe-Diele, a rustic pub-style place with wooden tables serving hearty platters of typical German fare, including pork cutlets, fish, Eisbein, and lentil soup. You'd be wise to call first to inquire about exact opening hours—they've been in flux since reunification.

OPERNCAFE, Opernpalais, Unter den Linden 5. Tel. 200 22 69.
   Cuisine: GERMAN/CONTINENTAL. **S-Bahn:** Friedrichstrasse or Französische Strasse, about a 10-minute walk. **Bus:** 100 to Staatsoper.
$ Prices: Main courses 10–20 DM ($6.25–$12.50). AE, DC, MC, V.

Open: Daily 8:30am–midnight.

The Operncafé is one of Berlin's most famous coffeehouses, occupying part of a palace originally built in 1733, destroyed during World War II, and recently renovated at a great cost. A sumptuous breakfast buffet is offered until noon for 16.50 DM ($10.30), followed by an all-you-can-eat salad bar for 14.50 DM ($9.05) and an à la carte menu offering filet mignon, pork médaillons, fish, and daily specials. As many as 25 different tortes are prepared daily. If the weather is fine, you may wish to dine on the outdoor terrace.

In addition to the Operncafé, the Opernpalais contains several other restaurants, all under the same management. Schinkelklause is a cafeteria offering Berliner specialties; Fridericus is a basement restaurant specializing in grilled fish; and Operntreff offers a Mediterranean-inspired buffet nightly from 5pm, as well as a limited menu, cocktails, and live music. If you feel like splurging, head for the first-floor restaurant, Königin Luise, which offers German fare at higher prices and a view of the famous Unter den Linden boulevard.

OREN, Oranienburger Strasse 28. Tel. 282 82 28.

Cuisine: KOSHER. **S-Bahn:** Oranienburger Strasse, a 3-minute walk.

$ Prices: Appetizers and soups 6–17 DM ($3.75–$10.60); main courses 11–22 DM ($6.85–$13.75). No credit cards.

Open: Daily 10am–midnight.

About a 6-minute walk north of Museumsinsel and located next to a towering gold-domed synagogue currently under renovation, this is eastern Berlin's first modern Kosher restaurant and is one of the city's most popular. Decorated in the fashion of a 1920s Berlin coffeehouse and catering to an intellectual crowd, it offers excellently prepared food, with an interesting menu that draws inspiration from Asia, the Middle East, and international vegetarian cuisines. Perhaps you'll want to start with the Russian borscht or lentil soup, followed by moussaka, vegetarian quiche, broccoli lasagne, potato and spinach casserole, or grilled fish. The Orient Express platter, with its assortment of Middle Eastern vegetarian food, is especially good.

WIENERWALD, Rathausstrasse 5. Tel. 242 32 91.

Cuisine: GERMAN. **S-Bahn and U-Bahn:** Alexanderplatz, a 1-minute walk.

$ Prices: Soups and salads 4–14 DM ($2.50–$8.75); main courses 11–17 DM ($6.85–$10.60). AE, MC, V.

Open: Daily 10am–midnight.

A successful chain of restaurants specializing in grilled chicken, this comfortable, family-style restaurant offers a variety of chicken dishes, fish, soups, and a salad bar. An especially good deal is the quarter chicken with french fries for less than $5. There's a no-smoking section. It's located just off Alexanderplatz, near a post office.

ZILLE STUBE, Forum Hotel, Alexanderplatz. Tel. 219 42 45.

Cuisine: GERMAN. **S-Bahn:** Alexanderplatz.

$ Prices: Soups and appetizers 4.50–10 DM ($2.80–$6.25); main courses 10–20 DM ($6.25–$12.50). AE, MC, V.

Open: Daily 11am–midnight.

Located on the first floor of this high-rise hotel in the middle of

Alexanderplatz but with its own entrance, this restaurant/bar resembles a Gaststätte, with golden-oak wainscoting and an ornate wooden bar. Best of all, it provides a good view of Alexanderplatz. Its menu offers traditional Berlin food, including Eisbein, as well as other dishes ranging from omelets and fish to a Bauernfrühstück (scrambled eggs with ham and pickles).

NEAR WILMERSDORFER STRASSE & BAHNHOF CHARLOTTENBURG

TEGERNSEER TÖNNCHEN, Mommsenstrasse 34. Tel. 323 38 27.

    Cuisine: GERMAN. **U-Bahn:** Wilmersdorfer Strasse, about a 4-minute walk.

$ Prices: Main courses 10–20 DM ($6.25–$12.50). No credit cards.

    Open: Daily 11:30am–midnight.

This typical Gaststätte near Bahnhof Charlottenburg specializes in local and Bavarian favorites. Its decor is traditional: a perfect match for such dishes as Berliner Eisbein with Sauerkraut, vegetables, and potatoes; Tafelspitz; Bavarian-style Leberkäs; Schweinshaxen; Würste salad; bloodwurst and liverwurst; and Schnitzel. Come with an appetite, because its platters of main courses, all with side dishes, are enormous.

TY BREIZH, Kantstrasse 75. Tel. 323 99 32.

    Cuisine: FRENCH. **U-Bahn:** Wilmersdorfer Strasse, about a 4-minute walk.

$ Prices: 8–27 DM ($5–$16.85). No credit cards.

    Open: Mon–Fri 5pm–midnight, Sat 6pm–midnight.

If you're craving French cuisine but on a budget, try Ty Breizh, which looks more like a campus pizza parlor than a restaurant specializing in dishes from Brittany. Owner/chef Patrick Mattei—fluent in English, German, Italian, and his native French—is outgoing and friendly, and has been known to perform magic tricks for his guests. For an appetizer, try Mattei's creation of mushrooms with shrimp and cheese; also recommended are casserole of eggplant, paprika, onions, and tomato; quiche; beef cooked in a rich Burgundy wine sauce with onions, carrots, and butter noodles; omelets; and crêpes. The fish soup is a specialty of the house; oysters are available in winter. This is a fun place to dine; the clientele ranges from the middle class to punks and the avant-garde. Even the bills are unusual—if he has time, Mattei illustrates each by hand with a tally of soups, main courses, and glasses of wine. A memo for your scrapbook.

UDAGAWA JAPAN IMBISS, Kantstrasse 118. Tel. 312 30 14.

    Cuisine: JAPANESE. **U-Bahn:** Wilmersdorfer Strasse, about a 3-minute walk.

$ Prices: 10–28 DM ($6.25–$17.50). No credit cards.

    Open: Wed–Mon 12:30pm–midnight.

This tiny, self-service restaurant offers Japanese food at reasonable prices, from about 15 DM to 20 DM ($9.35 to $12.50) for most dishes. An informal place with only a few counters and tables, it offers a wide selection, including teriyaki chicken, yakisoba (fried noodles) with chicken, tempura udon (deep-fried food served in broth), sashimi, nabe (stews), and complete set meals. Great food, great prices.

WILHELM HOECK, Wilmersdorfer Strasse 149. Tel. 341 31 10.
Cuisine: GERMAN. **U-Bahn:** Bismarckstrasse, about a 2-minute walk.
$ Prices: Soups and salads 3–5 DM ($1.85–$3.10); main courses 8–20 DM ($5–$12.50). No credit cards.
Open: Mon–Sat 11am–11pm.

If you're hungry and want a traditional meal at modest prices, head for this well-known establishment north of Bismarckstrasse. You'll find two doors at this address—the door on the left leads to the simple family-style restaurant; the one on the right leads to the bar, first opened in 1892. The bar has more character, but the restaurant isn't as smoky. In any case, both offer the same menu of home-cooked foods "from Grandmother's kitchen," including Sülze (jellied meat) with potatoes, Bratwurst (sausage) with Sauerkraut and potatoes, Schnitzel, Eisbein with kraut, puréed peas and potatoes, and Boulette. Most platters are priced between 10 and 15 DM ($6.25 to $9.35), but you can eat even more cheaply if you order sausages or Boulette, priced under 5 DM ($3.10).

NEAR SCHLOSS CHARLOTTENBURG

LUISEN-BRÄU, Luisenplatz 1. Tel. 341 93 88.
Cuisine: GERMAN. **Bus:** 109 from Bahnhof Zoo to Schloss Charlottenburg, then a half-minute walk.
$ Prices: 8–20 DM ($5–$12.50). No credit cards.
Open: Daily 11am–midnight.

Where better to round off a day of sightseeing than at a brewery—this one conveniently located southeast of Charlottenburg Palace, at the corner of Spandauer Damm. Nice, cheerful, and rustic, it has large windows and paneled walls—with stainless steel tanks of beer brewing at one end of the room. You sit at long wooden tables, which makes it easy to strike up conversations with those around you—especially after a few beers. Order your food from the self-service counter, where you are charged by the weight of the meat slice you order, just as in a butcher shop. Slices of Schweinebraten, Kasseler Rippenspeer, Leberkäs, Boulette, or Schweinshaxen are priced at 100-gram (3½ oz.) increments. There are also stews and salads, but if all you want is a beer, that's perfectly acceptable at this brewery. Beer is available only in small mugs, with the philosophy that it remains fresher that way. In summer there's outdoor seating.

IN DAHLEM

ALTER KRUG DAHLEM, Königin-Luise-Strasse 52. Tel. 832 50 89.
Cuisine: GERMAN. **U-Bahn:** Dahlem-Dorf, about a 2-minute walk.
$ Prices: Appetizers and soups 8–17 DM ($5–$10.60); main courses 18–39 DM ($11.25–$24.35). DC, MC, V.
Open: Mon–Wed and Fri–Sat noon–midnight, Sun noon–10pm.

Though more expensive than most of our restaurant listings, this pleasant restaurant is convenient if you're visiting the many museums in Dahlem. The yellow building with green shutters is easy to find; inside it's decorated in typical German fashion, with a low-beamed ceiling and ceramic-tile heater. In summer, there's seating in the backyard garden. The menu includes such favorites as turkey breast, trout, salmon, veal Schnitzel, beef Stroganoff, pork chops, and lamb cutlets. The salads are meals in themselves. As the restaurant does retail sales of wines from all over Germany, it keeps a large stock in supply. If you're interested in a specific wine from Baden, Württemberg, Franken, Mosel, Saar, Rheingau, or Rheinhessen regions, you might strike it lucky here.

IN KREUZBERG

GROSSBEERENKELLER, Grossbeerenkeller 90. Tel. 251 30 64.

   Cuisine: GERMAN. **U-Bahn:** Möckernbrücke, less than a 5-minute walk.

$ Prices: 14–30 DM ($8.75–$18.75). No credit cards.

   Open: Mon–Fri 4pm–2am, Sat 6pm–2am. **Closed:** Holidays.

There used to be hundreds of places like this in prewar Berlin—simple, smoky bars peopled by the famous and the infamous. Most were destroyed during World War II, but this one survived and is now more than a century old: evident in its aged walls, hardly visible with all the photos of theater personalities who have been here. Theatergoers still stop here for a late-night meal of home-style cooking. This basement establishment serves simple and inexpensive dishes such as Berliner Würste salad with grilled potatoes, Leberkäs, and Bauernfrühstück, as well as Schnitzel, Rumpsteak, fish, and Sülze. After 7pm, make a reservation.

---

3. SPECIALTY DINING

FAST FOOD & *IMBISSE*

If you're looking for the absolute cheapest food in town or want a meal on the run, your best bet is an *Imbiss*. An *Imbiss* is a food stand or a tiny locale, where food is served for take-out or to customers who eat standing up at chest-high counters. Würste, Berliner Boulettes, hamburgers, and french fries are common fare, along with such ethnic choices as pizza by the slice, Turkish pizza, gyros, doner kebab, and other finger foods. Of course, most *Imbisse* also sell beer, as well as soft drinks. You can easily dine for less than 5 DM ($3.10).

There are several *Imbisse* up and down the Ku'damm—where sausages or cans of beer are sold for about 3 DM ($1.85)—including stands on the corner of Fasanenstrasse across from the Bristol Hotel Kempinski, and on the corner of Uhlandstrasse. There are also *Imbisse* on Wittenbergplatz, Savignyplatz, Alexanderplatz, Pariser Platz near Brandenburger Tor, in Dahlem across from the U-Bahn station, in the Tiergarten park, and at Berlin's many markets. At the Turkish market, you'll find Turkish specialties in addition to the usual sausages and burgers. During my last visit to the weekend market on

---

Ⓕ FROMMER'S COOL FOR KIDS: RESTAURANTS

Jimmy's Diner *(see p. 90)* Is your teenager bugging you for a hamburger or some "real" food? Head for this '50s-style diner, which offers hamburgers, sandwiches, chicken, spaghetti, and Mexican food. The clientele—mainly Berlin teenagers striving for just the right look—are an entertaining eyeful.

Piccola Taormina Tavola Calda *(see p. 92)* You won't go broke feeding your whole family at this inexpensive Italian restaurant. You can order take-out or eat at one of the simple wooden tables.

Times Square *(see p. 104)* Although the sandwiches and Mexican food are pricey, this may be the place if your child refuses to eat one more dish of pork and Sauerkraut. You'll feel right at home here, with a menu serving everything from burgers to tacos. In warm weather, there's outdoor seating on the Ku'damm.

Zitadelle *(see p. 117)* Older kids love the drama of this place—a medieval setting in a 700-year-old fortress in Spandau, where you eat with your fingers as in the Middle Ages. Expensive, but an evening you won't forget.

Strasse des 17. Juni, I found stands selling everything from Turkish pizza to Würste, chili con carne, and hamburgers. Check the shopping chapter for more information on markets.

In addition, several inexpensive locales (described above in the restaurant section) serve take-out food or offer stand-up tables. These include Ashoka (Indian), Asia-Quick (Chinese), Einhorn (Vegetarian), Ihre Frisch-Backstübe (German), Joseph Langer (German), Karavan (Turkish), Nordsee (Seafood), Orient (Middle Eastern), Piccola Taormina Tavola Calda (Italian), Pizza Bleibtreu (Italian), and Rogacki (German). For exact page numbers, refer to "Restaurants by Cuisine" in the Index.

DINING CLUSTERS

As mentioned at the beginning of this chapter, the city's greatest concentration of restaurants is on or near the Ku'damm. Nowhere are they more numerous than in the nearby Europa-Center, which is easy to spot by the Mercedes-Benz logo that crowns its roof. This huge complex contains a number of German, Japanese, Swiss, and French restaurants, as well as fast food. During summer, Mövenpick on the ground floor spills over onto Breitscheidplatz with outdoor tables and colored umbrellas in the summer.

COFFEEHOUSES

Along with beer, wine, and bottled water, coffee is probably the most popular drink in Germany. Not only a breakfast drink, coffee is also the star of that national obsession—the afternoon coffee break: a wonderful opportunity to indulge in cakes, tortes, and desserts. Of course, you could always order sparkling water or a sparkling wine.

If you're on a budget, try **Tschibo,** which offers a cup of coffee for 1.20 DM (75¢), an espresso for 1 DM (60¢), and cappuccino for 1.95 DM ($1.20). You can drink it standing up at one of the chest-high tables. Two convenient locations are at Kurfürstendamm 11 (tel. 883 11 94), across from the Gedächtniskirche, and at Wilmersdorfer Strasse 117 (tel. 312 80 23). They're open Monday to Friday from 9am to 6:30pm, and on Saturday from 9am to 2pm (to 6pm the first Saturday of the month).

In addition to Berlin's famous coffeehouses presented below, see also the "Breakfast and Sunday Brunch" section later in this chapter for other cafés serving coffee, desserts, and breakfast.

ON OR NEAR THE KU'DAMM

CAFE KRANZLER, Kurfürstendamm 18–19. Tel. 882 69 11.

U-Bahn: Kurfürstendamm, less than a 1-minute walk.

$ Prices: Coffee from 3.50 DM ($2.15). AE, DC, MC, V.

Open: Daily 8am–midnight.

Most of the many cafés in Berlin were destroyed in World War II. One of the few to have survived is Café Kranzler, one of the city's most famous coffeehouses. Founded in 1825 and formerly located on Unter den Linden, today it now occupies a modern building on the Ku'damm—a premier people-watching spot, especially in summer when there are sidewalk tables. In winter, it's wonderful to sit near the huge floor-to-ceiling windows. Besides breakfasts and snacks, this café offers cakes and tortes, including *Sachertorte* (a Viennese chocolate cake).

LEYSIEFFER, Kurfürstendamm 218. Tel. 882 78 20.

U-Bahn: Uhlandstrasse or Kurfürstendamm, each less than a 2-minute walk.

$ Prices: Cup of coffee from 3.50 DM ($2.15) indoors, 4 DM ($2.50) outdoors. AE, DC, MC, V.

Open: Summer Mon–Sat 9am–10pm, Sun and holidays 10am–10pm; winter Mon–Sat 9am–8pm, Sun and holidays 10am–7pm.

Not far from Café Kranzler is this small café in what was formerly the Chinese embassy. On the ground floor is a shop selling bonbons, while the coffee shop upstairs resembles an art gallery, with a black-and-white tiled floor and an ornate ceiling. It's best known for its wonderful cakes, especially the exotic fruitcake and a butter cake with almonds. Some people rave about its *Rote Grütze,* cooked fruits with a vanilla sauce, a specialty of northern Germany. The miniature balcony has room for only a lucky few. There's also sidewalk seating, with slightly higher prices.

CAFE IM LITERATURHAUS, Fasanenstrasse 23. Tel. 882 54 14.

U-Bahn: Uhlandstrasse, a 1-minute walk.

$ Prices: Coffee from 3 DM ($1.85). No credit cards.

Open: Daily 10am–1am.

Just off the Ku'damm and away from the madding crowd is this refined oasis, a café above a bookstore in a neighborhood of restored turn-of-the-century villas, art galleries, and the

Käthe-Kollwitz Museum next door. In summer you can sit outside; in winter, in its greenhouselike room. It serves breakfast until 1pm to a decidedly artsy crowd, as well as salads and snacks, and such desserts as apple strudel with vanilla sauce, rice pudding with purée of kiwi, and *Rote Grütze*.

CAFÉ MÖHRING, Kurfürstendamm 213. Tel. 881 20 75.

U-Bahn: Uhlandstrasse, less than a 1-minute walk.

$ Prices: Coffee from 3.30 DM ($2.05). No credit cards.

Open: Daily 7am–midnight.

When Café Möhring first opened here in 1898, it was out in the countryside. Now, of course, it sits in one of the most exclusive neighborhoods; it was rebuilt after a fire in 1973. In addition to its coffees and cakes, including spiked coffees, it offers breakfasts starting at 5 DM ($3.10), daily specials, and a menu that lists soups, salads, and main courses.

There are two other locations of Café Möhring on the Ku'damm, one at no. 163 near Adenauerplatz, and the other across from the Gedächtniskirche at no. 234. The latter, which opened in 1977, took over a preexisting coffeehouse and restored it to its former glory—including a turn-of-the-century facade renovated according to old documents and photographs.

BERLIN-MITTE (EASTERN BERLIN)

OPERNCAFE, Opernpalais, Unter den Linden 5. Tel. 200 22 69.

U-Bahn: Friedrichstrasse or Französische Strasse, about a 7-minute walk. **Bus:** 100 to Staatsoper.

$ Prices: Cup of coffee 3.50 DM ($2.15). AE, DC, MC, V.

Open: Daily 8:30am–midnight.

Located on one of Berlin's most famous boulevards is this well-known café. It occupies part of a palace, the Opernpalais, originally built in 1733, destroyed during World War II and recently painstakingly and lovingly restored. Elegant with chandeliers and a panoramic mural of Berlin architecture, it offers a grand breakfast buffet for 16.50 DM ($10.30) daily until noon, as well as 25 different tortes made fresh daily. It's especially nice on the outdoor terrace underneath the trees of this pretty square.

NEAR NOLLENDORFPLATZ

EINSTEIN, Kurfürstenstrasse 58. Tel. 261 50 96.

U-Bahn: Nollendorfplatz, about a 3-minute walk.

$ Prices: Cup of coffee 3.90 DM ($2.45). AE, DC, MC, V.

Open: Daily 10am–2am.

Einstein probably wouldn't object to lending his name to this student's café, located in a beautiful high-ceilinged town house from the 1920s—the former residence of Henny Porten, one of Germany's first silent-film stars. Popular with Berlin's younger, yuppie generation, it's a good place for either a coffee or drinks; breakfast is served until 2pm, with prices ranging from about 8 DM ($5) to 17 DM ($10.60). There's also champagne, wine, and cakes. Similar to Viennese coffeehouses, newspapers and magazines are provided—many in English like *Time*. In summer, there's seating for as many as 180 outside. It's located on Kurfürstenstrasse (not to be confused with the Ku'damm), north of Nollendorfplatz.

BREAKFAST & SUNDAY BRUNCH

Many hotels and pensions in Berlin include breakfast in their rates. In case yours doesn't or you want to eat more cheaply elsewhere, here are some recommendations for both breakfast and Sunday brunch. In addition, the coffee shops listed in the section above offer breakfast.

ON OR NEAR THE KU'DAMM

EIERSCHALE, Rankestrasse 1. Tel. 882 53 05.
  Cuisine: BUFFET BREAKFAST. **U-Bahn:** Kurfürstendamm, about a 1-minute walk.
$ Prices: Fixed-price brunch 11.90 DM ($7.45); breakfast from 6.50 DM ($4.05). AE, MC, V.
  Open: Breakfast daily 8am–2pm.
Located right off the Ku'damm across from the Gedächtniskirche, this popular music house heralds every day with a breakfast brunch, which includes breads, croissants, marmalade, Würste, cheeses, eggs (soft-boiled, scrambled, or fried), ham, salad, and cereal. There are also breakfasts offered starting at 6.50 DM ($4.05) for bread, cheese, and an egg. On Sunday it's especially nice, with jazz, blues, and rock-and-roll bands playing from 10am through much of the day. No reservations are accepted, so get here early.

CAFE BLEIBTREU, Bleibtreustrasse 45. Tel. 881 47 56.
  Cuisine: BREAKFAST/SNACKS. **S-Bahn:** Savignyplatz, a 1-minute walk.
$ Prices: Coffee from 2.40 DM ($1.50); breakfast 6–10 DM ($3.75–$6.25). No credit cards.
  Open: Sun–Thurs 9:30am–1am, Fri–Sat 9:30am–2:30am.
This pleasant café/bar—with outdoor seating in summer—is popular with a 30-ish crowd for breakfast, served until 2pm (to 3pm Saturday and Sunday). Breakfasts range from the light Französisches Frühstück consisting of two croissants and marmalade, to the more substantial Frühstück Bleibtreu, which includes ham, Würste, cheese, honey, one egg, fruit, and orange juice.

SCHWARZES CAFE, Kantstrasse 148. Tel. 313 80 38.
  Cuisine: BREAKFAST. **S-Bahn or U-Bahn:** Savignyplatz or Uhlandstrasse, each about a 3-minute walk.
$ Prices: Coffee from 3 DM ($1.85); breakfast 8–30 DM ($5–$18.75). No credit cards.
  Open: Around the clock, except Tues 3am–5pm.
Just east of Savignyplatz, this unconventional café is popular with a hip, younger crowd; breakfasts are a specialty and available anytime—ranging from the simple continental to complete meals.

ZILLEMARKT, Bleibtreustrasse 48a. Tel. 881 70 40.
  Cuisine: BREAKFAST/SNACKS. **S-Bahn:** Savignyplatz, a 1-minute walk.
$ Prices: Breakfast 5.50–12 DM ($3.45–$7.50). No credit cards.
  Open: Daily 9am–1am.
This century-old building used to house an antiques and curio market—all that remains is the name Zillemarkt. Breakfast, which includes a variety of scrambled eggs, is served until 4pm. Summers are especially nice, when you can dine in the outdoor back garden or at one of the sidewalk tables.

NEAR NOLLENDORFPLATZ

CAFE SIDNEY, Winterfeldstrasse 40. Tel. 216 52 53.
   Cuisine: BREAKFAST/SNACKS. **U-Bahn:** Nollendorfplatz, about a 5-minute walk.
$ **Prices:** Breakfasts 6.50–15 DM ($4.05–$9.35). No credit cards.
   Open: Daily 9am–4am.
The best days to eat breakfast at this modern and breezy café/bar are Wednesday or Saturday, when you can also shop the morning market on Winterfeldplatz. Breakfast is served until 5pm.

IN KREUZBERG

ESPRESSOBAR ROXY, Südstern. Tel. 691 85 98.
   Cuisine: BREAKFAST. **U-Bahn:** Südstern, less than 1-minute walk.
$ **Prices:** Coffee 2.50 DM ($1.55); breakfast 6–13 DM ($3.75–$8.10). No credit cards.
   Open: Daily 10am–1am.
This sleek café/bar is known for its breakfasts, served until 3pm and attracting grandmothers to artists to yuppies. Decorated with pictures of Marilyn Monroe above the bar and chrome ceiling fans, it also serves espresso, cappuccino, cocktails, and ice cream. In summer you can sit outside.

YORCKSCHLÖSSCHEN, Yorckstrasse 15. Tel. 215 80 70.
   Cuisine: BREAKFAST. **Bus:** 119 from Kurfürstendamm to Grossbeerenstrasse. **U-Bahn:** Möckernbrücke or Mehring-damm.
$ **Prices:** 5–20 DM ($3.10–$12.50). No credit cards.
   Open: Breakfast daily 9am–3pm.
This is one of Berlin's most popular places to be on Sunday, when live Dixieland jazz serenades a largely young clientele from 2 to 6pm. Get there early, get a table and order breakfast, and then hang around for the music to start. It's a typical student bar, with a wooden plank floor, posters adorning the walls, and an outdoor beer garden. Continental breakfast, scrambled eggs, and fried eggs are among the breakfast options—and of course there's beer.

LATE-NIGHT DINING

If hunger strikes after midnight, there are a number of restaurants, bars, and cafés open to the early morning hours. These establishments listed in the paragraph below are described above in detail. For page numbers, turn to the "Restaurants by Cuisine" section in the Index. In addition, many bars listed in Chapter 9, "Berlin Nights," remain open to as late as 4am.

The following restaurants are all within walking distance of Ku'damm: Avanti (Italian), open to 2am; Ciao Ciao (Italian), open to 2am Sunday to Thursday, and to 3am on Friday and Saturday nights; Grung Thai (Thai food), open to 3am; Orient (Middle Eastern food), open to 3am; Piccola Taormina Tavola Calda (Italian), open to 2am; Athener Grill (Greek and Italian), open to 4am during the week, and to 5am on weekends; and Jimmy's Diner (American/Mexican), open to 4am during the week, and to 6am on Friday and Saturday nights.

Schwarzes Café, described above in the breakfast and brunch section, serves breakfast around the clock, with the exception of Tuesday from 3am to 5pm.

PICNIC FARE & WHERE TO EAT IT

All department stores have large food departments with counters serving prepared meats, salads, and take-out food. Two of the largest are KaDeWe (Kaufhaus des Westens), on Wittenbergplatz (tel. 212 10), with a huge food department on the sixth floor; and Wertheim, Kurfürstendamm 231 (tel. 88 20 61), with a food section in the basement. You can buy everything from cheese, bread, fruit, and wine to Leberkäs, grilled chicken, and casseroles. Both are open Monday to Friday from 9am to 6pm (KaDeWe is open until 6:30pm), and on Saturday from 9am to 2pm (to 6pm first Saturday of each month). In addition, restaurants listed above under "Fast Food and *Imbisse*" sell take-out foods that may be perfect for an afternoon picnic.

And where to eat your goodies? The largest and most convenient green space in the center of Berlin is the Tiergarten, just northwest of Bahnhof Zoo. This park stretches all the way to Brandenburger Tor, with ponds, woods, meadows, and trails throughout. If you don't feel like walking far from the Ku'damm, there are public benches on Breitscheidplatz in the shade of the Kaiser-Wilhelm Gedächtnis-kirche.

4. WORTH THE EXTRA BUCKS

ON OR NEAR THE KU'DAMM

FOFI'S ESTIATORIO, Fasanenstrasse 70. Tel. 881 87 85.
   Cuisine: GREEK. **Reservations:** Imperative. **U-Bahn:** Uhlandstrasse, a 1-minute walk.
$ Prices: Appetizers and salads 10–25 DM ($6.25–$15.60); main courses 28–45 DM ($17.50–$28.10). No credit cards.
   Open: Daily 7:30pm–12:30am (last order).

Fofi's is a wildly popular restaurant; it's got a good location—a stone's throw from the Ku'damm—good food, interesting interior, sidewalk tables, and a mothering Greek owner named Fofi who greets strangers as warmly as she does her many regulars. It's decorated with abstract art, and the background music is likely to be easygoing jazz. In summer, an outdoor table is a thing to covet.

The menu lists the usual national Greek dishes, including bean salad, *dolmades* (meat and rice rolled in grape leaves), *keftedes* (fried meatballs), and a Greek salad for appetizers. Main dishes range from grilled scampi and *moussaka* (eggplant and minced-meat casserole) to souvlaki, kebab, and lamb. There's also a changing menu with international dishes, as well as an abundant supply of Greek wines and spirits. The sign on the facade of this place is Estiatorio, but everyone calls it Fofi's.

LUTTER & WEGNER, Schlüterstrasse 55. Tel. 881 34 40.
   Cuisine: GERMAN/CONTINENTAL. **Reservations:** Impera-tive. **S-Bahn:** Savignyplatz, a 1-minute walk.
$ Prices: Soups and appetizers 10–20 DM ($6.25–$12.50); main courses 35–40 DM ($21.85–$25). AE.
   Open: Daily 6:30pm–3am (last order 11:30pm).

✪ Lutter & Wegner first opened its doors as a wine cellar in eastern Berlin in 1811, and this branch of the establishment still has an old-world style and grace. A combination restaurant and wine bar, it's unpretentious yet refined, with a dark-paneled wainscoting, candles, and pleasant background music. Catering to a professional and artistic crowd, it also has a small bar where you can come for a drink.

The menu changes often and always offers daily specials, which may include Tafelspitz, fish, or noodle casserole with cheese, mushrooms, and leeks. The salads are huge. Lutter & Wegner specializes in wines, and you can indulge in one of its selections from Franken, the Rhine area, Baden, Mosel Valley, or France. A glass of wine starts at about 8.50 DM ($5.30).

RISTORANTE TAVOLA CALDA, Leibnizstrasse 45. Tel. 324 10 48.

Cuisine: ITALIAN. **Reservations:** Imperative for lunch or dinner. **S-Bahn:** Savignyplatz, a 3-minute walk.

$ Prices: Pasta and pizza 11–15 DM ($6.85–$9.35); main courses 30–38 DM ($18.75–$23.75). No credit cards.

Open: Mon–Sat noon–11pm.

This one-room restaurant with a marble floor and abstract art is a great place for a romantic evening—even though it's small and the tables are close together. Its pasta and pizza are especially good, at moderate prices. If you opt for one of its higher-priced lamb, beef, or seafood dishes, however, you're in for a special treat. Attracting an artsy crowd, this place is trendy without being clichéed.

TAFELRUNDE, Nachodstrasse 21. Tel. 211 21 41.

Cuisine: GERMAN. **Reservations:** Recommended, especially on weekends and before Christmas. **U-Bahn:** Spichernstrasse, less than a 5-minute walk.

$ Prices: Fixed-price dinner 69.50 DM ($43.45). No credit cards.

Open: Daily 6pm–midnight.

Dining as it was in the Middle Ages—that's the theme of the Tafelrunde (the Roundtable). Diners are given only a special knife and are expected to eat with their fingers. Bibs are passed out just in case. The dining halls are in the spirit of the times, simple with long wooden tables and chairs, although the building itself is modern. It's located about a 15-minute walk south of the Ku'damm, or only one stop away by U-Bahn.

Only one fixed-price meal is served, changing several times a month: It's usually a seven-course meal, starting with a drink from a cow's horn and loaves of bread. Then comes a soup and appetizers, followed by a main course such as Spiessbraten (shish kebab) or Spanferkel (suckling pig), a surprise dish, and cheese and fruit. With entertainment provided by the staff.

IN KREUZBERG

HASENBURG, Fichtestrasse 1. Tel. 691 91 39.

Cuisine: GERMAN/FRENCH. **Reservations:** A must. **U-Bahn:** Südstern, about a 5-minute walk.

$ Prices: Appetizers 13–22 DM ($8.10–$13.75); main courses 39–45 DM ($24.35–$28.10); fixed-price dinners 75–90 DM ($46.85–$56.25). No credit cards.

Open: Mon–Sat 6:30pm–1am.

★ This upscale restaurant is proof that Kreuzberg is no longer just the playground of students. Serving what can best be described as nouvelle German cuisine influenced by French kitchens, it offers great food served by an earnest staff, who aren't afraid to advise against a dish when it's a bit off that night—which rarely happens anyway. An employee claims that he's never seen a more spotless kitchen and that the harmonious relationship between the kitchen and serving staff is reflected in the food and atmosphere. There's outdoor dining in fine weather, though traffic tends to be loud.

The menu changes daily depending on what's in season, offering such creative appetizers as rack of lamb on a bed of artichokes or salmon ravioli, and such main courses as breast of duck with a rhubarb and ginger sauce, grated filet of beef on a bed of potatoes and leeks with a truffle sauce, and Norwegian salmon with sour cream and caviar. Fixed-price menus are also offered nightly, ranging from four to six courses.

IN SPANDAU

ZITADELLE, Am Juliusturm, Spandau. Tel. 334 21 06.
   Cuisine: GERMAN. **Reservations:** Recommended, especially on weekends. **U-Bahn:** U-7 to Zitadelle.
$ **Prices:** Main courses 20–40 DM ($12.50–$25); fixed-price weekend banquet 69.50–80 DM ($43.45–$50). AE, DC, MC, V.
   Open: Tues–Sun 11am–11pm.

★ The Zitadelle, located in Spandau, operates on the same medieval principle as the Tafelrunde described above, but here it feels and looks like the real thing—because it is. It's located in a 700-year-old medieval fortress with stone walls, brick vaulted-ceilings, wooden tables, and an open fireplace.

On weekdays it offers an à la carte menu with typical German fare such as pork cutlet or trout. The real fun is on Friday, Saturday, and Sunday evenings, when there's a medieval banquet with ballad-singing and special entertainment: a fixed-price meal is served which includes a welcoming drink in a bull's horn, bread, appetizer, a main course such as Spiessbraten, and several other dishes. Although Spandau is on the outskirts of Berlin, it is easily reached by subway. Highly recommended.

CHAPTER 6

WHAT TO SEE & DO IN BERLIN

Berlin is sightseeing heaven for people who love museums—so spectacular that they alone are worth the trip to Berlin. The city's collections are richly diverse, ranging from Egyptian art treasures to contemporary art, from musical instruments to traditional German clothing, from architectural wonders to Islamic and African art. With more than 80 public museums and 200 galleries, Berlin offers something for everyone. You can't be bored here even for a minute.

Berlin has actively sought treasures from around the world since the early 1800s, when it first began developing a museum complex on Museumsinsel. After World War II, most of the city's treasures were divided between East and West; that's why there are two of almost everything, giving visitors a bewildering choice of museums with similar and overlapping collections. The city plans to merge some of its collections, once the more pressing unification problems are addressed.

Thankfully, museum-hopping in Berlin isn't the chore it can be in other major cities. The city is surprisingly compact—a savings in time and transportation costs. Furthermore, most of its major museums and attractions are clustered together in four distinct parts of the city—all conveniently reached by an efficient public transportation system and easily seen in a few days.

Of Berlin's four major museum centers, Museumsinsel in Berlin-Mitte is the oldest and best-known. This island in the middle of the Spree River is so laden with the treasures of the Pergamon Museum that I'm surprised it isn't sinking. Not to be outdone is Dahlem, which boasts the largest collection of museums in Berlin—including the famous Gemäldegalerie (Picture Gallery) and museums of non-European art. Charlottenburg is home of Schloss Charlottenburg (Charlottenburg Palace) and museums specializing in the antiquities, including the Ägyptisches Museum (Egyptian Museum) with the bust of Nefertiti. Finally, Berlin's newest museum area is in Tiergarten; still under construction, this region will eventually be the city's center for European art. Though not as important as the museum centers above, Kreuzberg also has some unique and valuable museums.

It makes sense to cover Berlin section by section, not only because it saves time but also because it saves money. Most of the museum clusters, including most of those in Dahlem, several on Museums-insel, and those in the Tiergarten, offer their own combination ticket (called a *Sammelkarte*), allowing entrance to several museums in the same geographic area at a reduced rate.

SUGGESTED ITINERARIES

To help you get the most out of your visit, here are some suggested itineraries to guide you to the most important attractions. Since the dining, nightlife, and sightseeing chapters are all arranged according to geographic locations, you can match your own choices in restaurants, attractions, and nightlife entertainment to the suggested itineraries below. Have fun!

IF YOU HAVE ONE DAY Berlin's three most famous treasures are the Pergamon Altar, the bust of Nefertiti, and the *Man with the Golden Helmet* (which nonetheless was painted by one of his students and not by Rembrandt himself). If you wish to see all three, get up early in the morning and head straight to Dahlem. (*Note:* Most museums in Dahlem are closed on Monday.) Among the half dozen museums here, most important is the Gemäldegalerie (Picture Gallery), with the *Man with the Golden Helmet* and other master-pieces from the 13th to 18th century, including works by Dürer, Brueghel, Botticelli, Raphael, Rubens, and Rembrandt. Since time is precious, concentrate on the artists you're most interested in.

From Dahlem, head to the Ägyptisches Museum (closed on Friday) in Charlottenburg, where Berlin's most beautiful woman holds court: Nefertiti. Across the street is Schloss Charlottenburg, Berlin's most beautiful baroque building. If you have time, visit its Knobelsdorff Flügel and the Schinkel Pavilion for a look at how Prussian royalty lived, or stroll its lovely gardens.

By mid-afternoon, head for the Brandenburger Tor (Brandenburg Gate), built in the 1780s as the grand finishing touch to Berlin's most famous boulevard, Unter den Linden. After Berlin became a divided city, the gate and boulevard ended up under East Berlin's jurisdiction and was inaccessible to West Berliners—making it a poignant symbol of Germany's division. With the fall of the Wall, it was here at the gate that many Berliners gathered to rejoice. Take a stroll down Unter den Linden, stopping off for a coffee at the famous Operncafé. By 5pm at the latest, you should be in the Pergamon Museum on Museumsinsel, with its incredible Pergamon Altar, Market Gate of Miletus, and Babylonian Processional Street leading to the Gate of Ishtar.

If you still have the energy for more sightseeing, round out your eastern Berlin experience with a trip to the Museum Haus am Checkpoint Charlie, which opened in 1961 with the sole purpose of documenting the Berlin Wall and the many attempts of East Berliners to escape to the West. Today it's the best place in the city to gain an understanding of what Berlin was like during the decades of division.

Finish off the day with a leisurely evening stroll along the Ku'damm, the showcase avenue with many shops and restaurants. Relax over coffee at one of the area's many coffeehouses, or order a drink at one of the bars—if it's summer, try to get a seat outdoors. Dine at a traditional German restaurant. And then start planning your next trip to Berlin.

DID YOU KNOW . . . ?

- Berlin has more than 6,000 restaurants, as well as 6,500 pubs and bars.
- There is no official curfew in Berlin; some bars remain open all night.
- Each year, Berliners and their guests drink the equivalent of Wannsee—in beer.
- Berlin claims to have more local rock groups than any other city in Europe—about 1,000.
- Berlin claims to have more dogs than any city in the world—about 200,000.
- 80,000 Berliners lost their lives in World War II—50,000 of them Jewish.
- From 1949 until the Wall went up in 1961, approximately 3 million East Germans fled their country.
- From 1961 to 1989, 78 East Berliners died trying to escape to West Berlin; most were shot by East German border guards.
- City officials expect Berlin's population to double to about 6 million by the year 2005.
- Greater Berlin is larger than Munich, Stuttgart, and Frankfurt combined.
- Einstein developed his theory of relativity in Berlin.

IF YOU HAVE TWO DAYS Day 1
Devote your entire morning to Dahlem as described above, first visiting the Gemäldegalerie. Add to it one or two of the museums that most interest you. The Museum für Deutsche Volkskunde (Museum of German Ethnology) has an excellent display of simple furniture and household items used by Germany's middle-class, peasants, and farmers. There are also fine museums of Asian art and one of the world's largest ethnological museums. If you're still in Dahlem during lunch time, you might wish to dine on traditional German cuisine at Luise or Alter Krug Dahlem. If you're on a budget or in a hurry, there's a thatched-roof *Imbiss* right across the street from the subway station, selling Würst, coffee, and beer.

In the afternoon head for Charlottenburg, where in addition to Schloss Charlottenburg and the Ägyptisches Museum, there's also the Museum of Greek and Roman Antiquities, the Museum of Pre- and Early History, and the wonderful Bröhan Museum with its art deco and Jugendstil collection. Just southeast of the palace is the Luisen-Bräu brewery, another good spot for a meal or a beer.

Day 2 Go to Berlin-Mitte in eastside Berlin. Have a look at Brandenburger Tor and stroll down Unter den Linden. Then visit the outstanding Pergamon Museum on Museumsinsel. If you have time, also see the National Gallery, or the Bode Museum. Finish the day with a walk to Alexanderplatz, once the heart of East Germany's capital and home of the towering TV tower, and the nearby Nikolai Quarter, a small neighborhood of restored buildings housing several pubs and restaurants.

At the end of the day, head for the Museum Haus am Checkpoint Charlie with its important collections documenting the history of the Berlin Wall.

In the evening, try to attend a performance at the Deutsche Oper, the Philharmonie, or—if you understand German—one of the several theaters.

IF YOU HAVE THREE DAYS Days 1–2 Spend days 1 and 2 as outlined above.

Day 3 On day 3, head for the Tiergarten museum complex (south of Tiergarten park); this is a newly developed center for European art, where you'll find the Neue Nationalgalerie (New National Gallery), which houses German and European artists of the 19th and 20th centuries. Nearby are the Kunstgewerbe Museum (Museum of Applied Arts), with its collections dating from the Middle Ages to the present day, and the Musikinstrumenten Museum (Museum of Musical Instruments).

Spend the rest of the day according to your own special interests. Good choices include the Berlin Museum (in Kreuzberg) for exhibits on the city's history; the Käthe-Kollwitz Museum (near the Ku'damm) with the artist's powerful drawings; the Bauhaus-Archiv and the Hansaviertel (Hansa Quarter) for architectural buffs; the Ku'damm and Wilmersdorfer Strasse for shopping. Be sure to visit KaDeWe department store's incredible food emporium on its top floor.

In the evening, take advantage of Berlin's active nightlife scene. Watch a rock, jazz, or blues concert at a live-music house or enjoy an evening of pub crawling.

IF YOU HAVE FIVE DAYS Days 1–3 Spend days 1–3 as outlined above. In addition, if you're in Berlin on a Saturday or Sunday, be sure to schedule a trip to the flea market held every weekend on Strasse des 17. Juni near Tiergarten park. It offers antiques, junk, and curios, as well as arts and crafts from Berlin's enterprising young artists. On a Tuesday or Friday afternoon, visit the fascinating Turkish Market in Kreuzberg.

Day 4 Pamper yourself with a day of relaxation. Take an excursion to Wannsee or Havel, where you can swim or board a pleasure boat. Alternatives include taking one of the suggested walking tours in the next chapter, heading for the Spreewald and a boat ride, or visiting all those other museums.

Day 5 Head for the quaint old city of Potsdam with the palace and gardens of Sanssouci.

1. THE TOP ATTRACTIONS

Since most of Berlin's top attractions are located near other worthwhile museums, be sure to read the next section, "More Attractions," to plan your day's itinerary. Near the Gemäldegalerie in Dahlem, for example, are no fewer than six other museums, each important in its own right.

IN BERLIN-MITTE (EASTERN BERLIN)

PERGAMON MUSEUM, Kupfergraben, Museumsinsel. Tel. 203 55-0.

✪ The Pergamon Museum houses Berlin's most valued cultural treasure, the Pergamon Altar. Essentially devoted to architecture, this museum was the first of its kind when it opened in 1930, and today ranks among the world's best for its collection of Greek, Roman, and Middle Eastern antiquities. It also contains Near Eastern and Asian art, Islamic art, and German folk art.

The Pergamon Altar, a magnificent masterpiece of Hellenistic art dating from 180 to 160 B.C., occupies a hall of its own. From a town in what is now Turkey, the altar was dedicated to Zeus and Athena and remains one of the architectural wonders of the ancient world. A seven-foot frieze along the base of the altar depicts the struggle of the Greek gods against the giants. Zeus and Athena are to be seen in the eastern frieze, across from the steps.

In the Roman Architecture Hall, you'll find the Market Gate of Miletus. Erected around A.D. 120, this two-story Roman gate provided access to a public market, but was also large enough to contain a few shops as well. The museum's third architectural gem is the dazzling Babylonian Processional Street, which leads to the Gate of Ishtar. Originally 990 feet long and twice as wide as reconstructed here, the street was used for religious processionals during the reign of Nebuchadnezzar II (605–562 B.C.). It is bordered by walls decorated with lions in stride, against a striking blue background. The gate itself is of blue and ocher tiles, with fanciful bulls and dragons.

Upstairs are the collections of Asian and Islamic art, including Chinese porcelain from the Stone Age to the 20th century, and significant pieces of Chinese sculpture. The Japanese department contains ceramics and porcelain, lacquerware, and woodblock prints by one of Japan's foremost artists, Hokusai (1760–1849). The highlight of the Islamic art department is the Facade from Mschatta, a desert palace built in the 8th century but never completed. Note the intricate designs carved in its walls, not unlike the designs of an elaborate carpet. Carpets, too, are a part of the museum's collection, many from the 13th to 15th centuries.

Note that the museum is entered via a bridge off a lane called Kupfergraben, behind and to the left of Das Alte Museum. Near the entrance to the Pergamon is a small café where you can have a cup of coffee and snacks.

Admission: 4 DM ($2.50) adults; 2 DM ($1.25) students and children. Free Sun and holidays.

Open: Daily 10am–6pm (Mon only for Pergamon Altar, Market Gate, and Gate of Ishtar). **Bus:** 100 to the Deutsche Staatsoper stop. **S-Bahn:** Hackescher Markt or Friedrichstrasse, each less than a 10-minute walk.

IN DAHLEM

GEMÄLDEGALERIE [Picture Gallery], Arnimallee 23-27. Tel. 8301-1.

✪ Considered Berlin's top art museum, the Gemäldegalerie offers a comprehensive survey of European painting from the 13th to 18th century—possessing more than 1,500 works. Stemming from the royal court collection with works added through the years, it first opened to the public in 1830 in the Altes Museum on Museumsinsel. After World War II, during which 400 major works were destroyed, the collection was divided between East and West Berlin. Even so, only half of the Gemäldegalerie's present works can be displayed at one time—this will be remedied if and when the gallery moves into new and larger quarters in the Tiergarten.

The museum's holdings are arranged historically and systematically, by schools and by periods. There are works by Dürer, Cranach, Holbein, Gainsborough, Brueghel, Titian, Botticelli, Raphael, Rubens, Vermeer, Murillo, El Greco, Goya, and Velázquez. It has an outstanding collection of Rubens, but the crowning achievement of

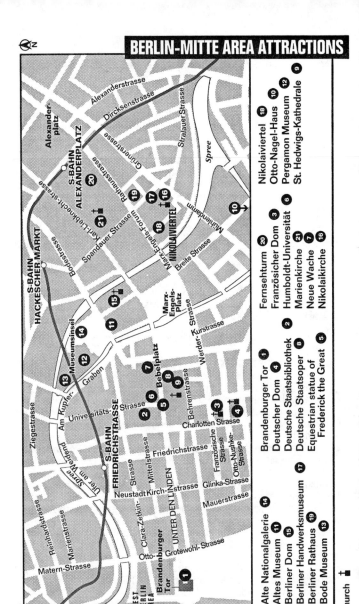

BERLIN-MITTE AREA ATTRACTIONS

Nikolaiviertel **18**
Otto-Nagel-Haus **10**
Pergamon Museum **12**
St. Hedwigs-Kathedrale **9**

Fernsehturm **20**
Französicher Dom **3**
Humboldt-Universität **2**
Marienkirche **21**
Neue Wache **7**
Nikolaikirche **16**

Brandenburger Tor **1**
Deutscher Dom **4**
Deutsche Staatsbibliothek **8**
Deutsche Staatsoper **8**
Equestrian statue of
Frederick the Great **5**

Alte Nationalgalerie **14**
Altes Museum **11**
Berliner Dom **15**
Berliner Handwerksmuseum **17**
Berliner Rathaus **19**
Bode Museum **13**

Church ✝ ■

the museum is probably its 20-some paintings by Rembrandt—one of the world's largest collections by this master. My personal favorite is his portrait of Hendrickje Stoffels and his common-law wife (note the intimacy of her gaze). The famous and striking *Man with the Golden Helmet*, though no longer attributed to Rembrandt but rather to one of his students, is nonetheless considered quite important.

Other must-see paintings include Botticelli's *Venus*, Dürer's portrait of a Nürnberg patrician, and Hans Holbein's portrait of merchant Georg Gisze. Brueghel the Elder's *The Netherlands Proverbs* illustrates more than 100 proverbs. Lucas Cranach's *Fountain of Youth (Der Jungbrunnen)* depicts old women being led to the fountain, swimming through it, and then emerging youthful and beautiful. Note that apparently only women need the bath—men in the painting regain their youth through relations with younger women.

Since this museum is large, pick up a map and pamphlet; you may want to concentrate on a particular period or school. The ground floor is devoted to German, Netherlandish, and Italian art from the 13th through 16th centuries, as well as to French and English paintings of the 18th century. Sixteenth-century German art is especially well represented, with works by Dürer, Altdorfer, and Baldung Grien.

The first floor has 17th- and 18th-century works, including Flemish, French, Dutch, and Spanish works, as well as baroque and rococo Italian paintings.

Admission: 4 DM ($2.50) adults, 2 DM ($1.25) students and children. Free Sun and holidays.

Open: Tues–Fri 9am–5pm, Sat–Sun 10am–5pm. **Closed:** Jan 1; Tues after Easter and Whitsunday; May 1; Dec 24, 25, and 31. **U-Bahn:** Dahlem-Dorf.

IN CHARLOTTENBURG

SCHLOSS CHARLOTTENBURG [Charlottenburg Palace], Luisenplatz and Spandauer Damm. Tel. 32 09 11.

Regarded as Berlin's most beautiful baroque building, Schloss Charlottenburg started out as something far less grand. First constructed in the 1690s as a small residence for Sophie Charlotte, wife of the future Prussian King Friedrich I, it was expanded in the 18th century into a palace fit for kings with extensions added by such renowned architects as Eosander von Göthe, Knobelsdorff, and Langhans. It served as the summer residence of almost all Prussian kings from Friedrich I to Friedrich Wilhelm IV, and today contains objects from the baroque to Biedermeier periods.

The first thing that catches your eye as you approach the front of the palace is the equestrian statue of the Great Elector (*Grossen Kurfürsten*). Designed by Andreas Schlüter, it was cast in one piece in 1700. Originally it stood on a famous bridge near the Berliner Schloss, which no longer exists. While being moved to a safe haven during World War II, it accidentally sank to the bottom of Tegel harbor, where it remained until the early 1950s when it was finally retrieved and placed here in 1952.

The central section of the palace, topped with a dome and a clock, holds the historical apartments. These served as the private living quarters of Sophie Charlotte and her husband; they contain rich furnishings, including a priceless Chinese porcelain cabinet and lacquered furniture. The historical apartments can be visited only on guided tours conducted solely in German (last tour at 4pm). At least, that was the case the last time I checked; you might check again to see whether this has changed. You may be better off skipping the apartments and heading instead to the New Wing, better known as the Knobelsdorff-Flügel and located to the right if you're facing the historical apartments.

On the ground floor of Knobelsdorff-Flügel are more royal living quarters, where visitors can wander unguided through rooms charmingly decorated in the Romantic and Biedermeier styles. Upstairs you'll find the Golden Gallery with its gold and green ornamentation, an impressive German rococo ballroom, and the state dining hall. Be sure, too, to walk through the Galerie der Romantik, a gallery of paintings from the German romantic period with works by C. D. Friedrich and Schinkel. Knobelsdorff-Flügel also contains Frederick the Great's art collection, including works by Watteau, Lancret, Pater, Chardin, Boucher, and Pesne.

Next head for the Schinkel Pavilion, located on the far east end of the palace, behind the Knobelsdorff-Flügel. This delightful summer house, built in 1825, was designed by Karl Friedrich Schinkel, one of Berlin's most respected architects. Resembling an Italian villa, it is decorated with sculptures and paintings from the early 19th century, including some works by Schinkel, who was also an accomplished fine artist. Given a choice, I'd much prefer living in the small and cozy rooms here than in the more pretentious Schloss Charlottenburg.

The park that stretches behind the palace was first laid out in 1697 in French style, then transformed into an English garden early in the 19th century. It was destroyed in World War II and restored to its original baroque form. Besides the Schinkel Pavilion, found in the park are two other important structures. The Mausoleum, located on the west end, contains the tombs of Queen Luise, King Friedrich Wilhelm III, Kaiser Wilhelm I, and Kaiserin Augusta. Designed by Schinkel and built in 1810, with its Doric columns it resembles an ancient temple. Belvedere, at the far end of the park near the Spree River, is a former teahouse that now contains Berlin porcelain of the 18th and 19th centuries, including some by KPM Berlin (Königliche Porzellan-Manufaktur).

Admission: Combination ticket covering all the above and guided tour, 8 DM ($5) adults, 3 DM ($1.85) students and children; Knobelsdorff Flügel, 3 DM ($1.85) adults, 1.50 DM (95¢) students and children; Schinkel Pavilion and Belvedere, 2.50 DM ($1.55) each adults, 1.50 DM (95¢) students and children; Mausoleum, 1 DM (60¢) adults, 50 Pfennig (30¢) students and children; Galerie der Romantik, 4 DM ($2.50) adults, 2 DM ($1.25) students and children.

Open: Tues–Fri 9am–5pm, Sat–Sun 10am–5pm. **Closed:** Mausoleum, Nov–Mar. **Bus:** 109, 145, or 204 to Charlottenburger Schloss. **U-Bahn:** Sophie-Charlotte-Platz or Richard-Wagner-Platz, each about a 10-minute walk.

ÄGYPTISCHES MUSEUM (Egyptian Museum), Schlossstrasse 70. Tel. 32 09 11.

✪ The Egyptian Museum is just across the street from Charlottenburg Palace in what was originally the barracks of the Royal Bodyguards. Here you'll find Berlin's most famous art object and probably the most well-known Egyptian artwork in the world: Queen Nefertiti (called *Königin Nofretete* in German). She's up on the first floor, in a dark room all to herself. Created more than 3,300 years ago, the bust never left the sculptor's studio and served only as a model for subsequent portraits of the queen. When the ancient city was later deserted, the bust was simply left on a shelf in the sculptor's studio. The studio eventually became buried—protecting the bust for more than 3,000 years, until it was unearthed early in this century by a team of German archeologists.

In adjoining rooms are smaller likenesses of her husband, King Ahkenaton, and her daughter, Princess Meritaton. Look also for Queen Tiyi, Akhenaton's mother, known for her shrewdness in politics. Also in this amazing museum are burial cult objects, a mummy and sarcophagi, a papyrus collection, everyday tools, and the Kalabasha Gate.

Admission: 4 DM ($2.50) adults, 2 DM ($1.25) students and children. Free Sun and holidays.

Open: Mon–Thurs 9am–5pm, Sat–Sun 10am–5pm. **Closed:** Jan 1; Maundy Thursday; May 1; Dec 24, 25, and 31. **Bus:** 109, 145, or 204 to Charlottenburger Schloss. **U-Bahn:** Sophie-Charlotte-Platz or Richard-Wagner-Platz, each about a 10-minute walk.

IN KREUZBERG

MUSEUM HAUS AM CHECKPOINT CHARLIE, Friedrich-strasse 44. Tel. 251 10 31.

Since the fall of the Wall, a visit to this significant museum is more important than ever, especially if this is your first trip to Berlin. Popularly known as the Museum of the Wall, it was established soon after the Wall went up in 1961, with the sole purpose of documenting the grisly events that were taking place because of the Wall. Located near what was once a major border check for foreigners entering East Berlin, Checkpoint Charlie, it manages to vividly convey what life was like during the grim decades of the Cold War, using photographs, items used in escapes and unsuccessful escape attempts (a hot-air balloon, cars with hidden compartments), and newspaper clippings. The museum also documents nonviolent revolutions that have taken place throughout the world, with information on Mahatma Gandhi, Lech Walesa, and the peaceful 1989 revolution in East Germany. A block farther north, on the original site of Checkpoint Charlie, is a continuation of the museum with an open-air exhibition that includes a guard tower, a section of the Wall, and other relics of the Cold War.

Admission: 7.50 DM ($4.70) adults, 4.50 DM ($2.80) students.

Open: Daily 9am–10pm. **U-Bahn:** Kochstrasse, a few minutes' walk.

2. MORE ATTRACTIONS

IN BERLIN-MITTE [EASTERN BERLIN]

The first three museums described here (and the Pergamon Museum under "The Top Attractions," above) are located in eastern Berlin on Museumsinsel, a museum complex that dates back to the 1820s when King Friedrich Wilhelm III decided to construct a home for art treasures collected through the ages by the royal family and make them available to the viewing public. During the next century—and particularly under the guidance of museum director Wilhelm von Bode—the museum collections grew with the express purpose of rivaling the other great museums of Europe, including the Louvre and the museums of London, Madrid, and Vienna. German archeologists combed the world for ancient artifacts, bringing back treasures from

Persia, Greece, and Egypt. Paintings from Europe's old masters rounded out the outstanding collections.

After World War II, most of the collections housed here were divided between east and west; many works originally displayed here are now in Dahlem, Charlottenburg, and the Tiergarten. However, Museumsinsel is still world renowned for its ancient architectural and sculptural wonders, particularly the Pergamon Altar.

Note that a *Sammelkarte,* or combination ticket, is available for several museums in Berlin-Mitte; the ticket costs 8 DM ($5) for adults and 4 DM ($2.50) for students and children. It allows entry to the Pergamon Museum, Bode Museum, Alte Nationalgalerie, and Otto-Nagel-Haus.

BODE MUSEUM, Bodestrasse 1-3 (entrance on Monbijou-brücke), Museumsinsel. Tel. 203 55-0.

Named after the former director responsible for bringing great works of art and fame to Museum Island, this is actually several museums under one roof. Here you'll find the Egyptian Museum with its Papyrus Collection, the Early Christian and Byzantine Collection, the Sculpture Collection, the Picture Gallery with art from the 13th to 18th century, and the Coin Cabinet. The majority of what used to be here in the Picture Gallery, however, is now in the museum complex in Dahlem.

On the ground floor you'll find the Ägyptische Museum (Egyptian Museum)—considered one of the world's best—with a lively presentation of the life and times of the Pharaohs. The Early Christian and Byzantine Collection includes a valuable 6th-century mosaic from the church of San Michele in Ravenna and a collection of icons. The Picture Gallery—many of its masterpieces ended up in Dahlem—has German, Dutch, Flemish, French, English, and Italian works—ranging from the 13th to 18th centuries. The Coin Cabinet boasts more than a half million coins, medallions, notes, and seals—one of the largest in the world.

Admission: 4 DM ($2.50) adults, 2 DM ($1.25) students and children. Free Sun and holidays.

Open: Wed–Sun 10am–6pm. **Bus:** 100 to Deutsche Staatsoper stop. **S-Bahn:** Hackescher Markt or Friedrichstrasse, each less than a 10-minute walk.

ALTE NATIONALGALERIE (Old National Gallery), Bodestrasse, Museumsinsel. Tel. 203 55-0.

Built in the style of a Corinthian temple, the Alte Nationalgalerie houses both paintings and sculpture, including classical, romantic, Biedermeier, impressionist, and expressionist works, mainly by German and French artists from the 19th and early 20th centuries. Among them are works by Schadow, Menzel, Degas, Cézanne, and Rodin; of special note are the German expressionist and impressionist departments on the upper floor, with works by Liebermann, Slevogt, Kirchner, Nolde, and Kokoschka.

Admission: 4 DM ($2.50) adults, 2 DM ($1.25) students and children. Free Sun and holidays.

Open: Wed–Sun 10am–6pm. **Bus:** 100 to Deutsche Staatsoper stop. **S-Bahn:** Hackescher Markt, about a 5-minute walk; Friedrichstrasse, about a 10-minute walk.

ALTES MUSEUM (Old Museum), Museumsinsel (entrance on Lustgarten). Tel. 203 55-0.

Built according to plans by Karl Friedrich Schinkel and considered one of his greatest works, this museum was the first one constructed on Museumsinsel. Easily recognized by its 18 Ionic columns, it offers changing exhibitions devoted mainly to ancient art. Refer to the monthly *Berlin Programm* for current exhibitions.

Admission: Varies according to exhibit.

Open: Wed–Sun 10am–6pm. **Bus:** 100 to Deutsche Straatsoper stop. **S-Bahn:** Hackescher Markt, about a 5-minute walk; Friedrichstrasse, an 8-minute walk.

MÄRKISCHES MUSEUM, Am Köllnischen Park 5. Tel. 270 05 14.

This museum concentrates on the history of Berlin from 1648 to 1815, including its cultural life. Displays include local archeological finds beginning with the Stone Age; models of the city around 1500 when it was just the two villages of Berlin and Cölln; as well as paintings, glassware, porcelain (including KPM Berlin), wrought-iron furniture, and wares produced in the city through the centuries. There's also a special section dedicated to Berlin theater, with pictures of famous actors, actresses, and directors of the Berlin stage.

Admission: 3 DM ($1.85) adults, 1.50 DM (95¢) students and children.

Open: Wed–Sun 10am–6pm. **U-Bahn:** Märkisches Museum, a few minutes' walk.

OTTO-NAGEL-HAUS, Märkisches Ufer 16-18. Tel. 279 14 02.

Located on the banks of a small canal, this small museum features German proletarian and antifascist art. Though there are some changing exhibitions, it is devoted primarily to Otto Nagel and his contemporaries. Born in Berlin, Nagel (1894–1967) chose as the subject of his paintings Berlin's working class during the 1920s and 1930s. His portrayals are hauntingly realistic. A very interesting museum.

Admission: 4 DM ($2.50) adults, 2 DM ($1.25) students. Free Sun and holidays.

Open: Sun–Thurs 10am–6pm. **U-Bahn:** Märkisches Museum, a few minutes' walk.

REICHSTAG [Parliament], Platz der Republik. Tel. 39 77-0.

Although technically in western Berlin, the Reichstag is most easily combined with a sightseeing trip to Berlin-Mitte. Completed in 1894, it is since reunification again used for sessions of the German Parliament. When sessions are not being held, the building is open to visitors. Of most interest is the exhibition "Fragen an die Deutsche Geschichte" (Questions of German History), with displays relating to German history from 1800 to the present. Since displays are in German only, be sure to rent a cassette in English and headphones for 2 DM ($1.25) which will guide you through the exhibits in about 45 minutes. Included are displays and photographs on workers' uprisings, the industrial age, Bismarck's reign, World War I, Hitler's rise to power, World War II, the division of Germany, and the events of 1989 that opened the East German border. The entrance to the exhibition is on the Reichstag's north side. Note, however, that the exhibition may close if the space it occupies is deemed necessary for administration purposes.

Admission: Free; English-language audiocassette rental 2 DM ($1.25).
Open: Tues–Sun 10am–5pm. **Bus:** 100 to Reichstag.

BRANDENBURGER TOR [Brandenburg Gate], Unter den Linden.

One of Berlin's best-known structures, the gate was built in 1788–91 by Carl Gotthard Langhans as the grand western entrance onto Unter den Linden. It is topped by a Quadriga created by Johann Gottfried Schadow that shows the goddess of victory in a chariot pulled by four steeds.

During the decades of the Wall, the Brandenburger Tor stood in a no-man's land, marking the boundary of East and West Berlin and becoming the symbol of a divided Germany. After the November 1989 revolution and the fall of the Wall, it was here that many Berliners gathered to rejoice and to dance together on top of the Wall.

S-Bahn: Unter den Linden. **Bus:** 100 to the Unter den Linden/Brandenburger Tor stop.

IN DAHLEM

You can reach the museums in Dahlem in about 20 minutes from the city center by taking U-Bahn 2 to Dahlem-Dorf station. At the station, there are signs pointing the direction of the various museums—most about a 5-minute walk. The Gemäldegalerie (described under "The Top Attractions," above) and museums for sculpture, ethnology, East Asian, Islamic, and Indian arts are all located in a huge sprawling complex with entrances on either Arnimallee and Lansstrasse. One admission price, 4 DM ($2.50) for adults and 2 DM ($1.25) for students and children, allows entry to all museums in the entire complex. Note that museums in Dahlem are closed on Monday.

Several of the Dahlem museums may eventually find new homes in the Tiergarten by the end of the 1990s. The Kupferstichkabinett (Museum of Prints and Drawings) has already closed and will reopen its doors in the Tiegarten by 1994 (check with the tourist office for the exact date and new address). The Gemäldegalerie was scheduled to move to the Tiergarten in 1995, to be followed by the Skulpturengalerie at the turn of the century. That was the plan prior to reunification: Now that Berlin's state museums have come under one administration and museums may combine collections, the future of the Tiergarten is in question. Should the Gemäldegalerie and Skulpturengalerie move, the Tiergarten will become a new center for European art, while Dahlem will continue to house collections of non-European art.

SKULPTURENGALERIE [Sculpture Gallery], Arnimallee 23-27. Tel. 830 11.

One of Germany's foremost sculpture collections, this gallery contains approximately 1,200 European works, dating from the early Christian and Byzantine periods to the late 18th century. Most notable are the works from the Italian Renaissance and German Gothic periods, including carvings by one of Germany's most famous artists, Tilman Riemenschneider. Also on display in the two-story gallery are wooden religious figurines, ivories, marble reliefs, and bronzes.

Admission: Combination ticket 4 DM ($2.50) adults, 2 DM ($1.25) students and children. Free Sun and holidays.

Open: Tues–Fri 9am–5pm, Sat–Sun 10am–5pm. **Closed:** Jan 1; Tues after Easter and Whitsunday; May 1; Dec 24, 25, and 31. **U-Bahn:** Dahlem-Dorf.

MUSEUM FÜR VÖLKERKUNDE [Ethnological Museum], Lansstrasse 8. Tel. 830 11.

This is one of the world's largest ethnological museums, with almost a half million objects from around the world in its possession.

To me, most fascinating is its display of boats and water crafts from the Pacific region in the Oceania Department. There are also original dwellings and facades from the Pacific islands, including a men's clubhouse from Palau and a hut from New Guinea. Equally impressive is the museum's fine collection of Pre-Columbian artifacts, especially its gold objects and Peruvian antiquities. Other departments center on religious life in China, the nomad cultures of Mongolia, shadow puppetry and marionette theaters of Asia, ceremonial masks, African sculpture, and musical instruments. In the Department of Music Ethnology, visitors can listen to recordings of folk music from around the world. A fascinating museum for adults and children alike.

Admission: Combination ticket 1 DM ($2.50) adults, 2 DM ($1.25) students and children. Free Sun and holidays.

Open: Tues–Fri 9am–5pm, Sat–Sun 10am–5pm. **Closed:** Jan 1; Tues after Easter and Whitsunday; May 1; Dec 24, 25, and 31. **U-Bahn:** Dahlem-Dorf.

MUSEUM FÜR DEUTSCHE VOLKSKUNDE [Museum of German Ethnology], Im Winkel 6-8. Tel. 839 01 01.

This ethnological museum focuses on handcrafted objects of the German-speaking people in Central Europe, from the 16th century to the present day. With an emphasis on rural culture before and during the early stages of the Industrial Revolution, the museum displays farm machinery, furniture, costumes, jewelry, religious ceremonial objects, items of leisure, and household goods. This is an interesting contrast to the extravagance of Charlottenburg Palace.

Note that this museum is *not* part of the Dahlem museum complex containing the Gemäldegalerie; it charges its own separate admission.

Admission: 4 DM ($2.50) adults, 2 DM ($1.25) students and children. Free Sun and holidays.

Open: Tues–Fri 9am–5pm, Sat–Sun 10am–5pm. **Closed:** Jan 1; Tues after Easter and Whitsunday, May 1; Dec 24, 25, and 31. **U-Bahn:** Dahlem-Dorf, a 5-minute walk.

MUSEUM FÜR INDISCHE KUNST [Museum of Indian Art], Lansstrasse 8. Tel. 830 11.

Quite simply, this is the most significant collection of Indian art in Germany. Its displays, covering a period of almost 4,000 years, reflect the spread of Indian culture throughout Southeast and Central Asia. Objects range from prehistoric terra-cotta and stone sculptures of Buddhist, Jainist, and Hindu divinities to finely crafted miniatures, ivories, and murals. Of special note is its Turfan Collection of frescoes from the 6th to 10th centuries depicting Buddhist legends. The museum is also famous for its collection of art from Buddhist

DAHLEM MUSEUMS

**TOP FLOOR
(not shown)**

UPPER FLOOR

3 Museum für Völkerkunde
   (South Seas)
4 Skulpturengalerie
5 Gemäldegalerie
7 Museum für Völkerkunde
   (Africa)
9 Museum für Islamische Kunst
10 Museum für Ostasiatische
    Kunst
11 Museum für Völkerkunde
    (Southeast Asia)
12 Special exhibitions

GROUND FLOOR

1 Museum für Indische Kunst
2 Museum für Völkerkunde
   (America)
3 Museum für Völkerkunde
   (South Seas)
4 Skulpturengalerie
5 Gemäldegalerie

LOWER FLOOR

A Lecture Room
B Young People's Museum
C Cafeteria
D Museum for the Blind

UPPER FLOOR

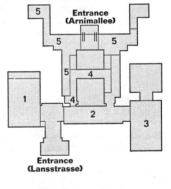

GROUND FLOOR

LOWER FLOOR

cave-monasteries from along the once legendary Silk Road. Not to be missed is the 9th-century stone sculpture of Shiva and his wife, considered a masterpiece of Nepalese art.

Admission: Combination ticket 4 DM ($2.50) adults, 2 DM ($1.25) students and children. Free Sun and holidays.

Open: Tues–Fri 9am–5pm, Sat–Sun 10am–5pm. **Closed:** Jan 1; Tues after Easter and Whitsunday; May 1; Dec 24, 25, and 31. **U-Bahn:** Dahlem-Dorf.

MUSEUM FÜR ISLAMISCHE KUNST [Museum of Islamic Art], Lansstrasse 8. Tel. 830 11.

All Islamic countries are represented in this important collection of art from the 8th to 18th centuries. Highlights include a Koran parchment from the 9th century, enameled Syrian glassware, as well as Egyptian, Turkish, and Iranian carpets.

Admission: Combination ticket 4 DM ($2.50) adults, 2 DM ($1.25) students and children. Free Sun and holidays.

Open: Tues–Fri 9am–5pm, Sat–Sun 10am–5pm. **Closed:** Jan 1; Tues after Easter and Whitsunday; May 1; Dec 24, 25, and 31. **U-Bahn:** Dahlem-Dorf.

MUSEUM FÜR OSTASIATISCHE KUNST [Museum of Far Eastern Art], Lansstrasse 8. Tel. 830 11.

The first of its kind in Germany when established in 1906, it offers a fine overview of Far Eastern decorative and religious art—from 3,000 B.C. to the present. Of note are a lacquered Chinese imperial throne dating from the 17th century with mother-of-pearl inlays, the collection of Japanese woodblock prints, and Japanese and Chinese paintings and scrolls. Because the paintings and scrolls are fragile, displays are changed every 3 months and center on different themes. On one of my visits, there was a special exhibition of 18th- and 19th-century woodblock prints depicting foreigners (who, despite their rounded eyes, still looked rather Asian).

Admission: Combination ticket 4 DM ($2.50) adults, 2 DM ($1.25) students and children. Free Sun and holidays.

Open: Tues–Fri 9am–5pm, Sat–Sun 10am–5pm. **Closed:** Jan 1; Tues after Easter and Whitsunday; May 1; Dec 24, 25, and 31. **U-Bahn:** Dahlem-Dorf.

BRÜCKE-MUSEUM, Bussardsteig 9. Tel. 831 20 29.

This small but important museum is dedicated to members of Die Brücke (The Bridge), a group of painters from Dresden credited with introducing expressionism to Germany. Among the oil paintings, sculptures, watercolors, graphic prints, and other works on display, look for Heckel's *Mann in jungen Jahren* (Man in his Younger Years), Nolde's *Feriengäste* (Vacation Guests), Pechstein's *Fischerboot* (Fishing Boat), and Kirchner's *Berliner Strassenszene* (Berlin Street Scene).

Note that this museum is not part of the Dahlem museum complex; it charges its own admission.

Admission: 4 DM ($2.50) adults, 2 DM ($1.25) students and children.

Open: Wed–Mon 11am–5pm. **U-Bahn:** Dahlem-Dorf, about a 15-minute walk. **Bus:** No. 115.

IN CHARLOTTENBURG

The Charlottenburg precinct's top two attractions, Schloss Charlottenburg (Charlottenburg Palace) and the Ägyptisches Museum (Egyptian Museum), are described above under "The Top Attractions." Near these two attractions are three other museums worth visiting: The Antikenmuseum (Museum of Antiquities), Museum für Vor- und Frühgeschichte (Primeval and Early History Museum), and the Bröhan Museum. If you plan to visit several of these museums, consider purchasing a combination ticket for 8 DM ($5), which allows entry to the Ägyptisches Museum, Antikenmuseum,

Museum für Vor- und Frühgeschichte, and the Galerie der Romantik (located in Schloss Charlottenburg). In addition, Charlottenburg Palace has its own combination ticket.

Other sights in Charlottenburg include the Kaiser-Wilhelm Gedächtniskirche (Kaiser-Wilhelm Memorial Church) and the Käthe-Kollwitz Museum, both located near the Ku'damm.

ANTIKENMUSEUM [Museum of Antiquities], Schlossstrasse 1. Tel. 32 09 11.

Standing directly across from the Egyptian Museum and also designed originally as barracks, this museum contains ancient Greek, Etruscan, and Roman treasures, including pottery, ivory carvings, glassware, jewelry, wood and stone sarcophagi, and small statuettes in marble. Particularly outstanding are the Attic red-figure vases of the 5th century, with their depictions of everyday life and the world of the gods. Most impressive is the *Schatzkammer,* with its silver collection and its exquisite jewelry from about 2000 B.C. to late antiquity.

Admission: 4 DM ($2.50) adults, 2 DM ($1.25) student and children. Combination ticket 8 DM ($5) adults, 4 DM ($2.50) students. Free Sun and holidays.

Open: Mon–Thurs 9am–5pm, Sat–Sun 10am–5pm. **Closed:** Jan 1; Maundy Thursday; May 1; Dec 24, 25, and 31. **Bus:** 109, 145, or 204 to Charlottenburger Schloss. **U-Bahn:** Sophie-Charlotte-Platz or Richard-Wagner-Platz, each about a 10-minute walk.

MUSEUM FÜR VOR- UND FRÜHGESCHICHTE [Primeval and Early History Museum]. Spandauer Damm. Tel. 32 09 11.

This museum is located in the west wing of Schloss Charlottenburg (to the left if you're facing the palace, outside the palace gate). It illustrates the history of humankind from the Stone Age through the Bronze Age and late Iron Age—with objects from prehistoric Europe and the Near East. Arranged in chronological order, the displays begin with Paleolithic cave paintings and idols; then continue with sections devoted to the creation of a written language, early agriculture, metalworking, Trojan antiquities, and items from the Pre-Roman Iron Age and early Germanic tribes. Also included are archeological finds from the Spandau district of Berlin. Spandau, first settled in the 7th to 12th centuries by Slavic people, remains Berlin's most extensively researched archeological site.

Admission: 4 DM ($2.50) adults, 2 DM ($1.25) students and children. Combination ticket 8 DM ($5) adults, 4 DM ($2.50) students. Free Sun and holidays.

Open: Mon–Thurs 9am–5pm, Sat–Sun 10am–5pm. **Closed:** Jan 1; Maundy Thursday; May 1; Dec 24, 25, and 31. **Bus:** 109, 145, or 204 to Charlottenburger Schloss. **U-Bahn:** Sophie-Charlotte-Platz or Richard-Wagner-Platz, each about a 10-minute walk.

BRÖHAN MUSEUM, Schlossstrasse 1a. Tel. 321 40 29.

This privately owned museum (located next to the Antikenmuseum) is named after Professor Karl Bröhan, who collected art nouveau (*Jugendstil* in German) and art deco pieces when others thought they were worthless and threw them away.

Pieces (exquisite vases, glass, furniture, silver, sculptures, and paintings) dating from 1889 to 1939 are beautifully arranged to resemble a salon or home of the period rather than a museum. Outstanding is the porcelain collection, including KPM Berlin, Meissen, and Royal Copenhagen, as well as the turn-of-the-century buffet created by Hector Guimard (1867–1942), who also designed the cast-iron entranceways of the Paris Métro. There's also glass by Emile Gallé, Bohemian iridescent glass, paintings by a group of artists known as the Berlin Secession, silver objects by Viennese artist Josef Hoffmann, and magnificent furniture crafted by Jacques-Émile Ruhlmann. In short, it's a joy; don't miss it.

Admission: 4 DM ($2.50) adults, 2 DM ($1.25) students and children.

Open: Tues–Sun 10am–6pm (Thurs to 8pm). **Bus:** 109, 145, or 204 to Charlottenburger Schloss. **U-Bahn:** Sophie-Charlotte-Platz or Richard-Wagner-Platz, each about a 10-minute walk.

KÄTHE-KOLLWITZ MUSEUM, Fasanenstrasse 24. Tel. 882 52 10.

Located just a minute's walk south of the Ku'damm is this significant museum, displaying the powerful drawings and sketches of Käthe Kollwitz (1867–1945). This Berlin artist was a genius in capturing the emotions of her subjects, from the tenderness of mothers to the despair of poverty and the horrors of war. The museum covers four floors of an old villa; the top floor displays some of Kollwitz's sculptures. Don't miss the opportunity to see her works—their power will stay with you long afterward.

Admission: 6 DM ($3.75) adults, 3 DM ($1.85) children, students, and senior citizens.

Open: Wed–Mon 11am–6pm. **U-Bahn:** Uhlandstrasse, a 1-minute walk.

KAISER-WILHELM GEDÄCHTNISKIRCHE (Kaiser-Wilhelm Memorial Church), Breitscheidplatz. Tel. 24 50 23.

This church, which marks the beginning of the Ku'damm, comes as something of a surprise in modern Berlin. First constructed in 1895, it was destroyed by bombs during World War II and was left in ruins as a visual reminder of the horrors of war. Underneath the skeletal remains of its war-damaged steeple is a small museum with displays related to war and destruction. Beside the Gedächtniskirche is a newer church, designed in the shape of an octagon by Professor Egon Eiermann and completed in 1961. A striking contrast to the ruined church beside it, it's made of blue glass plates from Chartres and includes a hexagonal tower. In the true Berliner style of nicknaming everything in sight, the new church is referred to as the "powderbox and lipstick."

Admission: Free.

Open: Ruined church, Tues–Sat 10am–5pm; new church, daily 9am–7:30pm. Services Sun and holidays 10am and 6pm; short services Mon–Fri 1, 5:30, and 6pm. Organ concerts Sat 6pm. **U-Bahn:** Kurfürstendamm or Bahnhof Zoo, each a 1-minute walk.

IN TIERGARTEN

South of Tiergarten park is Berlin's newest cultural center, the Kulturforum—home of the Philharmonie, the Neue Nationalgalerie, the Kunstgewerbe Museum (Museum of Applied Arts), and

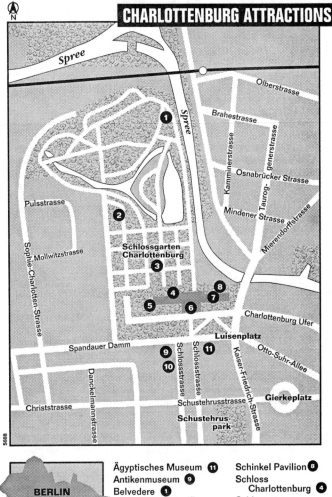

CHARLOTTENBURG ATTRACTIONS

BERLIN
Charlottenburg

Ägyptisches Museum ⑪
Antikenmuseum ⑨
Belvedere ❶
Bröhan Museum ⑩
Knobelsdorff-Flügel and
  Galerie der Romantik ❼
Mausoleum ❷
Museum für Vor- und
  Frühgeschichte ❺

Schinkel Pavilion ❽
Schloss
  Charlottenburg ❹
Schlossgarten
  Charlottenburg ❸
Statue of the
  Great Elector ❻

Musikinstrumenten Museum. Originally planned by West Berlin city planners as a modern counterpart to East Berlin's Museumsinsel, this cultural area was to serve as a center for European art. Since reunification, however, the purpose of Tiergarten has been open to question. If plans continue as scheduled, Tiergarten will eventually house several museums now in Dahlem: the Gemäldegalerie, the Skulpturengalerie, and the Kupferstichkabinett (Museum of Prints and Drawings). In fact, the Kupferstichkabinett is scheduled to open its new Tiergarten quarters by the end of 1994. Check with the Berlin tourist office for exact details. Note that a combination ticket allowing entry to the Neue Nationalgalerie, Kunstgewerbe Museum, and Musikinstrumenten Museum is available for 8 DM ($5) adults and 4 DM ($2.50) students and children.

NEUE NATIONALGALERIE [New National Gallery], Potsdamer Strasse 50. Tel. 266 26 63 or 2666.

The first museum to open in the Tiergarten cultural area, this gallery is called "new" to distinguish it from the much older Alte Nationalgalerie on Museumsinsel, from which it received more than 600 works. Designed by architect Mies van der Rohe and built in the 1960s, it's set in a vast square surrounded by a sculpture garden. Featuring art of the late 19th and 20th centuries, it has changing exhibitions on the ground floor, with the permanent collection on a lower floor. This gallery has the largest collection of works in the world by Berlin artist Adolph von Menzel, also represented are Beckmann, Corinth, Klee, Picasso, Munch, Monet, Manet, Pissarro, Renoir, Kokoschka, Kirchner, and Dali. This bright and airy museum is one of my favorites in Berlin. It's a good introduction to German artists of the past century.

Admission: Permanent collection, 4 DM ($2.50) adults, 2 DM ($1.25) students and children. Combination ticket 8 DM ($5) adults, 4 DM ($2.50) students. Free Sun and holidays. Temporary exhibits 4–8 DM ($2.50–$5).

Open: Tues–Fri 9am–5pm, Sat–Sun 10am–5pm. **Closed:** Jan 1; Tues after Easter and Whitsunday; May 1; Dec 24, 25, and 31. **U-Bahn:** Kurfürstenstrasse, then bus 148 or 248. **Bus:** 129 from Ku'damm.

KUNSTGEWERBE MUSEUM [Museum of Applied Arts], Tiergartenstrasse 6. Tel. 266 29 02.

Housed in a modern, red-brick building, just a 5-minute walk from the Neue Nationalgalerie, and next to the Philharmonie—this delightful museum displays European applied arts from the early Middle Ages to the present day. The oldest museum of its kind in Germany, it displays glassware, porcelain, beer steins, tableware, measuring instruments, and more. Particularly outstanding is its collection of medieval goldsmiths' works, including the *Guelph Cross* and the *Domed Reliquary*, considered among the richest ecclesiastical treasures in any German museum; an 8th-century *Burse-Reliquary*, associated with Charlemagne; and the baptism bowl of Emperor Barbarossa. Another priceless treasure is the *Lüneburg Town Hall Silver Plate*, which consists of 32 vessels and implements in gold-plated silver; it is regarded as one of the most valuable municipal treasures still in existence in Germany.

Admission: 4 DM ($2.50) adults, 2 DM ($1.25) students and children. Combination ticket 8 DM ($5) adults, 4 DM ($2.50) students. Free Sun and holidays.

Open: Tues–Fri 9am–5pm, Sat–Sun 10am–5pm. **Closed:** Jan 1; Tues after Easter and Whitsunday; May 1; Dec 24, 25, and 31. **U-Bahn:** Kurfürstenstrasse, then bus 148 or 248. **Bus:** 129 from Ku'damm.

MUSIKINSTRUMENTEN MUSEUM [Museum of Musical Instruments], Tiergartenstrasse 1. Tel. 25 48 10.

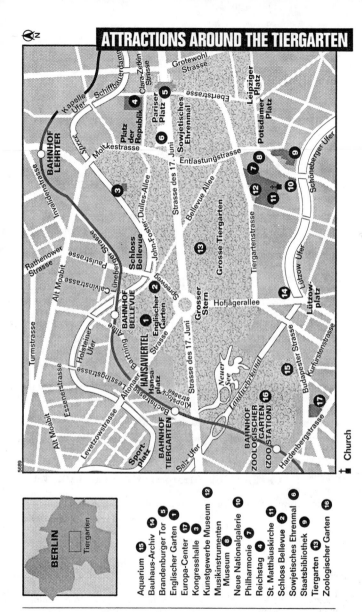

ATTRACTIONS AROUND THE TIERGARTEN

Aquarium **15**
Bauhaus-Archiv **14**
Brandenburger Tor **5**
Englischer Garten **1**
Europa-Center **17**
Kongresshalle **3**
Kunstgewerbe Museum **12**
Musikinstrumenten Museum **8**
Neue Nationalgalerie **10**
Philharmonie **7**
Reichstag **4**
St. Matthäuskirche **11**
Schloss Bellevue **2**
Sowjetisches Ehrenmal **6**
Staatsbibliothek **9**
Tiergarten **13**
Zoologischer Garten **16**

A small gray building overshadowed by the Philharmonie next door, the Musikinstrumenten Museum originated in 1888 but suffered greatly during World War II, losing more than 3,000 of its 4,000 pieces. Fortunately, the past decades have seen many new acquisitions of European musical instruments from the 16th century to the present day. On display are spinets, clavichords, violins, trumpets, flutes, alpenhorns, harps, zithers, guitars, and the now-forgotten glass harmonica, for which Mozart and others wrote compositions.

Admission: 4 DM ($2.50) adults, 2 DM ($1.25) students and children. Combination ticket 8 DM ($5) adults, 4 DM ($2.50) students. Free Sun and holidays.

Open: Tues–Fri 9am–5pm, Sat–Sun 10am–5pm. **Closed:** Jan 1; Tues after Easter and Whitsunday; May 1; Dec 24, 25, and 31. **U-Bahn:** Kurfürstenstrasse, then bus 148 or 248. **Bus:** 129 from Ku'damm.

IN KREUZBERG

Kreuzberg's most popular museum, Museum Haus am Checkpoint Charlie, is described above under "The Top Attractions." Unfortunately, no combination ticket is offered for Kreuzberg's museums.

BERLIN MUSEUM, Lindenstrasse 14. Tel. 258 62 839.

The Berlin Museum examines life in the city from the 17th century to the present, with emphasis on the 18th and 19th centuries. It's found in an impressive white-and-yellow baroque edifice that once housed the Supreme Court. Inside, displays include toys, furniture, paintings, and household objects. In addition, life during the Weimar Republic, the reign of the Nazis, World War II, and the Cold War are documented with paintings, artifacts, and newspaper clippings. One room is devoted to Jewish religious artifacts—of the 60,000 Jews living in Berlin in 1939, 50,000 were taken to concentration camps. (Since the museum lacks sufficient space, Jewish history displays continue in the Martin-Gropius-Bau, described below.) Although most explanations are only given in German, just looking at the exhibits is educational.

For refreshment after touring the museum, drop by the museum's Alt-Berliner Weissbier Stube, an Old Berlin-style pub, where a special wheat beer is served.

Admission: 4 DM ($2.50) adults, 2 DM ($1.25) students.

Open: Tues–Sun 10am–8pm. **U-Bahn:** Hallesches Tor, then bus 141 or a 10-minute walk. **Bus:** 129 from the Ku'damm to Charlottenstrasse stop, then a 10-minute walk.

MARTIN-GROPIUS-BAU, Stresemannstrasse 110. Tel. 25 48 60.

Designed by architect Martin Gropius in 1881, the Renaissance-style Martin-Gropius-Bau is beautiful inside and out and houses two museums: the Berlinische Galerie and the Jewish department of the Berlin Museum. The Berlinische Galerie features modern art, photography, and architecture, with changing exhibitions and a permanent display, with an emphasis on art of the 20th century. Though most of its works are by contemporary Berlin artists, it also shows international art.

Admission: 8 DM ($5) adults; 4 DM ($2.50) children, senior citizens, and students. Temporary exhibits cost extra.

Open: Tues–Sun 10am–8pm. **U-Bahn:** Kochstrasse, about a 5-minute walk. **S-Bahn:** Anhalter Bahnhof, about a 3-minute walk. **Bus:** 129 from the Ku'damm to Stresemannstrasse stop, then a 3-minute walk.

TOPOGRAPHIE DES TERRORS, Stresemannstrasse 110. Tel. 245 86-703.

Located beside the Martin-Gropius-Bau and easily overlooked, this museum documents Hitler's reign of terror and fittingly occupies what was once the site of Hitler's feared Gestapo headquarters. It was here that enemies of the state—Jews, Communists, Social Democrats, and members of resistance movements—were held for questioning and torture by the Third Reich's secret police. Through photographs and explanations, the museum depicts Hitler's rise to power, the fate of Jews and gypsies sent to concentration camps, the role of the Gestapo, and other grim statistics of Hitler's Third Reich. Unfortunately, most of the explanations are in German only, but a booklet in English is available for a small fee.

Admission: Free.

Open: Tues–Sun 10am–6pm. **U-Bahn:** Kochstrasse, about a 5-minute walk. **S-Bahn:** Anhalter Bahnhof, about a 3-minute walk. **Bus:** 129 from the Ku'damm to Stresemannstrasse stop, then a 3-minute walk.

IN FRIEDRICHSHAIN

EAST SIDE GALLERY, Mühlenstrasse.

✪ Formerly a part of East Berlin, Friedrichshain precinct bordered West Berlin, its western boundary marked by the Spree River and the Wall. In a surprise move, East German authorities decided in 1990 to leave a kilometer-long section of the Wall standing along Mühlenstrasse and invited artists from around the world to decorate it with murals (during a divided Germany, the East Berlin side of the Wall was always white and shiny—only in West Berlin could people approach it to paint). Since there is hardly any of the Wall remaining, this is bound to become a major tourist attraction. Look for my favorites: A Trabant (East German car) crashing through the Wall, and Brezhnev and Honecker kissing each other with the caption, "Will no one save me from this deadly love?"

Admission: Free.

Open: 24 hours a day. **S-Bahn:** Hauptbahnhof, a 2-minute walk. **U-Bahn:** Schlesisches Tor, a 5-minute walk.

IN ZEHLENDORF

MUSEUMSDORF DÜPPEL, Clauertstrasse 11. Tel. 802 66 71.

Open in summer only, this open-air reproduction of a medieval village that once occupied this site features thatched-roof houses and live demonstrations of woodworking, baking, weaving, plant cultivation, and other household and agricultural pursuits of medieval Germany. Explanations are in German only, but this is a pleasant trip in fine weather and a fun family outing.

Admission: 3 DM ($1.85) adults, 1.50 DM (95¢) children.

Open: Apr–Sept Sun and holidays 10am–5pm (enter before 4pm), Thurs 3–7pm (enter by 6pm). **Bus:** 211 to Lindenthaler Allee/Ecke Clauertstrasse; or 118 or 115 to Potsdamer Chaussee/Ecke Lindenthaler Allee.

IN KÖPENICK

KUNSTGEWERBEMUSEUM [Museum of Applied Arts], Schloss Köpenick, Schloss Insel. Tel. 657 26 51.

There's been a fortress on this island in the river ever since the 12th century, with the present baroque palace completed in the mid-17th century. Today it holds the Kunstgewerbemuseum, with

FROMMER'S FAVORITE BERLIN EXPERIENCES

Strolling the Ku'damm and Unter den Linden No trip to Berlin would be complete without a leisurely stroll down the Ku'damm, the city's showcase boulevard, and Unter den Linden, the historical heart of the city.

Café Life Cafés are where people meet friends, discuss the day's events, read the newspaper, or just sit at a sidewalk table and watch the never-ending parade.

A Picnic in the Tiergarten The Tiergarten in the heart of the city, home of the Berlin Zoo and Aquarium, is laced with hiking paths that skirt ponds and cut through meadows, a good place for a picnic or a leisurely walk.

Museum Hopping Since most museums in Berlin are located in clusters and offer combination tickets at a discount, you can literally race from one museum to the next, if only to see the great masterpieces.

The Food Emporium of KaDeWe With 1,000 different kinds of sausage, 500 different sorts of bread, 1,500 different types of cheese, and counters selling ready-to-eat dishes, this is a true culinary adventure and not to be missed.

Browsing the Market at Strasse des 17. Juni The best flea market in the city, with a wide variety of antiques, curios and junk, as well as handcrafted items such as jewelry and clothes. Held Saturday and Sunday only.

An Afternoon at the Turkish Market At the Turkish Market Tuesday and Friday afternoons, you'll find exotic spices and clothing; you'll think you've landed in Istanbul.

A Lazy Day at the Beach Europe's largest inland beach is at Wannsee, which boasts a children's playground, shops, and restaurants. A great place on a fine summer's day.

An Evening with the Berlin Philharmonic Orchestra Don't miss the chance of hearing one of the world's great orchestras at the fabulous Philharmonic Hall.

Pub Crawling 'til Dawn There are no mandatory closing hours for bars in Berlin, which means you can celebrate all night long. And if you stay out all night, you'll even find café/bars ready to serve you breakfast in the wee hours.

A Sunday Jazz Brunch Sunday brunch is very much in vogue in Berlin, and there are a number of places that offer a tempting buffet of goodies. Even more popular are those that offer live music as well, such as the Eierschale right off the Ku'damm.

displays covering the last 10 centuries of European applied art, including glass, ceramics, jewelry, tapestries, furniture, and silver and gold objects. What makes the contemporary collection particularly interesting is the presence of artists from eastern Berlin, Dresden, Leipzig, Erfurt, Weimar, and other cities formerly of East Germany, providing insight into the DDR art scene. Another highlight is the ornate Wappensaal (Coat of Arms Hall). Above the fireplace is the coat of arms of the Prussian Brandenburg State. Be sure to stroll the palace garden.

Admission: 4 DM ($2.50) adults, 2 DM ($1.25) students and children. Free Sun and holidays.

Open: Wed–Sun 9am–5pm. **S-Bahn:** Spindlersfeld, then a 15-minute walk; or S-Bahn to Köpenick, then tram 83 or 86 to Schloss Insel stop.

IN ORANIENBURG

NATIONALE MAHN- UND GEDENKSTÄTTE SACHSEN-HAUSEN [National Memorial Sachsenhausen]. Strasse der Nationen, Oranienburg. Tel. 03301/80 37 15.

Although not a part of Greater Berlin, Oranienburg is easily reached via S-Bahn and is an important destination for those who wish to know more about Hitler's death camps. Sachsenhausen was one of the most infamous concentration camps, in operation from 1936 to 1945 and responsible for 100,000 deaths. Since 1961 it has served as a memorial and contains original barracks and other camp structures and a museum complete with photographs. It is a sobering experience, and not recommended for children under 12.

Admission: Free.

Open: Tues–Sun 8:30am–4:30pm. **S-Bahn:** Oranienburg.

PANORAMAS

FERNSEHTURM [TV Tower], Alexanderplatz. Tel. 242 33 33.

From the time the Fernsehturm was completed in 1969 until the fall of the Wall 20 years later, this towering structure was popular in East Berlin for the view it afforded of West Berlin far in the distance, especially on clear days when there's a 24-mile visibility (an update of the day's visibility is posted on the outside door). Elevators whisk visitors to the 670-feet-high observation platform in 35 seconds. More than 1,200 feet tall, the tower is Berlin's tallest edifice and contains the revolving Tele-Café, which makes a complete turn every hour. Come for a cup of coffee on a clear day and enjoy the stunning views.

Admission: 5 DM ($3.10) adults, 2.50 DM ($1.55) children.

Open: Observation platform daily 9am–11:30pm; Tele-Café daily 9am–10:45pm. **Closed:** Until 1pm second and fourth Tues of every month. **S-Bahn or U-Bahn:** Alexanderplatz, a 1-minute walk.

RATHAUS SCHÖNEBERG, John F. Kennedy Platz. Tel. 7831.

It is from the steps of Rathaus Schöneberg that John F. Kennedy gave his famous "Ich bin ein Berliner" speech (see "For Visiting Americans," below). Should you choose to climb the 230-foot-high bell tower, you'll be rewarded with a good view of Schöneberg precinct.

Admission: Free.

Open: Wed and Sun 10am–3:30pm. **U-Bahn:** Rathaus Schöneberg, a 1-minute walk.

SIEGESSÄULE [Victory Column], Grosser Stern. Tel. 391 29 61.

Located in Tiergarten park in the middle of a traffic circle, the Siegessäule was dedicated in 1873 to commemorate three victorious wars. More than 220 feet high, it's topped by a gilded goddess of victory, as well as a 157-feet high observation platform, reached via 290 steps of a spiral staircase.

Admission: 1.50 DM (95¢) adults, 1 DM (60¢) children.

Open: Apr to mid-Nov Mon 1–5:45pm, Tues–Sun 9am–5:45pm. **Bus:** 100 to Grosser Stern stop.

ZOOS, PARKS & GARDENS

Most visitors to Berlin are surprised to learn that the city limits encompass a large area of woods and lakes. During the decades when West Berlin was surrounded by East Germany and the Wall, its green spaces and water, accounting for a full 30% of its total 190 square miles, served as an important emotional escape valve for city dwellers in need of nature.

THE TIERGARTEN, from Bahnhof Zoo to Brandenburger Tor.

Berlin's most convenient park, as well as the city's largest, is Tiergarten park. About two miles long and a half-mile wide, it stretches east from Bahnhof Zoo all the way to Brandenburger Tor. Originally used as a hunting reserve and then as the elector's private park, Tiergarten was opened to the public at the end of the 19th century. The park suffered damage during World War II, and then cold Berliners cut down most of its trees for firewood during the long postwar winters. Today trees have been replanted, and it's one of the most popular places in the city for picnics, jogging, sunbathing, and strolling. In addition to ponds, streams, a rose garden and an English-style garden, it also contains a zoo called the Zoologischer Garten (described below), located in the massive park's southwest corner.

ZOOLOGISCHER GARTEN [Berlin Zoo], Budapester Strasse 32 and Hardenbergplatz 8. Tel. 25 40 10.

Founded in 1841 and opened to the public in 1844, this is Germany's oldest and one of Europe's best zoos, with beautifully designed grounds. Located just a short walk from the Ku'damm or Bahnhof Zoo, it is home to more than 14,000 animals of almost 2,000 species. Probably the best-known and most-beloved resident is BaoBao, Germany's only panda. Also popular are the camels, kangaroos, antelopes, lions, tigers, and monkeys. There's a birdhouse (Europe's largest) with 720 species and a nocturnal house. The adjacent aquarium, built in 1913, has a collection of more than 6,000 fish, reptiles, and amphibians, including an impressive crocodile hall, and sea turtles, sharks, and snakes. A great escape from Berlin city life.

Admission: Combination ticket to zoo and aquarium, 12.50 DM ($7.80) adults, 11 DM ($6.85) students, 6 DM ($3.75) children; zoo only, 8 DM ($5) adults, 7 DM ($4.35) students, 4 DM ($2.50) children.

Open: Summer daily 9am–6:30pm; winter daily 9am–5pm. **U-Bahn:** Bahnhof Zoo, a 1-minute walk.

BOTANISCHER GARTEN [Botanical Garden], Königin-Luise-Strasse 6–8, Dahlem. Tel. 83 00 60.

Berlin's Botanischer Garten was laid out at the turn of the century and boasts 104 acres with 18,000 species of plants. Its 16 greenhouses contain plants from all the continents—from rain forests to deserts. Especially recommended are the great Tropenhaus, constructed in 1907 and one of the largest greenhouses in the world, and the orchid collection. Outdoor beds are arranged geographically, so that visitors can wander through landscapes that resemble the Alps, Japan, the Himalayas, South Africa, North America, and other regions. There's also a garden of medicinal plants, as well as a garden for the visually handicapped, where visitors can smell and touch the plants. The small Botanisches Museum displays the history and usage of various plants, but only in German.

Admission: 3 DM ($1.85) adults, 1.50 DM (95¢) students, free to children under 14 and the handicapped; Botanisches Museum, free.

Open: Botanischer Garten daily Nov–Feb 9am–4pm, Mar and Oct 9am–5pm, Apr and Sept 9am–7pm, May–Aug 9am–8pm; greenhouses daily Nov–Feb 10am–3:15pm, Mar and Oct 9am–4:15pm, Apr–Sept 9am–5:15pm; Botanisches Museum Tues–Sun 10am–5pm. **S-Bahn:** Botanischer Garten, then a 5-minute walk.

PFAUENINSEL AND SCHLOSS PFAUENINSEL [Peacock Island], Havel Lake. Tel. 805 30 42.

With an area of 185 acres, Pfaueninsel is the largest island in the Havel and has long been a popular destination for day-trippers. A nature reserve with many rare trees and birds, the island gets its name from a flock of 60 or so peacocks that has roamed here freely since 1795. But most famous on the island is Schloss Pfaueninsel, an artificial ruin built in the 1790s by Friedrich Wilhelm II for his mistress, the Countess Lichtenau. In contrast to his uncle, Frederick the Great—who spent much of his life waging wars and building empires—Friedrich Wilhelm II apparently preferred to spend his time building architectural fantasies. Schloss Pfaueninsel, later used by Friedrich Wilhelm III and Queen Luise as a summer residence, now contains a small museum with furnishings and artworks dating from 1795 to 1830.

As for the island itself, it's a great place to relax and escape from the hustle and bustle of the city—cars, dogs, portable radios, and smoking are forbidden. You can walk around the island in about an hour or two, though you'll probably want to make several stops along the way. Many rare trees and shrubs were planted here, including Weymouth and Arolla pines, sequoias, gingkos, and cedars. Other items of interest include the Schweizerhaus (Swiss Cottage), designed by Karl Friedrich Schinkel in 1825; the Kavaliershaus, built in 1804 and renovated by Schinkel in 1826, when he added the facade of a late-Gothic patrician home from Danzig; and the Meierei (Dairy Farm), located on the north end of the island and also built in the style of a ruin.

Admission: Pfaueninsel, free; Schloss Pfaueninsel 3 DM ($1.85) adults, 1.50 DM (95¢) students and children.

Open: Pfaueninsel, summer 8am–8pm; winter 10am–4pm. Schloss Pfaueninsel, Apr–Oct Tues–Sun 10am–5pm. **Directions:** Bus 116 or 216 to Pfaueninselchaussee, then by foot to Nikolskoer Weg, then ferry (2 DM, or $1.25, one way).

3. COOL FOR KIDS

MUSEUMS

Museum für Völkerkunde [Ethnological Museum] (see p. 130) One of the largest ethnological museums in the world, with a fascinating display of boats, canoes, masks, dwellings, weapons, clothing, and other objects. Fun and educational.

Museum Haus am Checkpoint Charlie (see p. 126) Older children will find this museum documenting the decades of the Berlin Wall fascinating. On display are vehicles used in daring escapes, including cars with hidden compartments and a hot-air balloon. With its many photographs, it is one of the best places to show your children what Berlin was like during the Cold War.

Museumsdorf Düppel (see p. 139) This is a re-created medieval village, complete with thatched-roof houses and live demonstrations of woodworking, baking, weaving, and other old-time pursuits. Fun for a family outing.

PARKS, THE ZOO & OUTDOOR ACTIVITIES

Zoologischer Garten and Aquarium (see p. 142) Who can resist BaoBao the panda, as well as the monkeys, lions, and camels? The Berlin Zoo, with more than 14,000 animals, and the adjacent aquarium with over 6,000 fish, are only minutes from the Ku'damm.

Botanischer Garten (see p. 143) Show your child that cocoa grows on trees and that there are such things as insect-eating plants. It has a special area for the visually handicapped, where visitors are encouraged to touch and smell the plants.

Tiergarten (see p. 142) Berlin's largest park, located in the heart of Berlin, is another good spot for an outing.

Boat Excursions (see p. 147) Fleets of ships await passengers wishing to travel the Spree River, the Wannsee, and other waterways of Berlin.

Wannsee Beach (see p. 148) A day at the beach is always fun; there's a playground with slides for the kids.

BLUB (see p. 148) This is Berlin's bathing paradise, a complex of indoor and outdoor pools, including a wave pool, a 396-foot super slide, a children's pool, and an outdoor heated pool open year round.

ENTERTAINMENT

Grips (Altonaer Strasse 22; tel. 391 40 04) is the undisputed champion of children's theater in Berlin, with shows that appeal to kids ages 7 to 100. If your child doesn't understand German, attend a production designed for a young age group—there's lots of action and the plot is easy to follow. There are performances throughout the year, usually at 10am or 3pm, with tickets averaging 9 DM ($5.60) for children and 13 DM ($8.10) for adults. It's located only a minute's walk from Hansaplatz U-Bahn station.

Berliner Kammerspiele (Alt-Moabit 99; tel. 391 55 43) is another good theater with programs appealing mainly to young children; it's near the Turmstrasse U-Bahn station. Check the *Berlin Programm* for information on current performances, times, and prices. Performances are usually at 10am.

4. SPECIAL-INTEREST SIGHTSEEING

FOR THE ARCHITECTURE LOVER Because Berlin suffered widespread destruction during World War II, the city is conspicuously devoid of the architectural gems that grace many other European cities. One notable exception is Schloss Charlottenburg, Berlin's most beautiful baroque structure and described above under "Top Attractions."

In addition, some buildings remain that were designed by Karl Friedrich Schinkel (1781–1841), one of Berlin's best-known architects. Among his surviving works are the **Schinkel Pavilion** on the grounds of Schloss Charlottenburg, the **Alte Museum** on Museum Island, and the **Schlossbrücke** that bridges Unter den Linden and the Lustgarten.

Most of Berlin's architecture is only a few decades old. The most famous postmodern buildings are those in the **Hansaviertel** (Hansa Quarter), which stretches along the northern border of Tiergarten park. It consists primarily of housing projects, from one-family dwellings to apartment buildings, along with two churches, a library, and school. The Hansaviertel is the result of an international gathering in 1957 by 48 leading architects from 13 countries, who were asked to design a community for Berliners still homeless as a result of World War II. Famous architects who participated include Walter Gropius, Alvar Aalto, Pierre Vago, Oscar Niemeyer, and Werner Düttmann. The closest subway stop is Hansaplatz station. For orientation, be sure to consult the outdoor map of the Hansaviertel, which lists each building and its architect. Incidentally, Le Corbusier's design turned out to be so large that it was built in the western end of the city near the Olympic Stadium. It's Berlin's largest housing project, with 530 apartments.

Another place of interest to architecture fans is the **Bauhaus-Archiv,** Klingelhöferstrasse 13-14 (tel. 2540 02-0). Located in a light, airy building constructed from plans designed by Walter Gropius, it is dedicated to preserving both the ideals and artifacts relating to the Bauhaus school of design. The Bauhaus, founded by Walter Gropius in Weimar in 1919 and disbanded in Berlin in 1933, revolutionized the teaching of architecture and industrial design, influencing modern design so greatly that its emphasis on aesthetics is still reflected in designs throughout the world.

The Bauhaus-Archiv contains a museum, an extensive collection of documents, and a library, and it stages special exhibitions and seminars throughout the year. The museum's collections, shown on a rotating basis, include architectural models, designs, paintings, drawings, and applied arts that adhere to Bauhaus principles, including architectural models and designs by Gropius, Hannes Meyer, Ludwig Mies van der Rohe, Marcel Breuer, and Ludwig Hilberseimer. In addition, paintings and drawings by Herbert Bayer, Lyonel Feininger, Johannes Itten, Wassily Kandinsky, Paul Klee, László Moholy-Nagy, Georg Muche, and Oskar Schlemmer are also sometimes on display. Note, however, that the small permanent display is sometimes removed to make way for temporary special exhibitions, which nevertheless also relate to the Bauhaus.

The Bauhaus-Archiv, which can be reached by taking bus no. 100, 106, 129, 219, or 341 to Lützowplatz, is open Wednesday to Monday from 10am to 5pm. Admission is 3.50 DM ($2.20) for adults and 1.50 DM (95¢) for students. On Monday, admission is free.

FOR VISITING AMERICANS More than 100 streets, boulevards, and squares are named after Americans—testimonial to the close tie with the United States. Most famous is probably **John F. Kennedy Platz,** the square in front of **Rathaus Schöneberg** (tel. 7831). It was here Kennedy gave his famous "Ich bin ein Berliner" speech on June 26, 1963, just months before he was assassinated. Of interest at the Rathaus is the huge Freedom Bell, given to Berlin by the American people in 1950. Located in a tower and modeled after the U.S. Liberty Bell, it's open for viewing, free, on Wednesday and Sunday only from 10am to 3:30pm (follow the signs that say "Zum Turm"). In the tower are some display cases on the history of the bell, including some of the signatures of Americans who pledged their support to Berlin by signing a "Declaration of Freedom." Altogether, there are 16 million American signatures, which are kept in a vault in the tower. To reach the tower, you have to climb a lot of steps, but the view is grand. To reach Rathaus Schöneberg, take U-4 to the U-Bahn station of the same name, from which it's a minute's walk.

Other streets and places named after Americans include Truman Plaza, Clayallee (named in honor of Gen. Lucius Clay for initiating the airlift of 1948–49), and the **John F. Kennedy School** (part of the Berlin school system but staffed by both American and German teachers).

5. ORGANIZED TOURS

In light of the many changes taking place in Berlin since reunification, companies are also redesigning their tours. In particular, tours to the surrounding environs of Berlin have increased greatly, so be sure to inquire for an update on tour offerings.

BUS TOURS With the aid of this book, you shouldn't have to spend the extra money to join a tour. However, you may wish to join a tour upon arrival, simply for orientation and to see the highlights. You can then return to the sights that interest you and visit them at your leisure.

There are a number of tour companies in Berlin, with most buses departing from the Ku'damm area. The biggest is **Severin + Kuhn,** Kurfürstendamm 216 (tel. 883 10 15), which is open daily from 9am to 6pm. Its 2½-hour tour of Berlin costs 30 DM ($18.75), while a 4-hour tour, with a stop at the Pergamon Museum on Museumsinsel, costs 45 DM ($28.10).

If you're in Berlin for several days, you may wish to take Severin + Kuhn's 7-hour trip to Potsdam, where you'll see Frederick the Great's rococo palace, Sanssouci, and its surrounding gardens. You'll also visit Schloss Cecilienhof, former home of the crown prince and his family; it was here that the 1945 Potsdam Agreement was signed. The tour, including lunch, costs 89 DM ($55.60) for adults and 44.50 DM ($27.80) for children.

From May through September, Severin + Kuhn offers a 5-hour trip to the Spreewald, including a boat ride, for 49 DM ($30.60). Another tour worth considering is its 10-hour trip to Dresden for 99 DM ($61.85). For more information, contact Severin + Kuhn.

Other tour companies include **Berolina**, with buses departing from the corner of Kurfürstendamm and Meinekestrasse (tel. 882 20 91), and **Berliner Bären Stadtrundfahrt,** Rankestrasse 35 (tel. 213 40 77). With prices similar to Severin + Kuhn, they also offer tours of the city, as well as tours of Potsdam, the Spreewald, and Dresden.

BOAT TRIPS   The Spree, a river that winds its way through the heart of Berlin, serves as a popular waterway throughout the year. Excursions of 1½, 3, and 4½ hours are offered throughout the year by **Horst Duggen** (tel. 394 49 54), with daily departures directly in front of the Kongresshalle north of the Tiergarten park (take bus 100 to the Kongresshalle stop). The 3-hour tour, which costs 12 DM ($7.50) for adults and 9 DM ($5.60) for children, travels along the Spree past the Reichstag building and Museumsinsel to Kreuzberg before returning to the Kongresshalle. The 1½-hour trip, costing 10 DM ($6.25) for adults and 7 DM ($4.35) for children, travels to Spandau and back. The 4½-hour trip travels to Müggelsee and back, passing through Berlin-Mitte, Kreuzberg, Köpenick, and other precincts. Cost of this tour is 15 DM ($9.35) for adults, 10 DM ($6.25) for children. All trips are free for children under 6.

Other companies offering trips along the Spree include **Stern and Kreisschiffahrt** (tel. 810 004-0) and **Berliner Wassertaxi Stadtrundfahrten** (tel. 972 61 24). Boats belonging to the latter depart from the Schlossbrücke, located in Berlin-Mitte at the eastern end of Unter den Linden in the shadow of Museumsinsel, for 1-hour trips through the historic heart of the city. Departing every half hour in summer and every hour in winter, the boats cost 9 DM ($5.60) for adults and 5 DM ($3.10) for students and children.

Stern and Kreisschiffahrt is the largest company, offering more than a dozen different trips in Berlin and beyond. City boat tours along the Spree are offered daily from April through October, with departures from either Schlossbrücke near Schloss Charlottenburg (Charlottenburg Palace) or from Jannowitzbrücke in eastern Berlin. Trips last approximately 3 hours and cost 18.50 DM ($11.55).

If you're in Berlin from April to the end of October, you can climb aboard one of the many boats plying the waters of Havel and Wannsee lakes. One of the most popular trips is from Wannsee, with boats departing from a pier near the Wannsee U-Bahn station, to Pfaueninsel and Potsdam and back, operated by Stern and

Kreisschiffahrt. There are also evening dancing cruises. For more information, contact Stern and Kreisschiffahrt.

In eastside Berlin, Stern and Kreisschiffahrt operates a 4-hour boat trip from Treptow to Müggelsee, Berlin's largest lake. The round-trip excursion runs through Köpenick, past the Altstadt (Old City) and Schloss Köpenick, to Friedrichshagen, a peaceful suburb, and then onto Müggelsee. The cost of the trip is 15 DM ($9.35).

For more information on these and other excursions, contact the boat companies directly or drop by the Berlin tourist office.

6. SPORTS & RECREATION

With approximately 6,000 sports grounds, 70 gyms, 60 indoor and outdoor public swimming pools, as well as numerous bowling alleys, tennis courts, and other sports facilities, Berlin offers a wide range of activities for the sports-minded visitor. If you'd rather watch sports instead of participate, check *Berlin Programm* for a day-by-day account of spectator events, from ice hockey and soccer to basketball and table tennis.

SWIMMING   Berlin may be landlocked, yet swimming is among the city's most popular summer recreations. Berliners and visitors alike flock to **Wannsee,** which boasts Europe's largest lake beach. On a warm sunny day, as many as 20,000 people will take advantage of its facilities, which includes a children's playground, slides, and a terrace with shops and restaurants. If you wish, you can rent one of those huge basketlike beach chairs common to northern Germany, which help shield against winds as well as the sun. The beach, open daily May through September from 7am to 8pm, costs 3.50 DM ($2.20) for adults and 2 DM ($1.25) for children. To reach it, take the S-Bahn to Nikolassee. Incidentally, don't be surprised to see topless bathing. Wannsee even has a section devoted to bathing au naturel.

If it's winter or you prefer swimming pools, you might try **BLUB,** Buschkrugalle 64, in Britz (tel. 606 60 60). This is a huge bathing-entertainment leisure complex, which contains a pool with 3-feet-high artificial waves, a 396-foot-long water slide (Europe's longest), bathing grottoes complete with mist and music, saunas, steam baths, and a heated outdoor pool open year round. There's also a children's area, two restaurants, and a bar. Admission is 20 DM ($12.50) for adults, 17 DM ($10.60) for students, and 15 DM ($9.35) for children, with a 4-hour limit. It's open daily from 10am to 11pm. The nearest U-Bahn station is Grenzallee.

Although it's expensive, you may wish to indulge in the hot baths and saunas of the **Thermen,** located in the Europa-Center but with its own entryway at Nürnberger Strasse 7 (tel. 261 60 31 or 261 60 32). Open Monday to Saturday from 10am to midnight, and on Sunday from 10am to 9pm, it charges 27 DM ($16.85) for 3 hours, which includes use of a thermal swimming pool with an outdoor lane, saunas, steam room, fitness room, TV room, table-tennis room, and a sunning terrace with 150 lounge chairs. If you wish to really pamper yourself and hang out all day, the cost is 32 DM ($20). Also available is a solarium, massage, and even a restaurant. Again, bathing is mixed; and in European style, visitors are required to go in the buff.

CHAPTER 7

STROLLING AROUND BERLIN

1. ALONG THE KU'DAMM
2. TIERGARTEN PARK
3. BERLIN-MITTE (EASTERN BERLIN)

Even though Berlin is a large city, most of its sights, shops, restaurants, and attractions are concentrated in specific neighborhoods—making the city easy to explore on foot. From my experience, visitors usually prefer walking wherever possible, simply because it's sometimes easier than figuring out which bus to take and it allows them to see something of the city en route. Natives, more likely to jump on the subway or bus, are often astounded at the great distances visitors are prepared to walk. How often have you been told by a native, "It's too far to walk," only to discover that it's actually only a 10- or 20-minute hike? If you're really in the mood to walk, you might consider combining walks 2 and 3—if you start out early in the morning.

WALKING TOUR 1 — ALONG THE KU'DAMM

Start: The Europa-Center on Tauentzienstrasse.
Finish: Wittenbergplatz.
Time: Allow approximately 3 hours, not including stops at museums, shops, and the zoo.
Best Times: Weekdays, when shops are open, or the first Saturday of the month, when shops stay open until 6pm.
Worst Times: Tuesday, when the Käthe-Kollwitz Museum is closed; or Sunday, when all shops are closed.

The Kurfürstendamm is Berlin's most famous boulevard, home to the city's most expensive shops, hotels, restaurants, bars, and nightclubs. No visit to Berlin would be complete without at least one stroll down the Kurfürstendamm, affectionately called the Ku'damm by Berliners—who in the same breath are also apt to complain about their beloved boulevard. It's too crowded with tourists, they say, and there are too many bad restaurants out to make a buck. But that doesn't stop them from coming here, especially when the weather's warm and they can sit at one of the outdoor cafés to watch the passing parade. And what a parade it is: tourists from around the world, street performers, shoppers, punks, bejeweled women. Never a dull moment on the Ku'damm.

By the way, the Ku'damm stretches 2½ miles, but don't worry—we'll cover only the more important eastern half of it, with excursions down the most interesting side streets along the way. It's a loop stroll, ending up at nearby Wittenbergplatz, home of the largest department store on the continent, KaDeWe.

FROM THE EUROPA-CENTER TO SAVIGNYPLATZ

1. The Europa-Center, easy to spot from far away because of the Mercedes-Benz logo at its top, is 22 stories high and contains offices, a hotel, more than 100 shops and restaurants, a movie theater, cabarets, and a casino. In the main atrium on the ground floor is a strange-looking contraption, measuring 42 feet high. It's a clock, showing the time by way of colored water passing through pipes, and is known as the *Fliessenden Uhr* (the "Running Clock"). At the Tauentzien-Strasse exit is a section of the Berlin Wall. Be sure to stop off at the Berlin tourist office, located in the Europa-Center but with its own separate entryway on Budapester Strasse, for maps and brochures on sightseeing.

Also on Budapester Strasse, across the street from the Europa-Center, is the:

2. Zoologischer Garten (Berlin Zoo) and Aquarium, Budapester Strasse 32. Founded in 1844, it boasts more than 14,000 animals, including a panda. (See "Zoos, Parks & Gardens" in Chapter 6, "What to See & Do in Berlin.")

It would be hard to miss the:

3. Kaiser-Wilhelm Gedächtniskirche, located on Breitscheidplatz next to the Europa-Center, so out of place does this ruined church look beside the modern high-rises that surround it. Left as a reminder of World War II and containing a small museum, it marks the beginning of the Ku'damm.

West of the Gedächtniskirche on Breitscheidplatz is the:

4. American Express office at Ku'damm 11, as well as:

5. Tschibo coffee shop, where you can drink a cup of coffee standing at one of its chest-high counters for 1.20 DM (75¢) a cup. Walking past Tschibo along the north side of the Ku'damm, you'll soon come to:

6. Café Kranzler, Ku'damm 18, one of Berlin's most famous coffee shops and a favored spot for people-watching at its sidewalk tables. Nearby is:

7. KPM, Ku'damm 26a, a shop that deals in the exquisite porcelain of the Königliche Porzellan-Manufaktur, one of Berlin's most famous products with a history dating back more than 200 years. (See Chapter 8, "Berlin Shopping.")

The next intersection is Fasanenstrasse, and if you turn right here and walk past the Bristol Hotel Kempinksi, within a minute you'll come to:

8. Zille Hof, Fasanenstrasse 14, a jumble of junk stalls underneath the S-Bahn tracks. Who knows, you might find a treasure here among the crowded and dusty shelves laden with plates, glasses, pots and pans, books, clothing, and odds and ends. If nothing else, its entryway is worth a photograph. (See Chapter 8, "Berlin Shopping," for more information.)

Back on the Ku'damm, continue heading west 1 block to the corner of Uhlandstrasse. Here, in the median that runs in the middle of the Ku'damm, you'll notice a futuristic-looking row of lights. Believe it or not, it's a:

9. Clock, and here's how it works. Every light of the top row represents 5 hours; the lights beneath it each represent 1 hour; the third row stands for 5 minutes, and the bottom-row lights each represent 1 minute. If you count them all together, they'll tell you the exact time. Thus, if you had two lights on the top

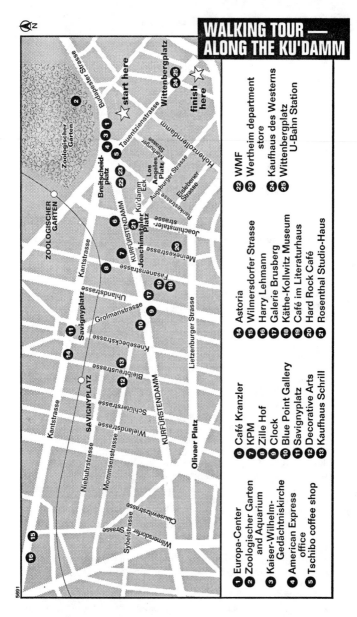

start here

finish here

Zoologischer Garten

Budapester Strasse

Wittenbergplatz

Tauentzienstrasse

Hohenzollerndamm

Breitscheid platz

Los Angeles Platz

Augsburger Strasse

KURFÜRSTENDAMM

Kurfürsten Damm Eck

Joachimstaler Platz

Joachimstaler strasse

Meinekestrasse

Fasanenstrasse

Rankestrasse

Eislebener Strasse

ZOOLOGISCHER GARTEN

Kantstrasse

Uhlandstrasse

Grolmanstrasse

Knesebeckstrasse

Savignyplatz

SAVIGNYPLATZ

Bleibtreustrasse

Schlüterstrasse

Lietzenburger Strasse

Olivaer Platz

Kantstrasse

Niebuhrstrasse

Wielandstrasse

Mommsenstrasse

KURFÜRSTENDAMM

Clausewitzstrasse

Wilmersdorfer Strasse

Sybelstrasse

5691

1 Europa-Center
2 Zoologischer Garten and Aquarium
3 Kaiser-Wilhelm-Gedächtniskirche
4 American Express office
5 Tschibo coffee shop
6 Café Kranzler
7 KPM
8 Zille Hof
9 Clock
10 Blue Point Gallery
11 Savignyplatz
12 Decorative Arts
13 Kaufhaus Schrill
14 Astoria
15 Wilmersdorfer Strasse
16 Harry Lehmann
17 Galerie Brusberg
18 Käthe-Kollwitz Museum
19 Café im Literaturhaus
20 Hard Rock Café
21 Rosenthal Studio-Haus
22 WMF
23 Wertheim department store
24 Kaufhaus des Westerns
25 Wittenbergplatz U-Bahn Station

row, followed by one light in the next row, three lights on the third, and then two, it would be 11:17am. Berliners consider this a child's game.

Just past the clock is the wonderful

10. Blue Point Gallery, Ku'damm 35. On the ground floor is a display of glass artwork, including vases, paperweights, perfume bottles, and plates; upstairs is a gallery featuring mostly Berlin artists but other European artists as well. Prices are a bit high for us, but it doesn't cost anything to look. (See Chapter 8, "Berlin Shopping," for more information.)

Continue walking west along the Ku'damm to the next street, Knesebeckstrasse, where you should turn right. Within 4 minutes, you'll find yourself on:

11. Savignyplatz, a grassy square lined with restaurants, bars, and turn-of-the-century apartment buildings. This is where you'll find some of Berlin's interesting nightlife, including trendy bars and restaurants, so you might want to return here after dark.

REFUELING STOPS Shell, on the north end of Savignyplatz at Knesebeckstrasse 22, is popular with young residents of the area, particularly for its international dishes, including light meals and vegetarian selections. Nearby is **San Marino,** Savignyplatz 12, an Italian pizzeria with outdoor seating in the square. If all you want is a drink, try **Zwiebelfisch,** Savignyplatz 7–8, open from noon to 6am, or **Cour Carrée,** Savignyplatz 5, recommended for its outdoor seating in the shade of spreading vines.

FROM SAVIGNYPLATZ TO WILMERSDORFER STRASSE Begin from Savignyplatz's southwest corner, where you'll find the overhead tracks of the S-Bahn. Beneath the arches of the tracks are a few interesting shops, bars, and restaurants, including a boutique devoted to lamps, gift shops, and an inexpensive Chinese eatery. At the end of the passage is Bleibtreustrasse, home to two interesting art deco shops. Take a left and walk 1 short block to the corner of Niebuhrstrasse, where you'll find:

12. Decorative Arts, a shop that specializes in glass and furniture, from art nouveau to art deco.

Across the street is:

13. Kaufhaus Schrill, Bleibtreustrasse 46, a wacky clothing store that sells costume jewelry, clothing, and hundreds—if not thousands—of unusual ties (not the kind you'd wear to impress an important business client).

If you backtrack and walk farther north on Bleibtreustrasse, within minutes you'll come to:

14. Astoria, Bleibtreustrasse 50, which deals in lamps, statues, jewelry, and some furniture—including antiques and reproductions. Take note that many antiques shops are open only in the afternoon.

You're now on the corner of Bleibtreustrasse and Kantstrasse. Head west on Kantstrasse for approximately 10 minutes, until you reach:

15. Wilmersdorfer Strasse. This is Berlin's main pedestrian shopping lane, where in quick succession you'll find such large department stores as Karstadt, Quelle, and Hertie. There are also a number of smaller shops and boutiques, as well as several restaurants. Just west of Wilmersdorfer Strasse is one of Berlin's most endearing institutions:

16. Harry Lehmann, Kantstrasse 106. This tiny, family-owned shop has been selling its own perfumes since 1926, using flowers, leaves, and grasses. A vial of perfume makes an inexpensive gift. (See Chapter 8, "Berlin Shopping," for details.) If you're tired or decide to spend the rest of the day shopping, you can return to your hotel by taking the subway from Wilmersdorfer Strasse station. Otherwise, take advantage of the many fast-food restaurants in the area, or head back down to the Ku'damm.

REFUELING STOPS There are a number of inexpensive eateries on Wilmersdorfer Strasse, including cafeterias and restaurants in the three department stores listed above. For a quick stand-up meal, try **Joseph Langer** at Wilmersdorfer Strasse 118, a butcher shop that also sells simple meals and Würste. Across the street is **Nordsee,** Wilmersdorfer Strasse 58, a fast-food fish restaurant.

If you prefer a more relaxed and less hectic environment where you can linger over a meal or drink, head to **Udagawa Japan Imbiss,** Kantstrasse 118, an informal Japanese restaurant serving everything from teriyaki and fried noodles to stews and tempura. **Athener Grill,** Ku'damm 156, near Adenauerplatz, is a cafeteria selling both Greek and Italian food, from moussaka to pizza. Next door is **Ciao Ciao,** a popular Italian restaurant with outdoor seating.

A popular watering hole in the area is **New York,** Olivaer Platz 15, where Berlin's trendy youth gather throughout the day and late into the evening.

FROM ADENAUERPLATZ TO RANKESTRASSE ON THE KU'DAMM Walking back in the direction of the Gedächtniskirche, this time on the south side of the Ku'damm, you'll again pass a number of shops. This, after all, is Berlin's most exclusive shopping street. Note the many freestanding display cases along the sidewalk, advertising the wares of nearby shops. During the evening, wares of a different sort are peddled, as the Ku'damm has long been a hot spot for the ladies of the night (prostitution, by the way, is legal in Germany).

Our first stop on this leg of our journey is the:

17. **Galerie Brusberg,** located on the corner of Uhlandstrasse at Ku'damm 213. The gallery, located up on the first floor of a beautiful century-old patrician home, represents such famous artists as Salvador Dali, Bernhard Dörries, Max Ernst, Joan Miró, and Picasso, in a setting as good as any museum. Entry is free, so it's worth a spin through. (See Chapter 8, "Berlin Shopping," for hours.)

A block farther east on the Ku'damm brings you to Fasanenstrasse, where you should turn right. This is where you'll find the:

18. **Käthe-Kollwitz Museum,** located at Fasanenstrasse 24, one of my favorite museums in Berlin. A Berliner, Kollwitz was a genius in capturing human emotions in her portraits. I feel she deserves more worldwide recognition. (See "More Attractions" in Chapter 6, "What to See & Do in Berlin," for details.) Beside the museum is a charming coffeehouse,

19. **Café im Literaturhaus,** where you can linger over a cup of coffee in its outdoor garden or, in winter, in its greenhouse.

Returning to the Ku'damm and walking one block farther east brings you to the next side street, Meinekestrasse, where you'll find the:

20. Hard Rock Café, Meinekestrasse 21, a worldwide chain featuring rock 'n roll memorabilia and burgers and beer. Prices are a bit high, so stop here to buy your T-Shirt and then move on to:

21. Rosenthal Studio-Haus at Ku'damm 226, which sells porcelain, Boda crystal, and Rosenthal porcelain. A good place to shop for a wedding gift. Ordinary and not-so-ordinary cookware and tableware is featured at:

22. WMF, Ku'damm 229, a well-known chain throughout Germany. (See Chapter 8, "Berlin Shopping," for details.)
    Next door is:

23. Wertheim department store, Ku'damm 231, convenient for stocking up on sundry items, film, or a souvenir of Berlin.

REFUELING STOPS Down in the **basement of Wertheim department store**—next to the grocery section—is an informal cafeteria with various counters devoted to different foods: from salads and stews to chicken and beer. Just around the corner from Wertheim is **Eierschale,** Rankestrasse 1, a popular bar with live jazz in the evenings.

FROM RANKESTRASSE TO WITTENBERGPLATZ

Tauentzienstrasse runs from the Ku'damm and the Europa-Center to Wittenbergplatz. It's lined with a number of inexpensive and expensive clothing stores, appealing to shoppers of all ages. Since many of the shops are open-fronted, it may be difficult to refrain from the temptation of giving the sales racks a once-over. If you can resist, however, within minutes you'll find yourself at Wittenbergplatz, home of:

24. Kaufhaus des Westens, popularly called KaDeWe. It's the star of this walk, and not to be missed is its food department on the sixth floor—lavishly stocked with gourmet foods. There are more than 1,000 different kinds of sausages alone. A true culinary adventure. (See Chapter 8, "Berlin Shopping," for more information.) Also on Wittenbergplatz is the:

25. Wittenbergplatz U-Bahn Station, one of Berlin's most beautiful stations, with art nouveau grillwork and oak ticket booths. In front of the station is a large black-and-gold sign that lists "Places of terror we should never be allowed to forget," including Auschwitz, Dachau, and Bergen-Belsen, all World War II concentration camps. It's a strange place for a memorial, as commuters and shoppers rush by, seemingly oblivious to the sign and its message.

   Inside the station you'll find an odd electromechanical scale, one of 55 such mechanical treasures dating from the 1920s still in operation in Berlin's subways. It's on Bahnsteig (platform) I, down the escalator (you need a valid subway ticket to enter the platform). By inserting a 10-Pfennig coin and stepping onto the weighing platform, you'll receive a card printed with your weight in kilos and the date.

FINAL REFUELING STOPS The **KaDeWe's food emporium** on the sixth floor is also a good place to dine as well as shop. There are separate counters with stools spread throughout, each specializing in a different food or drink: Choose from pasta, potato dishes, grilled chicken, wines, and much more. You can order take-out and eat your goodies on one of the benches on Wittenbergplatz. Another good place for take-out food—especially if you're vegetarian—is **Einhorn,** Wittenbergplatz 5–6, on the opposite end of the square from KaDeWe. A natural foods shop, it also offers daily specials ranging from vegetarian lasagne or spinach casserole to vegetarian moussaka. **Lekkerbek,** Ansbacherstrasse 11, is a pleasant cafeteria offering more than a dozen different types of sandwiches at inexpensive prices.

WALKING TOUR 2 — TIERGARTEN PARK

Start: Tiergarten S-Bahn Station.
Finish: Reichstag building.
Time: Allow approximately 1½ hours, not including stops along the way.
Best Times: Saturday and Sunday, when the market on Strasse des 17. Juni takes place.
Worst Times: Mondays, when the Reichstag is closed.

Take this stroll when you need a break from museums and want to spend the day out of doors. You'll pass through Tiergarten park all the way to Brandenburger Tor with several interesting stops along the way. If you really want to make an outing of it, pack a picnic lunch. There aren't many possibilities for refreshment on this walk.

FROM TIERGARTEN S-BAHN STATION TO THE SIEGES-SÄULE   If it's the weekend, head straight for the:

1. **Flea market** west of Tiergarten station (you can see the market from the station's platform) on Strasse des 17. Juni. This is one of my favorite places to shop in all of Berlin—not only for all the antiques, but for young people selling jewelry, drawings, clothing, and other crafts. I've picked up some great gifts here for friends. The crafts section is separated from the antique stalls by a bridge and a large stone gate: Don't miss it.

REFUELING STOPS   There are a number of **food stalls** (called *Imbisse*) at the above market, where you can eat everything from sausage and french fries to Turkish pizza and beer. If you'd rather sit down, backtrack under the elevated platform of the S-Bahn station, where on the east side you'll find a small white building called **Berlin Pavilion,** on Strasse des 17. Juni. There's a small café here, with tables outside in summer—and toilet facilities.

If you take this walking tour on a weekday when there's no market, you'll exit from the Tiergarten S-Bahn station and head east (in the direction of the huge column rising from the middle of the street in the distance). Almost immediately to your left, past the Berlin Pavilion, is a street called Klopstock. Turn left on Klopstock, where you'll soon find yourself in the midst of the:

2. **Hansaviertel** (Hansa Quarter). This area was developed in the late 1950s during a competition, in which 48 architects from 13 countries participated—with each architect designing one building in his own style. Most are apartments, since Berlin was still suffering from a housing crunch following the war. On your right as you walk north on Klopstock, you'll see a map of the area indicating the various buildings and their designers. Building 22, by Alvar Aalto, won the competition. It's the blue, green, and white apartment building and will be to your right as you continue walking north on Klopstock. What strikes me most about the entire Hansaviertel, however, is how ordinary the buildings seem—what was revolutionary in the 1950s now appears rather commonplace.

At the next big intersection, Hansaplatz, take a right onto Altonaer Strasse, heading towards that huge column rising from the middle of the street in the distance. It is encircled by a huge rotary called:

3. **Grosser Stern** (which translates as Great Star because of the many roads leading away from it). It was laid out in 1938 under orders from Hitler. Note the beautiful gas lamps surrounding the Grosser Stern. Berlin still has 40,000 gas lamps and 100 full-time employees to clean all those lamps and make sure they're still burning. In the middle of the traffic circle is a huge column, called the:

4. **Siegessäule** (Victory Column). Erected in the 1870s, it commemorates three victorious wars: against Denmark in 1864, against Austria in 1866, and against France in 1870–1871. More than 220 feet high, it's topped by a gilded goddess of victory. In the summer months from April to mid-November, visitors can climb the 290 steps of a spiral staircase to an observation platform 157 feet high, for wonderful views of the city. The Siegessäule is reached via pedestrian tunnels under Grosser Stern.

FROM THE SIEGESSÄULE TO THE REICHSTAG The Grosser Stern is surrounded by the:

5. **Tiergarten park,** Berlin's largest city park. Filled with ponds, wide grassy fields, and wooded areas, it stretches about 2 miles from Bahnhof Zoo all the way to Brandenburger Tor. It's a popular weekend destination for family picnics. You might wish to stop too for a picnic.

Next head northeast on Spreeweg, where to your left you'll see the French baroque–style:

6. **Schloss Bellevue** (Bellevue Palace), built in 1785 as a summer residence for Frederick the Great's youngest brother. Today it serves as the private residence of the German president and is not open to the public. You can, however, visit its attached:

7. **Englischer Garten** (English Garden) whenever the president is out of town. It was reconstructed after the war with donations from England. Continue walking down Spreeweg, taking a right onto John-Foster-Dulles-Allee (named after the former U.S. secretary of state), where to your left you'll soon see the:

8. **Kongresshalle,** built in 1957 by American Hugh A. Stubbins as part of the Hansaviertel architectural competition. Unfortu-

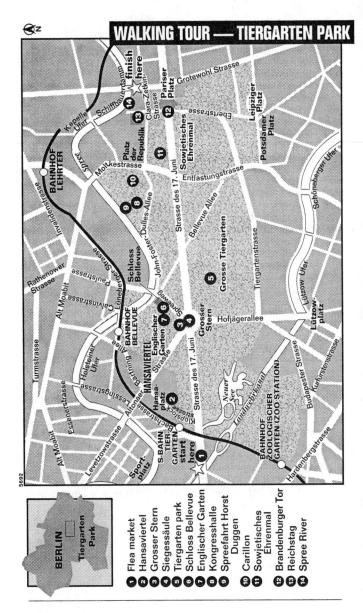

finish here

Grotewohl Strasse

Pariser Platz

Clara-Zetkin Strasse

Leipziger Platz

Schiffbauerdamm

Ebertstrasse

Sowjetisches Ehrenmal

Potsdamer Platz

Kapelle Ufer

Spree

Platz der Republik

Molkestrasse

Strasse des 17. Juni

Entlastungsstrasse

Schöneberger Ufer

Invalidenstrasse

BAHNHOF LEHRTER

John-Foster-Dulles-Allee

Schloss Bellevue

Bellevue Allee

Tiergartenstrasse

Grosse Tiergarten

Lützow Ufer

Rathenower Strasse

Paulstrasse

Linienstrasse

Calvinstrasse

Bartning Allee

Englischer Garten

Bauhaus

Spree

Grosser Stern

Hofjägerallee

Lützow platz

Turmstrasse

Alt Moabit

Holsteiner Ufer

BAHNHOF BELLEVUE

HANSAVIERTEL

Strasse des 17. Juni

Budapester Strasse

Kurfürstenstrasse

Essener Strasse

Levetzowstrasse

Altonaerstrasse

Hansa platz

Lessingstrasse

Klopstock Strasse

Neuer See

Landwehrkanal

Alt Moabit

Sport platz

S-BAHN TIER GARTEN

start here

BAHNHOF ZOOLOGISCHER GARTEN (ZOO STATION)

Hardenbergstrasse

5692

BERLIN

Tiergarten Park

1. Flea market
2. Hansaviertel
3. Grosser Stern
4. Siegessäule
5. Tiergarten park
6. Schloss Bellevue
7. Englischer Garten
8. Kongresshalle
9. Spreefahrt Horst Duggen
10. Carillon
11. Sowjetisches Ehrenmal
12. Brandenburger Tor
13. Reichstag
14. Spree River

nately, its roof collapsed in 1980, but no one was hurt; it has since been rebuilt. Because of its form, Berliners have nicknamed it the "Pregnant Oyster." There's a statue by Henry Moore in front of the building. Behind the Kongresshalle is the Spree River, from which the company:

9. Spreefahrt Horst Duggen offers boat trips through Berlin, lasting 45 minutes to 4½ hours, throughout the year. (See "Organized Tours" in Chapter 6, "What to See & Do in Berlin," for more information on boat trips.) Beside the Kongresshalle is a:

10. carillon, one of Europe's tallest. More than 130 feet high, it has 68 bells with a range of 5½ octaves. The carillon is played twice daily, at noon and 6pm, for five minutes.

Past the carillon is a busy street, Entlastungsstrasse, where you should take a right and then a left back onto Strasse des 17. Juni, where you will see the Brandenburger Tor. Immediately to your left, before the gate, you'll see the:

11. Sowjetisches Ehrenmal (Soviet Memorial) to your left on Strasse des 17. Juni. Erected after the war from marble of Hitler's chancellery, it is a memorial to the 20,000 Soviet soldiers who lost their lives in the war—guarded by two Russian soldiers.

And here we are at the:

12. Brandenburger Tor. Modeled after the propylaea in Athens, the gate was built by Carl Gotthard Langhans in 1788–91 as the west entrance onto Under den Linden. The only remaining city gate of 14, it is topped by a Quadriga created by Johann Gottfried Schadow, which consists of the goddess of victory in a chariot pulled by four steeds. After Napoléon's triumph over Prussia, the Quadriga was carted off to Paris by the French in 1806, where it remained until Marshal Blücher retrieved it in 1814. It was severely damaged in the war but has since been restored.

After the Wall went up in 1961, the Brandenburger Tor became inaccessible from West Berlin, making it a symbol of a divided Berlin. After the November 1989 revolution, it was here that many Berliners, from both East and West, gathered to rejoice and to dance together on top of the Wall. I myself witnessed part of the celebration in the months that followed, as people from around the world chiseled at the Wall for a piece of history. At the end of February 1990, the East German government began tearing down the Wall in anticipation of a united Germany. Finally, for the first time in decades, people could pass freely from Strasse des 17. Juni past the Brandenburger Tor to Unter den Linden in East Berlin.

To the left of the Brandenburger Tor is a large, solemn-looking building, the:

13. Reichstag (Parliament). Completed in 1894 in Neo-Renaissance style to serve the needs of Bismarck's united Germany, it had its darkest hour on the night of February 17, 1933, when a mysterious fire broke out. The Nazi government blamed the German Communist party for setting the blaze, and used the incident as a reason for arresting Communist party members and other opponents, thus abolishing such basic democratic rights as personal liberty and freedom of the press. Damaged in World War II, the Reichstag was restored with the exception of its dome. Since 1971, the north end of it has been used for an exhibition called "Fragen an die Deutsche Geschichte" (Questions of German History), with displays relating to German history from 1800 to the Cold War. In the wake of reunification, this exhibit, which has always been only in German but which offers earphones in English, may not continue (see "More Attractions" in Chapter 6, "What to See & Do in Berlin," for details on the museum). On October 4, 1990, the

German parliament (both East and West) met in the Reichstag for its first joint session after more than four decades of separation.

Behind the northeast corner of the Reichstag is the:

14. Spree River, which once formed part of the border between the two Berlins. East German soldiers, armed with guns and binoculars, used to keep watch from a guard tower here—a sight that always caused me anxiety even though I was on the lucky side of the Wall. There is a row of white crosses here, a memorial to people who were not so fortunate and who lost their lives as they attempted to flee to the West. Also behind the Reichstag is a flat, 60-foot-long concrete marker on Ebertstrasse, showing the exact former location of the Wall.

At the south end of the Reichstag is a bus stop; bus 100 travels between the Europa-Center and Alexanderplatz.

FINAL REFUELING STOPS Inside the Reichstag building, at the north entryway near the exhibition, is the informal **Cafeteria** serving one-pot stews (Eintöpfe), Gulaschsuppe, Würste, coffee, beer, and soft drinks. Down the corridor is the **Café-Stube,** a self-service café offering coffee, tortes, and other desserts.

WALKING TOUR 3 — BERLIN-MITTE (EASTERN BERLIN)

Start: Unter den Linden at Brandenburger Tor.
Finish: Nikolaiviertel.
Time: Allow approximately 2 hours, not including stops along the way.
Best Times: Weekdays when museums aren't as crowded; or Sunday when they're free.
Worst Times: Monday and Tuesday when some museums are closed.

This stroll brings you through what used to be the heart of old Berlin before World War II, later serving as East Germany's capital. From the historic boulevard Unter den Linden, you'll pass Museumsinsel and end your tour at the Nikolaiviertel (Nikolai Quarter), a restored neighborhood of restaurants and pubs.

FROM BRANDENBURGER TOR TO SCHLOSSBRÜCKE
This tour starts in front of Brandenburger Tor (described in Walking Tour 2, above), marking the west end of:

1. Unter den Linden. The Elector used to pass this way to the Tiergarten to hunt, and by 1675 this was a paved road. In the centuries that followed, it was the lifeline of old Berlin: the city's most fashionable and liveliest boulevard. Today, after decades of being cut off from western Berlin by the Wall at Brandenburger Tor, the tree-lined Unter den Linden is once again the center of a reunited Berlin. From here you have a view of the front of

Brandenburger Tor, topped by the Quadriga. Unter den Linden is 200 feet wide and stretches seven-tenths of a mile, from Brandenburger Tor to Schlossbrücke (formerly Marx-Engels-Brücke).

With the Brandenburger Tor behind you, walk east on Unter den Linden (which means Under the Lime Trees). After a couple blocks, you'll reach:

2. Friedrichstrasse, an important thoroughfare. Before World War II, this was Berlin's busiest intersection, and Café Kranzler, now on the Ku'damm, used to sit on this corner. At this point, Berlin's grand old buildings begin—most from the 1800s and now painstakingly restored.

Take a left onto Friedrichstrasse and walk a couple minutes north to the overpass of the S-Bahn. Here, underneath the arches of the track to the right, is the:

3. Berliner Antik- und Flohmarkt (Berlin Antique and Flea Market), where about 60 vendors sell everything from glassware and lamps to porcelain, jewelry, books, pocketwatches, canes, and odds and ends. Prices aren't cheap, but it's fun walking through. (The market is open Wed–Mon 11am–6pm.) Here, too, is the:

4. Heinrich-Zille-Museum, featuring drawings and personal items of one of Berlin's most well-known and beloved graphic artists and caricaturists. A chronicler of turn-of-the-century Berlin life, Zille is particularly known for his sketches of the poor and working class, which he depicted with compassionate humor. Back on Unter den Linden, continue walking one block east, taking a right onto Charlottenstrasse. After a few short blocks, you'll soon find yourself at the historic:

5. Gendarmenmarkt, once considered one of Berlin's most attractive squares and formerly the site of Berlin's main market. Totally destroyed during World War II, it has been painstakingly restored and features three neoclassical buildings. Most important is the Schauspielhaus, designed by Karl Friedrich Schinkel in 1821 and now a concert house that is flanked by the German and French cathedrals. Returning to Unter den Linden via Charlottenstrasse and turning right, you will immediately pass the neobaroque:

6. Deutsche Staatsbibliothek (National Library; formerly Prussian State Library), containing more than five million volumes, and the neoclassical:

7. Humboldt-Universität (Humboldt University), where Hegel, Marx, and the Brothers Grimm taught. In the median in front of the university is an:

8. equestrian statue of Frederick the Great. Just past the statue, to your right, is a square called:

9. Bebelplatz, dominated by St.-Hedwigs-Kathedrale. On May 10, 1933, the Nazis staged a massive book-burning here, destroying books deemed offensive to the regime, including works by Thomas Mann, Sigmund Freud, and Albert Einstein. At the east end of Bebelplatz is the:

10. Deutsche Staatsoper, designed by Georg Wenzeslaus von Knobelsdorff in the 1740s and rebuilt after the war. Today it serves as a venue for opera, ballet, and concerts. Next on Unter den Linden, to your left, is the:

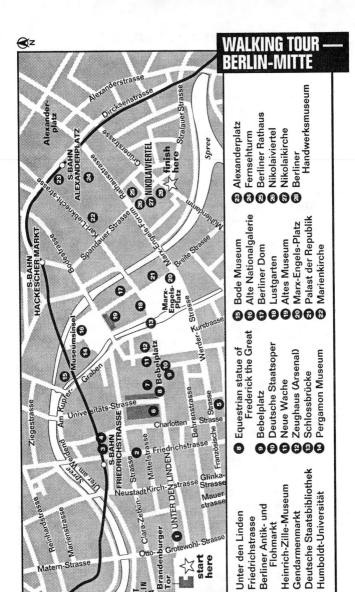

⊛z

Alexanderstrasse

Dircksenstrasse

Alexander-
platz

Stralauer Strasse

**finish
here**

S-BAHN
ALEXANDERPLATZ

NIKOLAIVIERTEL

Spree

Mühlendamm

Mühlendamm

Karl-Liebknecht-Strasse

Rathausstrasse

Spandauer Strasse

Marx-Engels-Forum

Breite Strasse

HACKESCHER MARKT

Bodestrasse

S-BAHN

Grunerstrasse

Kurstrasse

Marx-
Engels-
Platz

Werder-Strasse

Am Kupfer-
graben

Museumsinsel

Ziegestrasse

Universitäts-Strasse

FRIEDRICHSTRASSE

S-BAHN

Charlotten Strasse

Behrenstrasse

Strasse

Franzosische Strasse

Reinhardtstrasse

Marienstrasse

Spree

Spreekanal

Unter den Linden

Friedrichstrasse

Mittelstrasse

Neustadt-Kirch-strasse

Glinka-
Strasse

Mauer-
strasse

Clara-Zetkin-

UNTER DEN LINDEN

Neustädtische Kirchstrasse

Brandenburger
Tor

Otto-Grotewohl-Strasse

Matern-Strasse

WEST
BERLIN
AREA

☆ **start
here**

5693

① Unter den Linden
② Friedrichstrasse
③ Berliner Antik- und
    Flohmarkt
④ Heinrich-Zille-Museum
⑤ Gendarmenmarkt
⑥ Deutsche Staatsbibliothek
⑦ Humboldt-Universität

⑧ Equestrian statue of
    Frederick the Great
⑨ Bebelplatz
⑩ Deutsche Staatsoper
⑪ Neue Wache
⑫ Zeughaus (Arsenal)
⑬ Schlossbrücke
⑭ Pergamon Museum

⑮ Bode Museum
⑯ Alte Nationalgalerie
⑰ Berliner Dom
⑱ Lustgarten
⑲ Altes Museum
⑳ Marx-Engels-Platz
㉑ Palast der Republik
㉒ Marienkirche

㉓ Alexanderplatz
㉔ Fernsehturm
㉕ Berliner Rathaus
㉖ Nikolaiviertel
㉗ Nikolaikirche
㉘ Berliner
    Handwerksmuseum

11. Neue Wache (New Guardhouse). Easy to spot with its
columns resembling a Greek temple—built by architect Karl
Friedrich Schinkel in 1816–18—today it serves as a memorial to
victims of fascism and militarism. Inside is an eternal flame,
which burns for the Unknown Soldier and Unknown Resistance
Fighter.

Beside the Neue Wache is the baroque:

12. Zeughaus (Arsenal) at Unter den Linden 2. Built in the 17th century as an arsenal for the Prussian army, today it serves as a museum of German history with changing exhibits. *Note:* In 1993 the museum closed for renovation, with reopening expected at the end of the decade.

Unter den Linden terminates at the:

13. Schlossbrücke (Palace Bridge), designed by Schinkel. Its eight statues, also by Schinkel, are goddesses and warriors from Greek mythology. At the base of the bridge, to the left, is one of several companies offering 1-hour sightseeing tours of Berlin by boat. (See "Organized Tours" in Chapter 6, "What to See & Do in Berlin," for more information on boat trips.)

REFUELING STOPS Across the street from the Neue Wache and Zeughaus is the equally famous **Opernpalais** (Unter den Linden 5), which contains several eating establishments under one roof. Occupying part of a palace originally built in 1733 and faithfully restored after World War II, it is best-known for the ground-floor **Operncafé,** a coffeehouse offering more than 50 varieties of tortes and with indoor dining or outdoor seating in a pretty square. There's also an outdoor *Imbiss* (food stall) here serving snacks and drinks. Another good place for budget dining is the **Casino** in the Staatsbibliothek (Unter den Linden 8). This inexpensive cafeteria, located in the National Library, offers a limited number of soups, salads, and daily specials.

MUSEUMSINSEL Rather than crossing Schlossbrücke, take a left on Kupfergraben and walk to the second bridge. This is the entrance to the:

14. Pergamon Museum, the most important and famous museum on Museumsinsel. Named after its most prized treasure, the Pergamon Altar (160–180 B.C.), this museum of architectural wonders also contains art from Asia, the Near East, the Middle East, and German folk art. Don't miss it. (See "The Top Attractions" in Chapter 6, "What to See & Do in Berlin," for details.) Beside the Pergamon you'll find the:

15. Bode Museum, which contains the Egyptian Museum, the Early Christian and Byzantine Collection, Museum for Primeval and Early History, the Sculpture Collection, and the Picture Gallery with art from the 14th to 18th century. (See "More Attractions" in Chapter 6 for details.)

Behind the Pergamon is the:

16. Alte Nationalgalerie (Old National Gallery), which features art from the 19th and 20th centuries. (See "More Attractions" in Chapter 6.)

From the Nationalgalerie, walk south on Museumsinsel in the direction of the huge church. That's the:

17. Berliner Dom (Berlin Cathedral), erected at the turn of the century in Italian Renaissance style. Its crypt contains sarcophagi of Prussian royalty. It faces a tree-lined square called the:

18. Lustgarten (Pleasure Garden), once the site of the royal botanical garden but paved by the Nazis for parades and rallies. Also facing the Lustgarten is the:

19. Altes Museum (Old Museum), which stages changing exhibitions devoted to art and objects of ancient times. Built from plans by Schinkel, it features 18 Ionic columns and resembles a Greek temple.

REFUELING STOPS   There are two **cafeterias** on Museumsinsel, one in the Altes Museum and one in the Pergamon Museum. Both offer snacks, cakes, tortes, sandwiches, daily specials, and drinks.

FROM MUSEUMSINSEL TO ALEXANDERPLATZ   Opposite the Lustgarten is the:
20. **Marx-Engels-Platz,** filled with drab socialist architecture. The most conspicuous building here is the:
21. **Palast der Republik** (Palace of the Republic), once popular in East Berlin for its various concert halls and restaurants. Insulated with asbestos, it is now closed, its future undecided. It occupies the former site of Berlin's royal palace, once the largest baroque structure north of the Alps. Although what remained after World War II could have been salvaged, the Politbüro dynamited it in 1950 as a symbol of "Prussian imperialism."
     With the Lustgarten on your left and the Palast der Republik on your right, walk past the Berliner Dom, cross the Spree River, and continue down Karl-Liebknecht-Strasse. After crossing Spandauer Strasse, you'll see a small, brick church on your right; it looks rather out of place here with the huge TV Tower rising behind it. This is the:
22. **Marienkirche** (Church of St. Mary), the second-oldest church in Berlin. First constructed in the 13th century and then added to through the centuries, it's noted for its marble baroque pulpit by Andreas Schlüter. Take a look at the *Dance of Death* mural in its tower hall at the back of the church. Painted in the 15th century, the mural was subsequently covered up until it was rediscovered in 1860. The church is open Monday through Thursday from 10am to noon and 1 to 5pm and on Saturday from noon to 5pm.
     Behind the church sprawls:
23. **Alexanderplatz.** Named after Czar Alexander I, it served as an oxen market and an exercise field in Berlin's early days, becoming the center of government during the decades of Communist rule. Its landmark is the towering:
24. **Fernsehturm.** At 1,200-feet-high, the television tower is the tallest structure in Berlin; it contains an observation platform and a revolving restaurant. On fine days, there can be long lines waiting for the 35-second elevators that whisk visitors to the top. Before the Wall fell, of course, this was one of the few opportunities East Germans had for a panoramic glimpse of the West—and it's still a popular attraction. If the sky is clear, the view is stupendous. (See "More Attractions" in Chapter 6, "What to See & Do in Berlin," for information.) If you're tired, you can take the S-Bahn from Alexanderplatz to Bahnhof Zoo and beyond.

REFUELING STOPS   The **Tele-Café,** a revolving café 650 feet above ground in the Fernsehturm, is a great—though slightly expensive—place for a snack. Making a complete turn every hour, it offers unparalleled views of Berlin and a limited menu of coffee, cakes, ice cream, beer, wine, and warm and cold dishes. More affordable is **Wienerwald,** Rathausstrasse 5, located just off Alexanderplatz near a post office. It specializes in grilled chicken at modest prices.

FROM ALEXANDERPLATZ THROUGH THE NIKOLAI-VIERTEL At the southwestern end of Alexanderplatz, on the corner of Rathausstrasse and Spandauer Strasse, is an imposing red-brick building topped with a tower. This is the:
25. Berliner Rathaus (City Hall). Built in the 1860s, it served as the seat of Berlin's municipal administration—and since reunification has the same function. Note its frieze around the entire building: It's a stone chronicle of the history of Berlin.

Walk past the Rathaus, cross Spandauer Strasse, and to your left you'll see a small side street, Am Nussbaum, leading to church spires. This is the beginning of the:
26. Nikolaiviertel (Nikolai Quarter), a re-created neighborhood of Berlin as it was centuries ago. In the center is the:
27. Nikolaikirche (St. Nicholas' Church), regarded as Berlin's oldest church even though it was destroyed during World War II and was for the most part rebuilt. It dates back to 1230 but its architectural style has changed several times since then.

The buildings you see around the church are all new—many built by craftspeople according to plans of earlier buildings that existed elsewhere. Facing the church, walk around it to the right, where you'll see several shops selling handcrafted items. Take the first right behind the church, it will bring you to a busy street called Mühlendamm. Here, at Mühlendamm 5, you'll find the:
28. Berliner Handwerksmuseum (Berlin Crafts Museum), a tiny museum that features changing displays of items produced in Berlin in the past. During one of my visits, I saw hats, pottery, and jewelry. It's open every day except Monday from 9am to 5pm.

As the Nikolaiviertel is a small district of mostly apartments and bars, explore it at your leisure—stopping off for a meal or a beer at one of the places below.

FINAL REFUELING STOPS Among the best-known Gaststätte in the Nikolaiviertel are **Zur Rippe,** on the corner of Mühlendamm and Poststrasse; **Zum Paddenwirt** on Eiergasse; and **Zum Nussbaum** on Propstrasse beside the Nikolaikirche. The **Nikolai Café,** across the street from the church at Am Nussbaum, is a good place for coffee and desserts.

CHAPTER 8

BERLIN SHOPPING

1. THE SHOPPING SCENE

2. SHOPPING A TO Z

If it exists, you can find it in Berlin. However, you may not find it at bargain rates, especially with today's dollar exchange rate. Germany is not a shopper's paradise for travelers on a budget, but that doesn't mean you won't find a few treasures here and there. It just means you have to search for them, and recognize them when you see them.

But even if you don't buy anything, looking is half the fun. Window-shopping on the Ku'damm is a favorite Berliner pastime, and who could resist a whirl through the KaDeWe department store? There are also markets, specialty shops, clothing boutiques, art galleries, and antique shops, where you can lose yourself for hours or days.

1. THE SHOPPING SCENE

Only you can judge whether a purchase is a true bargain, but if you're making a major purchase be sure to comparison shop. Many European products, including clothing, kitchenware, and linen, are now readily available in U.S. stores. It may not be worth it to buy that German comforter, for example, and pay the expense of shipping it home, only to find you've saved all of $5 for your efforts.

BEST BUYS If souvenirs make your heart beat faster, you'll delight in porcelain freedom bells (fashioned after the one hanging in Schöneberg Rathaus), ashtrays illustrated with Brandenburger Tor, and the *Berliner Bär* (the Berlin Bear), the city's mascot. If kitsch doesn't appeal to you, Berlin is also good hunting grounds for kitchen gadgets and cutlery, linens, those luxuriously fluffy *Federbetten* (literally "feather beds," or down comforters), binoculars and telescopes, cameras, and toys (including model trains, tin soldiers, and building blocks). If you like porcelain, look for Rosenthal, antique Meissen, and Berlin's own Königliche Porzellan-Manufaktur—assuming, of course, you have a Swiss bank account.

Another good purchase in Berlin is original artwork. There are so many galleries in the city that you could easily spend an entire lifetime making the rounds of changing exhibits. If you don't have the money for a major purchase, a good place to look for handmade arts and crafts is the weekend fleamarket on Strasse des 17. Juni, where young Berliners hawk their wares, including jewelry, sketches, and clothing.

For clothing, there's everything from designer fashions to punk, funk, and the ordinary. Finally, antiques are also in abundant supply in Berlin, evident by the city's several antique flea markets.

GREAT SHOPPING NAMES Berlin and the Kurfürstendamm are synonymous. Two-and-a-half miles long, the Kurfürstendamm, called Ku'damm by the locals, is the city's showcase—quite literally. Up and down the sidewalks are freestanding display cases containing goods of surrounding stores, just a little something to whet your shopping appetite. Along the boulevard are boutiques and shops selling clothing, accessories, porcelain, kitchenware, eyeglasses, and art. But don't neglect the side streets, since they're a virtual treasure trove of antique shops, more art galleries, bookstores, and clothing shops. Bleibtreustrasse and neighboring streets, for example, has a number of shops specializing in art deco. Tauentzienstrasse is good for inexpensive and fun fashions.

The other big name in shopping streets is Wilmersdorfer Strasse, a pedestrian-only lane lined with department stores, boutiques, and restaurants. This is where the locals come to shop, both for essentials and such nonessential essentials as yet another skirt. Since there is a large concentration of shops here, you can cover a lot of ground in a short amount of time—simply take the U-Bahn to Wilmersdorfer Strasse.

Other places for a concentrated shopping effort include the Europa-Center, department stores, and markets, described below. In fact, probably the best place to begin your shopping expedition is KaDeWe, the largest department store on the European continent. Come here for everything from bedsheets, comforters, fabrics, and clothing to souvenirs and even sausages. After that it's an easy walk to the Ku'damm.

HOURS, TAXES & SHIPPING   Most shops and businesses are open Monday through Friday from 9 or 10am to 6 or 6:30pm and on Saturday from 9am to 2pm. On the first Saturday of the month (called *langer Samstag*), shops remain open until 6pm in winter and until 4pm in summer. In addition, some shops remain open longer on Thursday, until 8:30pm. Note, however, that some of the smaller shops, especially art galleries and antique shops, are open only in the afternoons. Be sure to check individual listings, therefore, to avoid disappointment.

If you purchase more than 60 DM ($37.50) worth of goods from any one store and you're taking your purchases out of the country, you're entitled to a recovery of the Value-Added Tax (VAT), which is 15% in Germany and is called the *Mehrwertsteuer*. Note, however, that you will not receive the total 15% refund. Rather, depending on the item you purchased, you will receive a refund of 6% to 11% of the purchase price. If you've purchased an object of considerable worth,

---

IMPRESSIONS

. . . Berlin is all show, a forced place, having little commerce, and less content; no smiling faces—no mediocrity, that happiest of all conditions. Berlin contains nothing but the most hardened military despots, and is, in short, a mere Court; though it contains two hundred thousand inhabitants. I saw no modes of gaining a livelihood, or even of passing time honestly. Billiards, cards, dice, succeed to the spectacle of the parade, and the streets present nothing but sentinels on guard.
—CAPTAIN JOHN DUNDAS COCHRANE, 1824

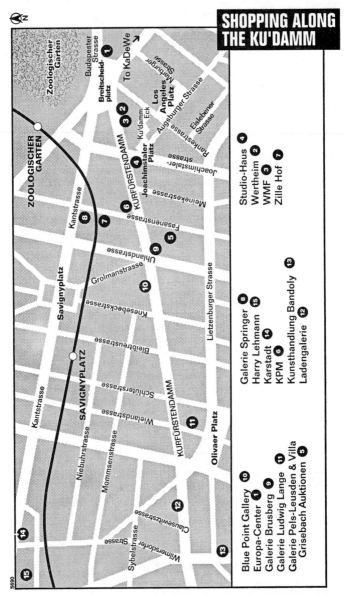

SHOPPING ALONG THE KU'DAMM

Studio-Haus ④
Wertheim ②
WMF ③
Zille Hof ⑦

Galerie Springer ⑧
Harry Lehmann ⑮
Karstadt ⑭
KPM ⑥
Kunsthandlung Bandoly ⑬
Ladengalerie ⑫

Blue Point Gallery ⑩
Europa-Center ①
Galerie Brusberg ⑨
Galerie Ludwig Lange ⑪
Galerie Pels-Leusden & Villa Grisebach Auktionen ⑤

even this can add up to a savings. When shopping, look for shops that display the "Tax-Free" sticker.

In any case, the procedure for obtaining the VAT refund is the same. All department stores and most major shops will issue a Tax-Free Cheque at the time of your purchase. Simply fill in the reverse side, and upon leaving Germany, present the Tax-Free Cheque, receipt from the store, and the purchased goods (which cannot be used prior to departure) to the German Customs official, who will stamp your check. If you're leaving Germany from Berlin's Tegel Airport, you can receive your cash refund immediately at the Berliner Bank counter in the Main Hall. In Frankfurt, you can receive an immediate tax refund at the International Departure Hall B Transit. Remember to show your purchases to the Customs officials before checking your luggage, unless you are hand-carrying your purchase. If you're leaving Germany by train, ask the Customs official who comes into your train to stamp your check.

You may wish to ship your purchases home, especially if you've gone overboard and can no longer carry everything with a reasonable semblance of dignity. Most shops used to dealing with tourists will ship your purchases home, which may be the easiest route to take. Your Tax-Free Cheque will indicate that the goods have already left the country; in some cases you may even receive an immediate refund of the VAT at the store.

If you wish to send home a package yourself, you can do so at all major post offices. All you have to do is show up with your goods, since post offices sell boxes complete with string and tape. Boxes come in five sizes and range in price from 1.10 DM (70¢) to 3.60 DM ($2.25). If you're sending a purchase for which you are entitled to a refund of the VAT, be sure to have an official at the post office stamp your Tax-Free Cheque (which you can then later present at the airport for an immediate refund).

Keep in mind, however, that there is a limit to the amount of duty-free goods you can bring back with you to the United States. If you're sending a package, it will automatically go to Customs upon arrival in the United States. If the total value of the goods acquired from abroad is less than $50, the package is sent on to the post office and is delivered to you by your mail carrier. If the value is more than $50, the amount you owe will be collected by your mail carrier upon delivery of your package. Note that it is illegal to mail liquor to the United States.

As for hand-carried items, you are allowed to bring back free of duty $400 worth of personal and household goods obtained abroad. Anything above this $400 personal exemption is charged a flat 10% on the next $1,000. That means the most you will have to pay on purchases valued at $1,400 (your $400 personal exemption plus the next $1,000) is only $100.

Unfortunately, you are not allowed to import any meat products into the United States—which means you cannot bring any of those wonderful German sausages home with you.

2. SHOPPING A TO Z

In addition to the specialty stores listed below, the single best source for most needs is a large department store, several of which are listed below.

ANTIQUES

The best place to search for antiques and curios is at one of Berlin's several **flea markets.** Not only is the atmosphere festive, but the range of goods offered by the various vendors is usually much more extensive than that offered by a single store. The most easily accessible and my favorite is the flea market held every Saturday and Sunday on Strasse des 17. Juni, where vendors sell porcelain, coffee grinders, glassware, brass, door knockers, lamps, clothing, and a seemingly endless supply of junk, as well as handmade arts and crafts. More upscale is the Berliner Antik- und Flohmarkt, an indoor market open six days a week at the Friedrichstrasse S-Bahn station.

Check the "Markets" section below for more information.

ZILLE HOF, Fasanenstrasse 14. Tel. 881 95 09.
Hard to believe that this quirky place exists in the middle of Berlin near the exclusive Bristol Hotel Kempinski just off the Ku'damm—it looks like an abandoned junkyard. Occupying a little courtyard that spreads beside and under the elevated tracks of the S-Bahn, this is a good place to browse through shelves of plates, glasses, rusted pots and pans, furniture, dusty books, old postcards, secondhand clothing, and piles upon piles of junk. If nothing else, this place is worth a photograph. Open: Mon–Fri 8:30am–5:30pm, Sat 8:30am–1pm. U-Bahn: Uhlandstrasse, a 2-minute walk.

ART GALLERIES

There are so many art galleries in Berlin that it's almost epidemic—albeit a very nice one. One pamphlet lists more than 175 galleries; the city magazine *zitty* lists about 125. In any case, there are far too many to mention here. The ones below, all within easy walking distance of the Ku'damm, offer a varied assortment of contemporary art. You won't be able to indulge in a shopping spree on a $50 a Day budget, but enter them with the same philosophy as you enter a museum—worth the experience of looking. Be sure to check *zitty* for a more complete listing.

BLUE POINT GALLERY, Kurfürstendamm 35. Tel. 883 61 37.
Easily found on the Ku'damm, this small shop features glassware on the ground floor, including delicately crafted vases, paperweights, and perfume bottles. Upstairs is the gallery, featuring mainly Berlin artists. Open: Mon–Fri 10am–6:30pm, Sat 10am–2pm. U-Bahn: Uhlandstrasse, a 1-minute walk.

GALERIE BRUSBERG, Kurfürstendamm 213. Tel. 882 76 82.

IMPRESSIONS

Public courtesans are more numerous here than in any town in Europe, in proportion to the number of inhabitants. They appear openly at windows in the day-time, beckon to passengers as they walk in the streets, and ply for employment in any way they please, without disturbance from the magistrate.
—JOHN MOORE, 1779

Located on the first floor of a turn-of-the-century patrician home, this is undoubtedly one of Berlin's best-known galleries. It represents the works of Dali, Bernhard Dörries, Max Ernst, Miró, and Picasso, as well as lesser-known artists of considerable talent. The gallery is light and airy, with enough space to properly display its paintings and sculpture. With its museumlike quality, it's definitely worth a stop, and it doesn't cost anything to look. Open: Tues–Fri 10am–6:30pm, Sat 10am–2pm. U-Bahn: Uhlandstrasse, less than a 1-minute walk.

LADENGALERIE, Kurfürstendamm 64. Tel. 881 42 14.

This small, one-room gallery specializes in one-person shows by contemporary German artists. Recent exhibitions, for example, have included Sarah Schumann's "Travels in the DDR," with her artistic presentation of former East Germany, and Helga Ginevra's portraits of women. The displays are always interesting, making it worth a spin through. Open: Mon–Fri 10am–6:30pm, Sat 10am–2pm (to 6pm first Sat of the month). U-Bahn: Adenauerplatz, a 2-minute walk.

GALERIE LUDWIG LANGE, Wielandstrasse 26. Tel. 881 29 26.

Located on the ground floor of an ornate turn-of-the-century building, this is a beautiful gallery inside and out. Although it also features paintings, its main emphasis is German sculpture and includes the works of Berliner Waldemar Grizmek. It even has a charming sculpture garden in the back, not to be missed. Open: Tues–Fri 11am–6pm, Sat 10am–2pm. U-Bahn: Adenauerplatz, a 6-minute walk.

GALERIE PELS-LEUSDEN AND VILLA GRISEBACH AUKTIONEN, Fasanenstrasse 25. Tel. 882 68 11.

Villa Grisebach is a beautiful restored villa built a century ago as the home of architect Hans Grisebach. Located next to the Käthe-Kollwitz Museum, it now serves as a gallery of contemporary art. In addition, twice a year in June and November, it also serves as the stage for the Villa Grisebach Auction, during which international art of the 19th and 20th century is sold, including paintings, graphic art, and sculpture. Former auctions have dealt with works by Adolph von Menzel, Franz Marc, Erich Heckel, Paul Klee, Emil Nolde, Georg Kolbe, Jean Dubuffet, and Christo, drawing art dealers from around the world. Open: Mon–Fri 10am–6:30pm, Sat 10am–2pm. U-Bahn: Uhlandstrasse, a 1-minute walk.

GALERIE SPRINGER, Fasanenstrasse 13. Tel. 31 70 63.

Located near the elevated tracks of the S-Bahn, this gallery has none of the highbrow looks of most of the other galleries, yet it has long remained on the crest of Berlin's artistic waves by recognizing young local talent and then sending them on to fame. Its exhibitions range from the avant-garde to photography. Open: Mon–Fri 10am–7pm, Sat 11am–2pm. U-Bahn: Uhlandstrasse, about a 3-minute walk.

CRAFTS

For handmade arts and crafts, the best place to look is the **weekend market held on Strasse des 17. Juni** just west of the Tiergarten S-Bahn station. Many young entrepreneurs and artisans set up shop here, selling sketches, jewelry, batik clothing, and other items they've made themselves. In addition, check with the Berlin tourist office to see whether any other special crafts fairs are being held.

DEPARTMENT STORES & MALLS
THE EUROPA-CENTER AREA

EUROPA-CENTER, Tauentzienstrasse and Budapester Strasse.

This is Berlin's largest indoor shopping center, with approximately 70 shops on its first three floors. Located near the Ku'damm and Bahnhof Zoo, it's a good place to explore on a cold or rainy day, where you can shop for everything from records and cassettes to clothing, shoes, and accessories. There are also plenty of cafés, restaurants, and bars where you can stop for refreshment. Open: Shops Mon–Fri 10am–6pm, Sat 10am–2pm (to 4pm first Sat of the month in summer, 6pm in winter); Europa-Center to 3am. U-Bahn: Kurfürstendamm or Bahnhof Zoo, each a 2-minute walk.

KADEWE, Wittenbergplatz. Tel. 21210.

The KaDeWe rates as one of Berlin's major tourist attractions and is worth the trip, even if you don't plan on buying anything. The largest department store on the European continent, it occupies 51,600 square yards of selling space with an inventory of 250,000 items and employs a staff of 3,000. In addition to shopping its seven floors, customers can eat, buy theater tickets, have their shoes repaired, their marriages and vacations planned, their hair done, their dogs shampooed, their money exchanged, their purchases wrapped and shipped abroad, their pictures taken, and—if necessary after all that—have first aid administered.

Officially known as Kaufhaus des Westens (which means "department store of the West") but popularly referred to as KaDeWe, it sells about anything you might imagine, including perfume, cosmetics, jewelry, watches, shoes, gloves, hats, luggage, umbrellas, housewares, carpets, office supplies, toys, leather goods, musical instruments, furs, wigs, porcelain, glassware, antiques, and much more. Souvenirs of Berlin are sold on the fourth floor, including beer steins and ashtrays stamped with the Berliner Bär.

But by far the biggest attraction of KaDeWe is its sixth-floor food emporium. There are 1,000 different sorts of sausage, 500 different kinds of bread, 1,500 different types of cheese, and gourmet items from around the world. There are exotic teas, coffees, liquors, wines, jams, sweets, vegetables, fruits, spices, canned goods, and fresh seafood, including eels, lobster, and fish still swimming around in tanks. Since few people eat as much pork in so many different ways as the Germans, it's no wonder that KaDeWe's pork section is one of the world's largest. If all this food makes you hungry, you can dine at one of the many counters spread throughout the sixth floor, offering everything from soups and salads to fresh seafood. You could easily get lost and spend the rest of your days here—but there are certainly worse things in life. The KaDeWe is located just a 5-minute walk from the Ku'damm and the Gedächtniskirche. Open: Mon–Wed and Fri 9am–6:30pm, Thurs 9am–8:30pm, Sat 9am–2pm (to 6pm first Sat of the month in winter, to 4pm first Sat of the month in summer). U-Bahn: Wittenbergplatz, a 1-minute walk.

WERTHEIM, Kurfürstendamm 231. Tel. 88 20 61.

This department store is conveniently located at the eastern end of the Ku'damm, across from the Gedächtniskirche. It's good for basic needs such as shampoo, film, or picnic supplies, but also has good clothing, porcelain, and housewares departments. It also has a souvenir department. Open: Mon–Wed and Fri 9am–6pm, Thurs 9am–8:30pm, Sat 9am–2pm (to 6pm first Sat of the month in winter, to 4pm first Sat of the month in summer). U-Bahn: Kurfürstendamm, a 1-minute walk.

ON WILMERSDORFER STRASSE

HERTIE, Wilmersdorfer Strasse 118–119. Tel. 311 050.

Hertie department store, together with Quelle across the street, is a good medium-price store, serving the basic needs of families. Stop here for those traveling necessities. Open: Mon–Wed and Fri 9:30am–6:30pm, Thurs 9:30am–8:30pm, Sat 9am–2pm (to 4pm first Sat of the month in summer, to 6pm first Sat of the month in winter). U-Bahn: Wilmersdorfer Strasse, a 1-minute walk.

KARSTADT, Wilmersdorfer Strasse 109–111. Tel. 31 891.

Located at the corner of Kantstrasse and Wilmersdorfer Strasse, this large department store chain can be found all over Germany and is slightly more upper-scale than other competing chains. A good place to look for clothing and accessories. Open: Mon–Wed and Fri 9:30am–6:30pm, Thurs 9:30am–8:30pm, Sat 9am–2pm (to 4pm first Sat of the month in summer, to 6pm first Sat of the month in winter). U-Bahn: Wilmersdorfer Strasse, less than a 1-minute walk.

QUELLE, Wilmersdorfer Strasse 54. Tel. 320 050.

The last of the three big department stores on Wilmersdorfer Strasse, it has much of the same merchandise and comparable prices. Quelle is a good place to stock up on film, and there's a good cafeteria on the second floor. Open: Mon–Wed and Fri 9am–6:30pm, Thurs 9am–8:30pm, Sat 9am–2pm (to 4pm first Sat of the month in summer, to 6pm first Sat of the month in winter). U-Bahn: Wilmersdorfer Strasse, a 1-minute walk.

IN BERLIN-MITTE (EASTERN BERLIN)

KAUFHOF, Alexanderplatz. Tel. 21 64 000.

Occupying the former East German Centrum department store, this German chain offers the usual goods and services, including toys, clothing, household goods, food, and shoe repair. Open: Mon–Wed and Fri 9am–6:30pm, Thurs 9am–8:30pm, Sat 9am–2pm (to 6pm first Sat of the month in winter, to 4pm first Sat of the month in summer). U- and S-Bahn: Alexanderplatz.

FASHIONS

The best places to check for clothing and accessories are the many department stores listed above, where there are various departments for men, women, children, and teenagers. In addition, there are many boutiques in the Europa-Center, as well as open-fronted shops along the Ku'damm, Tauentzienstrasse, Bleibtreustrasse, and Wilmersdorfer Strasse selling young, fun fashions at inexpensive prices. Finally, clothing is also sold at the weekend market on Strasse des 17. Juni, including ethnic clothing from Bali, batik scarves and shirts, and original, handmade jackets, hats, and accessories.

FOOD

Almost all department stores in Germany have food departments, usually in their basements. In Berlin the ultimate in food emporiums is the sixth floor of the KaDeWe department store on Wittenbergplatz, with an incredible stockpile of gourmet foods (see "Department Stores and Malls," above). If it's to be found anywhere in Berlin, KaDeWe is the place.

If your tastes run more towards natural foods, across the square from KaDeWe is a small shop called Einhorn, Wittenbergplatz 5–6 (tel. 24 63 47). In addition to ready-made vegetarian dishes, the shop also sells *Müsli,* breads, jams, juices, organic fruits and vegetables, nuts, and more. It's open Monday through Friday from 9am to 6pm and on Saturday from 10am to 1:30pm. A second Einhorn is located at Mommsenstrasse 2 (tel. 881 42 41), a minute's walk north of the Ku-Damm, with the same open hours.

GIFTS/SOUVENIRS

The largest selection of gifts and souvenirs can be found in Berlin's department stores, particularly KaDeWe and Wertheim, which are used to a steady flow of tourist traffic. Other places to look for unique gifts include the weekend crafts market on Strasse des 17. Juni, where young entrepreneurs sell their creations; and Harry Lehmann, listed below, which has been selling perfume for 65 years; and Studio-Haus and WMF, described below under "Kitchenwares."

BERLIN-GRAFIK, Spandauer Damm 1. Tel. 342 85 44.
Located across from Schloss Charlottenburg, this tiny shop sells original drawings and reproductions, many of famous Berlin architecture. Engravings of Berlin begin at 20 DM ($12.50). Open: Mon–Fri 11am–6pm, Sat 11am–2pm. Bus: 109 or 145.

BERLINER ZINNFIGUREN, Knesebeckstrasse 88. Tel. 31 08 02.
This small family-owned shop, located just north of Savignyplatz, has been producing and selling handcrafted pewter figures since 1934. Approximately 10,000 various figures are for sale, including more than 1,000 animals alone. Some are collectors items; others are appropriate as toys. Most popular are characters of Berlin, including the Potsdamer Soldat (soldier), the Blumenfrau (Flower Vendor), and Frederick the Great playing the flute. Flat, unpainted figures begin at only 1.50 DM (95¢), a great souvenir of Berlin. Open: Mon–Fri 1–6pm (Thurs to 8:30pm), Sat 10am–1pm. S-Bahn: Savignyplatz, about a 4-minute walk.

KUNSTHANDLUNG BANDOLY, Brandenburgische Strasse 27. Tel. 881 49 10.
This shop deals in reproductions of famous paintings, small etchings of Berlin, and copperplate prints. Many of its copperplate prints depict the architecture of old Berlin, while small etchings of such sights as the Brandenburger Tor can be purchased for as little as 15 DM ($9.35). It's a good place to purchase a small souvenir of Berlin. Open: Mon–Fri 10am–1pm, and 3–6pm, Sat 10am–1pm. U-Bahn: Adenauerplatz, a 3-minute walk.

BERLIN SOUVENIRS, Wertheim, Kurfürstendamm 231. Tel. 88 20 61.

The easiest place to shop for a souvenir of Berlin. With its own sidewalk entrance, it's located in the Wertheim department store right on the Ku'damm across the street from the Gedächtniskirche. Berlin bears, T-shirts, postcards, glasses, mugs, and city sketches are among the items for sale. Open: Mon–Wed and Fri 9am–6:30pm, Thurs 9am–8:30pm, Sat 9am–2pm (to 6pm first Sat of the month in winter, to 4pm first Sat of the month in summer). U-Bahn: Kurfürstendamm, a 1-minute walk.

KITCHENWARES

STUDIO-HAUS, Kurfürstendamm 226. Tel. 881 7051.

This smart-looking shop sells a wide range of decorative and functional items for the home, including Rosenthal porcelain, Boda glass, tableware, and chrome kitchenware. Prices are high, but if you're looking for a wedding gift, this is a good place to start. The adjoining In-Shop sells more items for the kitchen and table. Open: Mon–Fri 9am–6:30pm, Sat 9am–2pm (to 6pm first Sat of the month in winter, to 4pm first Sat of the month in summer). U-Bahn: Kurfürstendamm, less than a 1-minute walk.

WMF, Kurfürstendamm 229. Tel. 882 39 41.

WMF, a chain found all over Germany, specializes in both tableware and cookingware, from chrome eggcups and coffee-pot warmers to pots and pans—sleek, functional, and sturdy. If you're looking for something inexpensive and easily transportable, you might check the store's wonderful kitchen gadgets, ranging from bottle stoppers and can openers to hardboiled-egg slicers. Open: Mon–Wed and Fri 9:30am–6:30pm, Thurs 9:30am–8:30pm, Sat 9am–2pm (to 6pm first Sat of the month in winter, to 4pm first Sat of the month in summer). U-Bahn: Kurfürstendamm, a 1-minute walk.

MARKETS

Some of Berlin's best buys can be found at its many antique and flea markets. Some are indoor and are held almost daily. Others are outdoors and are open only 1 or 2 days a week. Altogether there are more than 70 weekly markets, 9 market halls, and 10 flea markets spread throughout the city. Below are a few of the best; for information on other markets, drop by the Berlin Verkehrsamt in the Europa-Center.

MARKET AT STRASSE DES 17. JUNI, Strasse des 17. Juni. Tel. 322 81 99.

This is my favorite market, and one I never miss when I'm in Berlin. Stretching just west of the Tiergarten S-Bahn station, this weekend market offers a staggering variety of antiques, including silverware, books, china, glass, jewelry, clothing, kitchenware, and junk. Don't miss the second half of the market (past the stone portal and on the other side of the bridge)—it features original arts and crafts, including funky and ethnic jewelry, clothing, hats, sketches, and innovative artwork. It's a good place to hunt for gifts, and prices are very reasonable. Don't miss it. Open: Sat–Sun 10am–5pm. S-Bahn: Tiergarten, a minute away.

BERLINER ANTIK- UND FLOHMARKT [Berlin Antique and Flea Market]. Georgenstrasse, Friedrichstrasse S-Bahn Station. Tel. 215 02 129.

Located at the eastern end of Friedrichstrasse S-Bahn station, under the arches of the elevated track, this upscale market features more than 60 vendors selling antiques and curios, including jewelry, porcelain, glassware, pocketwatches, canes, books, lamps, and odds and ends. It's Berlin's largest permanent flea market, and during warm weather additional vendors open shop outside along Georgenstrasse. Prices are relatively high, but who knows, you may find a bargain. For refreshment, drop by Zur Nolle, a pub decorated in the style of 1920s Berlin. Open: Wed–Mon 11am–6pm. S-Bahn: Friedrichstrasse, less than a minute away.

TURKISH MARKET, Bank of Maybachufer, Kreuzberg. Tel. 6809 29 26.

Kreuzberg is home of much of the city's Turkish population, so little wonder that it's here you'll also find Berlin's best Turkish market. Spread along the bank of a canal, this market offers a taste of the exotic, with both German and Turkish vendors selling vegetables, sheep's cheese, pita bread, beans, rice, noodles, spices, clothing, and Turkish fast food. Try a Turkish pizza, a *donner kebab,* or a felafel. If you like color, activity, the smell of spices, and being outdoors, you'll love this place. Friday's markets are livelier, with more vendors. Open: Tues and Fri noon–6:30pm. U-Bahn: Kottbusser Tor, about a 5-minute walk.

WEIHNACHTSMARKT, Breitscheidplatz and from Nürnberger Strasse to Joachimstaler Strasse.

Every December from the beginning of the month to Christmas Eve, there's a traditional Christmas market in the inner city. It radiates out from the Gedächtniskirche on Breitscheidplatz to Wittenbergplatz, particularly on Nürnberger Strasse and Joachimstaler Strasse. Colorful stalls sell those wonderful German Christmas ornaments, candies, cookies, sausages, and other goodies, including *Glühwein* (spiced mulled wine). Incidentally, there are also other Christmas markets in Berlin, including Spandau's Altstadt (Old City) and on Marx-Engels-Platz in Berlin-Mitte. Open: Dec 1–24 daily 11am–9pm. U-Bahn: Kurfürstendamm, Bahnhof Zoo, or Wittenbergplatz.

WINTERFELDPLATZ MARKET, Winterfeldplatz, Schöneberg.

Founded more than 80 years ago, this is Berlin's largest weekly market selling fruits, vegetables, meat, flowers, clothing, and accessories, and is lively with vendors hawking their wares at the top of their lungs. It's located just a 5-minute walk south of Nollendorfplatz on a pretty square lined with old Berlin buildings and is where Berliners come to do their shopping, whether it's for cabbage, olives, basil, mozzarella, or flowers. And of course, they also come to meet their friends and exchange the latest gossip. After making their purchases, many of the younger shoppers retire to Slumberland or Café Sidney, two bars on Winterfeldplatz. Saturday is the busier day. Open: Wed and Sat dawn–1pm. U-Bahn: Nollendorfplatz, a 5-minute walk.

PERFUME

For the big names in perfume from around the world, head for the ground floor of KaDeWe, described above under the department store section.

However, if you're looking for a scent unique to Berlin or an inexpensive and unusual gift, try **Harry Lehmann,** Kantstrasse 106 (tel. 324 35 82). This tiny, family-owned shop has been selling its own concoctions of scents since 1926, with approximately 50 scents now available made from flowers, leaves, and grasses. Scents, ranging from lavender and jasmine to magnolia, are sold by the weight, starting at 3.50 DM ($2.20) for 10 grams. Customers can either bring their own perfume bottle or purchase one of the inexpensive vials starting at 1.50 DM (95¢), a concept begun by Harry Lehmann in 1926 when he decided it was a shame that pretty bottles had to be discarded when the perfume ran out. In addition to its scents, the shop, now in its third generation of owners, also sells Kölnisch Wasser and other colognes, as well as after-shave lotion for men. Don't be put off by the fake flowers in the shop; just one of the idiosyncrasies of this charming little establishment, they're available scented with the real thing. How about a fragrant bouquet of fake roses? This shop is located a stone's throw west of the Wilmersdorfer Strasse pedestrian lane. Open: Mon–Fri 9am to 6:30pm, Sat 9am–2pm (to 4pm the first Sat of the month in summer, to 6pm first Sat of the month in winter). U-Bahn: Wilmersdorfer Strasse, a 2-minute walk.

PORCELAIN

KPM, Kurfürstendamm 26a. Tel. 881 18 02.

The Königliche Porzellan-Manufaktur (KPM) is a Berlin tradition, with a history stretching back more than 225 years. In 1763, Frederick the Great acquired a preexisting porcelain company, renamed it the Königliche Porzellan-Manufaktur, and made it the royal porcelain manufacturer for his Prussian government. Since then, monarchs and heads of state from around the world have been owners of KPM pieces, including Catherine II of Russia, Louis XVI of France, Elizabeth II of England, Princess Diana, Margaret Thatcher, Henry Kissinger, and Ed Koch. Although the official name was changed in 1918 to Staatliche Porzellan-Manufaktur, pieces are still identified with the KPM mark and everyone simply calls it KPM.

KPM pieces today include table settings, vases, baskets, figurines, and art pieces. All decorations and floral designs are handpainted. For tourists, the most popular KPM pieces include reproductions of the Liberty Bell in Rathaus Schöneberg, white statues of the Berliner Bär, and Christmas plates issued each year.

Although not as centrally located, the main shop of KPM is at Wegelystrasse 1 (tel. 39 00 90). Open: Ku'damm branch, Mon–Fri 9:30am–6:30pm, Sat 9:30am–2pm (to 6pm first Sat of the month in winter, to 4pm first Sat of the month in summer); main shop, Mon–Fri 9:30am–6pm, Sat 9:30am–2pm. U-Bahn for Ku'damm branch: Uhlandstrasse, a 1-minute walk. S-Bahn for main shop: Tiergarten, a 1-minute walk.

BERLIN NIGHTS

Berlin has no mandatory closing hours for nightclubs, bars, and discos, so many of these places stay open all night—making it the most popular German city with Europe's younger set of travelers. As one native told me, "The reason everyone comes to Berlin is its nightlife." When I pointed out that it could also be Berlin's wealth of museums, it seemed a possibility he hadn't considered. The action starts late; some travelers—those who are in bed each night by 11pm—may remain unaware of the city's garish nighttime transformation. Perhaps blissfully so: There's something to be said for early curfews.

Yet it would be difficult to remain completely naive of the city's after-dark activities. Signs of it are everywhere: The wicked exists beside the innocent; the tawdry, beside the deluxe. On a street off the Ku'Damm, there may be a first-class hotel and a haute cuisine French restaurant, yet there may also be a strip joint, peep show, and porn shop. At night even the elite boulevard itself is the domain of dolled-up hookers. It's this juxtaposition that makes Berlin fascinating; and it's this tolerance that makes the city what it is today.

You don't have to be a night owl to enjoy evenings in Berlin. There are cabarets, wine cellars, live music houses, and gambling casinos, as well as opera, chamber music, two world-renowned orchestras, and classical and contemporary theater.

To find out what's going on in the traditional performing arts, pick up a copy of *checkpoint Berlin* (an English monthly) or *Berlin Programm;* both give a daily schedule of events in all the city's opera, theater, and concert halls. Rock concerts, experimental theater, and avant-garde happenings are covered in more detail in city magazines *tip* and *zitty* (but these are printed only in German).

If you don't mind paying a commission, convenient ticket outlets can be found at **Centrum,** Meinekestrasse 25 (tel. 882 76 11); the **Europa-Center,** Tauentzienstrasse 9 (tel. 261 70 51); **KaDeWe** department store, Wittenbergplatz (tel. 218 10 28); and **Wertheim** department store, Kurfürstendamm 231 (tel. 882 53 54).

You'll save money, however, by buying your ticket directly from the theater or concert hall during box-office hours or an hour before the performance begins. The Deutsche Oper and state theaters give students discounts for unused tickets on the night of the performance. At the renowned Schiller-Theater, for example, students can get half-price tickets with their student card, 30 minutes before the performance—assuming, of course, there are still tickets available.

1. THE PERFORMING ARTS

CLASSICAL MUSIC

PHILHARMONIE, Mattäikirchplatz 1. Tel. 254 88-0.

This is Berlin's most famous concert hall, home of the world-renowned **Berlin Philharmonic Orchestra.** Located on the southern edge of the Tiergarten district and designed by architect Hans Scharoun in 1963, the Philharmonie is an asymmetric structure with a tentlike roof. Its main hall seats more than 2,200—with the conductor and orchestra placed in the very center—and no concertgoer is more than 100 feet from the podium. The acoustics are said to be nearly perfect.

Founded in 1882, the Berlin Philharmonic Orchestra has been led by some of the world's greatest conductors. It gained acclaim under the baton of the late Herbert von Karajan—acclaim that continues unabated under the skillful direction of conductor Claudio Abbado. Leading guest conductors and soloists regularly join the Berlin Philharmonic, including such notables as Sir Yehudi Menuhin, Zubin Mehta, Christoph von Dohnányi, Sir Georg Solti, and Seiji Ozawa.

The Philharmonic performs approximately 100 times in Berlin during its August-through-June season, attracting more than 220,000 people annually. It also performs 20 to 30 concerts around the world each year. Because the Berlin Philharmonic is so popular, tickets often sell out 2 months in advance. If you're able to procure one, consider yourself very lucky.

The Philharmonie is also the venue of the **Radio Symphony Orchestra Berlin,** the **Symphonic Orchestra Berlin,** and the **Berlin Philharmonic Choir.** There are also many guest performances by visiting groups and musical events such as the Berlin Jazz Festival. In addition to the main hall, there's also a smaller Kammermusiksaal (Chamber Music Hall). **Bus:** 129, 148, or 248.

Tickets: 12–100 DM ($7.50–$62.50) for Berlin Philharmonic Orchestra.

Open: Box office open Tues–Fri 3:30–6pm, Sat, Sun, and holidays 10am–2pm.

SCHAUSPIELHAUS BERLIN, Gendarmenmarkt, Berlin-Mitte. Tel. 20 90-21 29 (information), 20 90-21 56 (tickets).

MAJOR CONCERT & PERFORMANCE HALLS

Deutsche Oper Berlin, Bismarckstrasse 35, tel. 34 381
Deutsche Staatsoper, Unter den Linden 7, tel. 200 47 62
Deutschlandhalle, Messedamm 26, tel. 303 81
Internationales Congress-Centrum (ICC), Am Messedamm, tel. 303 81
Metropol, Nollendorfplatz 5, tel. 216 41 22
Philharmonie, Mattäikirchplatz 1, tel. 254 88-0
Schauspielhaus Berlin, Gendarmenmarkt, tel. 20 90-21 56
Waldbühne, Ruhleben, Charlottenburg, tel. 852 40 80

Located on the historic Gendarmenmarkt, this was originally a theater house, designed by Schinkel in 1819–1821 and restored after World War II. Now used for concerts, it was here that the late Leonard Bernstein conducted a performance of Beethoven's Ninth Symphony in celebration of the fall of the Wall. It features concerts by both the Radio Symphony Orchestra, the Berlin Symphonic Orchestra, and guest orchestras and ensembles. It has both a large music hall and a chamber-music hall. **U-Bahn:** Französische Strasse, Hausvogteiplatz, or Stadtmitte. **Bus:** 100.

Tickets: 8–70 DM ($5–$43.75).

Open: Box office Tues–Sat 2–6pm.

OPERA, OPERETTA & BALLET

DEUTSCHE OPER BERLIN, Bismarckstrasse 35, Charlottenburg. Tel. 34 381 (information), 341 02 49 (tickets).

Whereas most of Europe's opera houses are grand edifices from another era—the Deutsche Oper Berlin, rebuilt after World War II, is intentionally plain and modern with a stark street-side wall designed to shut out traffic noise. Seating 1,900, it features performances of opera or ballet almost every night. The Deutsche Oper Berlin attained worldwide success in the 1920s under such great conductors as Richard Strauss, Bruno Walter, Leo Blech, Wilhelm Furtwängler, Erich Kleiber, and Otto Klemperer. **U-Bahn:** Deutsche Oper.

Tickets: 12–130 DM ($7.50–$81.25); 50% reductions for students on unsold tickets 30 minutes before performance beings.

Open: Box office Mon–Sat 11am–7pm, Sun 10am–2pm.

DEUTSCHE STAATSOPER, Unter den Linden 7, Berlin-Mitte. Tel. 200 47 62.

The German State Opera—located on the famous Unter den Linden boulevard in Berlin-Mitte—has long been one of Berlin's most famous opera houses. Although its present building dates only from the 1950s, its facade is a faithful copy of a pre-existing structure first erected in the 1740s by Knobelsdorff and then renovated in 1927. Now under the musical direction of Israeli conductor Daniel Barenboim, it features opera, ballet, and concerts, with an emphasis on classical German operas and German operas of the 20th century. **U- and S-Bahn:** Friedrichstrasse. **Bus:** 100.

Tickets: 6–125 DM ($3.75–$78.10); 50% reductions for students on unsold tickets on evening of performance.

Open: Box office Mon–Sat noon–6pm, Sun and holidays 2–6pm.

KOMISCHE OPER, Behrenstrasse 55–57, Berlin-Mitte. Tel. 229 25 55.

Although Komische Oper translates as "comic opera," this innovative opera company serves as an alternative to the grander, more mainstream productions of Berlin's two other opera houses, above. It presents a varied program of light opera, operetta, and ballet, with productions ranging from Mozart's *The Marriage of Figaro* to Sergei Prokofiev's ballet *Romeo and Juliet*. **S- and U-Bahn:** Französische Strasse. **Bus:** 100.

Tickets: 5–60 DM ($3.10–$37.50).

Open: Box office Mon–Sat noon–5:30pm, Sun 10am–1pm.

THEATER

With a long tradition behind it, Berlin has played a leading role in the history and development of German theater. Hauptmann, Ibsen, Strindberg, and Brecht all left their mark on Berlin's stages, as did such well-known directors as Max Reinhardt, Erwin Piscator, and Gustaf Gründgens.

Today the theater is still going strong, and Berlin still plays center stage as one of the leaders for productions in the German language. You'll be at a disadvantage if you don't speak German, but if you do, you're in for a treat.

SCHILLER-THEATER, Bismarckstrasse 110, Charlottenburg. Tel. 312 65 05.

Of Berlin's many theaters, this is the best-known, noted for its playfully light interpretations of classical productions. Germans come from all over the country to watch its performances of classical and modern drama, both German and foreign. Built in 1951 from the ruins of an older theater destroyed in World War II, it has 1,065 seats. A smaller stage, called the Schiller-Theater Werkstatt (Workshop) is used for experimental pieces. **U-Bahn:** Ernst-Reuter-Platz.

Tickets: 9–55 DM ($5.60–$34.35); 50% reduction for students on unsold tickets, available 30 minutes before that night's performance.

Open: Box office daily 10am–7pm.

SCHAUBÜHNE AM LEHNINER PLATZ, Kurfürstendamm 153, Wilmersdorf. Tel. 89 00 23.

Located on Ku'damm near Lehniner Platz, this is one of Berlin's leading venues for drama and experimental theater. Although the original art deco facade from the 1920s has been preserved, inside is the latest in modern theatrical technology and three stages where plays can be given simultaneously. **U-Bahn:** Adenauerplatz. **Bus:** 119, 129, 219.

Tickets: 15–50 DM ($9.35–$31.25).

Open: Box office Mon–Sat 11am–6:30pm, Sun and holidays 3–6:30pm.

BERLINER ENSEMBLE, Am Bertolt-Brecht-Platz, Berlin-Mitte. Tel. 282 31 60.

Bertolt Brecht and Helene Weigel founded this remarkable theater in 1949, and it has been staging Brecht's works ever since. Even when the Wall cut off the Berliner Ensemble from Western eyes, it maintained an estimable reputation in West Germany. Also features works by guest playwrights. **S-Bahn:** Friedrichstrasse.

Tickets: 12–40 DM ($7.50–$25).

Open: Box office Mon–Sat 11am–6:30pm, Sun and holidays 3–6:30pm.

IMPRESSIONS

He said that in Berlin, if you wanted to make a scandal in the theatre, you had to have a mother committing incest with two sons; one wasn't enough.
—ARNOLD BENNETT, quoting RUDOLF KOMMER, 1925

THEATER DES WESTENS, Kantstrasse 12, Charlotten-burg. Tel. 319 03 193.
Built in 1896 and occupying a prime spot near the Ku'damm and Bahnhof Zoo, this is the place to go for popular productions, musicals, spirited revues, and frivolous comedies. Recent productions have included *La Cage aux Folles* and *Grand Hotel*. **S-Bahn or U-Bahn:** Bahnhof Zoo.
Tickets: 15–67 DM ($9.35–$41.85).
Open: Box office Mon–Sat 10am–6pm, Sun 3–6pm.

SCHLOSSPARK-THEATER, Schlossstrasse 48, Steglitz. Tel. 793 15 15.
The Schlosspark-Theater, built in 1920 as part of the Schloss Steglitz palace, is a state-owned theater known for its classical and modern productions. **S-Bahn:** Steglitz. **U-Bahn:** Rathaus Steglitz.
Tickets: 10–51 DM ($6.25–$31.85); student reduction of 50% for unsold tickets, available 30 minutes before each performance.

2. THE CLUB & MUSIC SCENE

CABARET & REVUES

Liza Minnelli sang to her old chums that life is very much like a cabaret, and nowhere is this more true than in Berlin. Granted, the old days of stinging political satires are long gone, which in any case required an excellent command of the German language to under-stand. Some nightclubs do offer political commentary, but mostly you'll find music and dance, including transvestite shows.

DIE STACHELSCHWEINE, basement of Europa-Center, Tauentzienstrasse and Budapester Strasse, Char-lottenburg. Tel. 261 47 95.
This is one of Berlin's old-timers, a cabaret with more than 40 years under its belt. Its name means "Porcupine," and it continues to make political commentaries, so you'll need a good understanding of German to appreciate it. Tickets sell out quickly, so come here immediately upon arrival in Berlin to procure a ticket. The box office is open Monday to Friday from 4 to 7pm and Saturday from 6 to 7pm. Performances are held Monday through Saturday, usually at 7:30pm. **U-Bahn:** Bahnhof Zoo or Kurfürstendamm, each less than a 2-minute walk.
Tickets: 22–38 DM ($13.75–$23.75).

CHEZ NOUS, Marburger Strasse 14, Charlottenburg. Tel. 213 18 10.
This is a cabaret of a different sort: With a bevy of transvestites, the shows here have been titillating audiences for more than 30 years. The elaborate costumes and the song and dance numbers make this a Berlin institution; it offers two shows nightly and is located just a minute's walk from the Europa-Center, about a 4-minute walk from either the Kurfürstendamm or Augsburger U-Bahn stations.

Admission: 15 DM ($9.35), plus a 20 DM ($12.50) drink minimum per person Sunday through Thursday, 35 DM ($21.85) Friday and Saturday.

WINTERGARTEN, Potsdamer Strasse 96, Tiergarten. Tel. 2 62 90 16.

One of the biggest entertainment names prior to World War II, Wintergarten reopened its doors in 1992, in a beautiful art deco building in the Tiergarten. It stages nightly variety shows, with a healthy mix of theater, revue, circus, cabaret, magic shows, and parody. Shows are nightly at 8:30pm; the box office opens at 10am. **U-Bahn:** Kurfürstenstrasse, less than a 4-minute walk. **Bus:** 129, 142, 148, 187, 248, or 341.

Tickets: 30–58 DM ($18.75–$36.25).

ROCK CONCERTS & OTHER SHOWS

If you buy tickets to one of Berlin's premier rock concerts, you'll probably be heading toward one of these major concert halls. For local bands and live music houses that offer nightly entertainment, refer to the section that follows, "Live Music Houses." Also check *checkpoint Berlin, tip,* or *zitty* for the latest concert information.

METROPOL, Nollendorfplatz 5, Schöneberg. Tel. 216 41 22.

A disco on weekends, the Metropol offers some of the best in contemporary music on weekday evenings. Not large enough to accommodate the big names—you can catch your favorite lesser-known artists here before they make it big. Johnny Clegg & Savuka and David Sanborn have played here on my visits. There's a smaller, separate stage in Metropol called Loft, which features punk rock to rhythm and blues in a more intimate setting (see "Live Music Houses"). **U-Bahn:** Nollendorfplatz. **Open:** Box office Mon–Fri 11am–6pm.

TEMPODROM, Tiergarten. Tel. 394 40 45.

Tempodrom is a huge tent right in the middle of the city, which provides alternative performances on a permanent site. The program includes circus shows, theater, music, and revues. Consult *checkpoint Berlin, tip, zitty,* or the *Berlin Programm* for current programs. The tent is located near the Kongresshalle at the north end of the Tiergarten, not far from the Reichstag building. **Bus:** 100 to Kongresshalle. **Open:** Performances May through October.

WALDBÜHNE, Ruhleben, Charlottenburg. Tel. 852 40 80.

Beautifully situated in a wooded ravine near the Olympiastadion (Olympic Stadium), the Waldbühne is Germany's largest open-air

---

IMPRESSIONS

In the Berlin cafés and restaurants the busy time is from midnight on till three. Yet most of the people who frequent them are up again at seven. Either the Berliner has solved the great problem of modern life, how to do without sleep, or, with Carlyle, he must be looking forward to eternity.
—JEROME K. JEROME, 1900

arena. It's Berlin's best-loved spot for rock, pop, and folklore concerts held in summer. Although concerts usually feature popular rock-and-roll performers, the Berlin Philharmonic Orchestra has been known to give concerts here as well. Be sure to pack a picnic and a warm blanket, and rain gear just in case. **U-Bahn:** Ruhleben, then a 20-minute walk through a park, or Olympiastadion. **Open:** Performances May through October.

DEUTSCHLANDHALLE, Messedamm 26. Tel. 303 81.

With 14,000 seats, this is Berlin's largest arena. In addition to occasional rock concerts (Metallica, James Brown, the B52's), it is also used for conventions, horse shows, some sporting events, and other events with mass attendance. It's located on the grounds of the city's largest conference and convention center, near the International Congress Centrum (ICC) and Radio Tower. **U-Bahn:** Kaiserdamm. **S-Bahn:** Westkreuz. **Bus:** 219, 149. **Open:** Box office Mon–Fri noon–6pm, Sat 10am–2pm.

INTERNATIONALES CONGRESS-CENTRUM (ICC), Am Messedamm. Tel. 3038-0 or 3038-44 44.

Opening in 1979, the ICC Berlin, right next to the Radio Tower, is massive, with 80 lecture halls, conference and meeting rooms, as well as two main halls (one with 2,000 seats, the other with 5,000 seats) used for both conferences and concerts of jazz, country, and rock music. **Bus:** 104, 105, 110, 149, or 219. **Open:** Box office Mon–Fri noon–6pm, Sat 10am–2pm.

LIVE MUSIC HOUSES

A-TRANE, Bleibtreustrasse 1, Charlottenburg. Tel. 313 25 50.

Located on the corner of Bleibtreustrasse and Pestalozzistrasse not far from Savignyplatz, this classy jazz venue opened in 1992, with the aim of putting Berlin on the map as a city offering first-rate jazz. Featuring local and international talent, it opens its doors nightly at 9pm and music begins at 10pm. A glass of wine begins at 3.50 DM ($2.20). **S-Bahn:** Savignyplatz, a 2-minute walk.

Admission: Usually 15 DM ($9.35), more for big names.

EIERSCHALE, Rankestrasse 1, Charlottenburg. Tel. 882 53 05.

Conveniently located just off the Ku'damm across the street from the Gedächtniskirche, this popular music house and bar offers live music nightly starting at 8:30 or 9pm—primarily traditional jazz and blues. With outdoor sidewalk seating in the summer, it's also a good place to come for breakfast, especially on Sunday when there's live music all day long. Beer costs 4.60 DM ($2.85) when there isn't a band, rising to 5.80 DM ($3.60) when there's live entertainment. **U-Bahn:** Kurfürstendamm, a 1-minute walk.

Admission: 4 DM ($2.50) when there's live music, which goes toward the first drink.

EWIGE LAMPE, Niebuhrstrasse 11a, Charlottenburg. Tel. 324 39 18.

This small and popular jazz bar features bands primarily from the United States, Germany, and Holland and can get pretty crowded. Either buy your ticket in advance or get there early. It's open Tuesday

to Sunday from 8pm to 2am; the music begins at 9pm. A large beer costs 5.50 DM ($3.45). **S-Bahn:** Savignyplatz, a 2-minute walk.
Admission: 10–20 DM ($6.25–$12.50).

GO-IN, Bleibtreustrasse 17, Charlottenburg. Tel. 881 72 18.

✪ The Go-In was my introduction to Berlin nightlife when I first visited the city as a student in the early 70s, and I'm happy to report that the place is still going strong. Its clientele (appreciative of folk music) seems to have grown older along with the Go-In. Opened in 1968, it offers jazz, blues, bluegrass, Spanish flamenco, Greek, German, and international folk, to name only some of the music heard here. It's located a few minutes' walk north of the Ku'damm or about a 2-minute walk from the Savignyplatz S-Bahn station, with performances beginning nightly at about 9pm. It's open from 8pm to 5am. Beer prices start at around 4.50 DM ($2.80).
Admission: 5–10 DM ($3.10–$6.25).

LOFT, Nollendorfplatz 5, Schöneberg. Tel. 216 10 20.

Located in the massive building that houses the Metropol disco, the Loft serves as a smaller arena for everything from punk rock to rhythm and blues, with concerts held two to four times a week. It features musicians from around the world and bands from the United States and Great Britain; if there's an opening act, it's likely to be one of Berlin's own. **U-Bahn:** Nollendorfplatz, a 1-minute walk.
Admission: 10–20 DM ($6.25–$12.50) depending on the group.

QUASIMODO, Kantstrasse 12a, Charlottenburg. Tel. 312 80 86.

✪ This basement establishment—in a small building dwarfed by the large Theater des Westens next door—features contemporary jazz and rock groups and is considered one of the best places in town to hear live music. Performances begin at 10pm, doors open at 9pm; check *checkpoint Berlin, tip,* or *zitty* for concert information. A beer costs 5 DM ($3.10). **U-Bahn:** Bahnhof Zoo.
Admission: 10–25 DM ($6.25–$15.60), depending on the band.

DANCE CLUBS & DISCOS

BIG EDEN, Kurfürstendamm 202, Charlottenburg. Tel. 882 61 20.

Right on the Ku'damm, this disco opened in 1968 and proudly displays photographs of celebrities who have come here such as Klaus Kinski, Roman Polanski, Telly Savalas, and Paul McCartney. Its days of being the hottest thing in town have long gone, but the Big Eden still attracts young visitors of every nationality. Teenagers crowd the dance floor until midnight; after the teens catch the last subway home, revelers in their 20s and 30s take over. In addition to a large dance floor, the place also has pool tables and pinball machines. It maintains a strict front-door policy and won't admit anyone who even looks like they're drunk. Opening nightly at 8pm, it closes at 5am Sunday to Thursday, at 6am Friday and Saturday. Beer prices begin at around 8 DM ($5). **U-Bahn:** Uhlandstrasse, about a 3-minute walk.
Admission: Sun–Thurs 4 DM ($2.50), Fri–Sat 7 DM ($4.35); unaccompanied women admitted free.

CAFE KEESE, Bismarckstrasse 108, Charlottenburg. Tel. 312 91 11.

A unique Berlin institution, it's the women who ask the men to dance here (except for the hourly "Men's Choice," when the green light goes on). Seating 700, it's popular with the middle-aged set, though there are some curious 20- and 30-year-olds. It opened in 1966, a companion to one in Hamburg since 1948: Both claim that in the past 40-some years more than 95,000 couples have met on their dance floors and married. No jeans or tennis shoes are allowed; most men are in jacket and tie, and women are dressed up. If you're over 30, you'll probably get a kick out of this place. It's open Monday to Thursday from 8pm to 3am, Friday and Saturday from 8pm to 4am, and Sunday from 4pm to 1am. A live band plays most evenings. It's located about a 15-minute walk north of the Ku'damm. A small beer costs 8 DM ($5). **U-Bahn:** Ernst-Reuter-Platz.

Admission: Free, but there's a minimum drink charge of 8 DM ($5) Sun–Thurs, 16 DM ($10) Fri–Sat and holidays.

FAR OUT, Kurfürstendamm 156, Charlottenburg. Tel. 320 00 723.

This disco has several things going for it—for one thing, it's easy to reach, on the side street between Ciao Ciao restaurant and the Schaubühne am Lehniner Platz theater, toward the western end of the Ku'damm. It's also modern, spacious, clean, and laid-back, featuring rock and roll from the 1970s and '80s and catering to a sophisticated crowd in their 20s and 30s. And wonder of wonders, it features a no-smoking night Tuesday evenings. If you want to see it at its roaring best, don't even think about showing up before midnight. Opening at 10pm, it closes at 4am weekdays and at 6am Friday and Saturday. It's closed on Monday. Beer starts at 4.50 DM ($2.80). **U-Bahn:** Adenauerplatz, a couple minutes' walk.

Admission: Sun, Tues–Thurs 5 DM ($3.10); Fri–Sat 10 DM ($6.25).

METROPOL, Nollendorfplatz 5, Schöneberg. Tel. 216 41 22.

Housed in a colossal and striking building that once was a theater, the Metropol has been one of the most popular and innovative establishments on the Berlin scene for years. Staging live concerts on weekdays, it serves as a disco every Friday and Saturday, from 9pm to 6am. It's a massive place, with three different dancing areas and eight bars, and all the latest in laser and electric technology. Every other Sunday night, from 7pm to 1am, there's the Gay Tea Dance, the hippest and wildest place to be for Berlin's gay community and featuring "techno" (read loud) music. It's open to people of all sexual persuasions and is usually packed. **U-Bahn:** Nollendorfplatz, a 1-minute walk.

Admission: 10 DM ($6.25).

---

3. THE BAR SCENE

ON OR NEAR THE KU'DAMM

AX BAX, Leibnizstrasse 34. Tel. 313 85 94.

For a thirtysomething Berliner out on the town, Ax Bax is likely to be on the evening's agenda. This is a popular watering hole for writers and personalities in the film industry, and the average age is 35 to 40. From Vienna, this combination restaurant/bar offers a changing selection of Viennese specialties, which may include a meat-and-vegetable strudel, Viennese salad, or marinated beef. Earlier in the evening people come to eat; after 10pm they usually come to drink, though food is served until a late 1am. Beer prices start at 5 DM ($3.10) for .4 liters. Open Tuesday to Sunday from 7pm to 3am, it's located a few minutes' walk west of Savignyplatz, off Kantstrasse. **S-Bahn:** Savignyplatz, less than a 4-minute walk.

CAFE BLEIBTREU, Bleibtreustrasse 45. Tel. 881 47 56.

Located a short walk north of the Ku'damm on a side street noted for its bars and restaurants, this is one of my favorite cafés, day or night. One of the first so-called café/bars to open in Berlin, it has a cordial atmosphere and sidewalk seating in summer. It's popular with the 30-ish crowd and serves breakfast until 2pm. A glass of wine is 4.80 DM ($3), beer starts at 4.50 DM ($2.80) for a half liter. It opens daily at 9:30am, closing at 1am Sunday to Thursday, and stays open until 2:30am Friday and Saturday. **S-Bahn:** Savignyplatz, a 1-minute walk.

COUR CARREE, Savignyplatz 5. Tel. 312 52 38.

One of several bars clustered around Savignyplatz, a small square just a 5-minute walk north of the Ku'damm, Cour Carrée offers outdoor seating beneath a canopy of spreading vines. Come in the summertime, and watch the world go by. Beer prices start at 4.50 DM ($2.80) for a half liter. It's open daily from noon to 2am. **S-Bahn:** Savignyplatz, about a 2-minute walk.

DICKE WIRTIN, Carmerstrasse 9. Tel. 312 49 52.

Dicke Wirtin is named for the "fat barmaid" who used to run this place, but she's long gone and so are the days when this was the hottest bar around. Still, it's one of the old-timers near Savignyplatz and continues to draw a faithful clientele. I've never been here in the wee hours of the night, but judging from the serious beer drinkers who are already here by early evening, things can only get rowdier. This old-style German pub is known for its hearty stews; it occupies part of the ground floor of a beautiful but neglected and bullet-ridden building, recently earmarked for renovation: From the looks of things, it could take years. Stews start at 4.50 DM ($2.80); beer at

---

IMPRESSIONS

Aside from the theaters and movie houses; aside from the elegant hotels, the restaurants, cafés, and confectionary shops; aside from the countless bars, dance halls, and cabarets, which only a thick tome could list; aside from the light-flooded Friedrichstrasse, and Kurfürstendamm, and the places on Jäger and Behrensstrasse, where you find a night club in every house . . . where admission is free and a thousand shapely legs are displayed . . . aside from all this, there are two kinds of places: those one talks about and those one doesn't talk about, but frequents just the same.
—EUGEN SZATMARI, 1927

3.90 DM ($2.45). It's open daily from noon to a late 4am. **S-Bahn:** Savignyplatz, about a 3-minute walk.

DIENER, Grolmanstrasse 47. Tel. 881 53 29.

This is a typical German *Kneipe,* or bar, but it's been here for decades and is named after a former champion boxer named Franz Diener. On the walls are photographs of famous people who have dropped in, including theater and film stars. Otherwise it's an unpretentious-looking place, the service is friendly, and it serves German soups and snacks. A good place for a bit of old Germany away from the glitz of the Ku'damm. It's open daily from 6pm to 1am and serves beer starting at 4.50 DM ($2.80) a glass. **S-Bahn or U-Bahn:** Savignyplatz or Uhlandstrasse, both about a 3-minute walk.

HARD ROCK CAFE, Meinekestrasse 21. Tel. 884 62 20.

You know Berlin is in when a Hard Rock Café moves to town. Opened in 1992, this worldwide chain features the usual rock 'n' roll memorabilia, T-shirts for sale, hamburgers, and beer. Be forewarned, however, that the music is loud and prices for food are high. If you must, come for a beer, which starts at 4.50 DM ($2.80) for a half liter, and a T-shirt. Located just south of the Ku'damm, it's open daily from noon to 3am. **U-Bahn:** Kurfürstendamm, a couple minutes' walk.

KU'DORF, Joachimstaler Strasse 15. Tel. 883 66 66.

Located in a basement, the Ku'Dorf is a sprawling underground "village," which consists of several "lanes" lined with one tiny bar after another. In fact, there are 18 different bars here, each with a different theme. At one end of the village is a disco; at the other, the Carrousel, popular with a middle-aged crowd and featuring music of the 1950s through the 1970s. Everybody in the Ku'Dorf is likely to be a tourist, the majority still in their teens; if you want to be among Berliners, go someplace else. There's a cover charge of 4 DM ($2.50), and a half liter of beer costs 6.70 DM ($4.20). Closed on Sunday, it opens the rest of the week at 8pm, staying open until 2am weekdays and a late 4am on weekends. **U-Bahn:** Kurfürstendamm, about a 2-minute walk.

NEW YORK, Olivaer Platz 15. Tel. 883 62 58.

Casual and trendy, this is one of the "in" places for people in their 20s and 30s. Even in the middle of the day people hang out here, read the newspaper, and shoot pool—a good place for an afternoon drink, especially on a sunny day when you can sit outside. A café by day, by midnight it looks more like a bar; breakfast is served from 2am on Friday and Saturday. Located on a square south of the Ku'damm near Adenauerplatz, it opens at 10am, closing at 4am Sunday through Thursday, and at a very late 6am on the weekends. Beer starts at 4 DM ($2.50), while wine starts at 6 DM ($3.75). **U-Bahn:** Adenauerplatz.

SCHWARZES CAFE, Kantstrasse 148. Tel. 313 80 38.

Schwarz means "black," and true to its name, the front room of this unconventional café is painted black. If you find black rooms depressing, head upstairs to a more cheerful surrounding, where the only black in sight is the furniture. Breakfast is the specialty, available anytime, ranging from 7 DM ($4.35) for a continental to 30 DM ($18.75) for the works. There's also a large selection of coffees, including spiked coffees starting at 8 DM ($5). A simple cup of coffee is 3 DM ($1.85). Open round the clock, except Tuesdays from 3am to 6pm. **S-Bahn or U-Bahn:** Savignyplatz or Uhlandstrasse, each about a 3-minute walk.

WIRTSHAUS WUPPKE, Schlüterstrasse 21. Tel. 313 81 62.

This is a working man's neighborhood pub—plain, unrefined, and blackened from years of cigarette smoke. Most people come to drink, but there are also daily specials written on a blackboard, including hearty stews and salads. For entertainment, there's a pinball machine. Beer starts at 3.50 DM ($2.20) for .4 liter. It's open daily from 10am to 3am (in winter from noon to 3am). **S-Bahn:** Savignyplatz, about a 2-minute walk.

WIRTSHAUS ZUM LÖWEN, Hardenbergstrasse 29. Tel. 262 10 20.

Located just north of the Gedächtniskirche tucked behind a plaza, this beer hall is reminiscent of those in Munich. There's outdoor seating in summer, but even in winter you feel as if you're in a beer garden: the interior resembles a tree-filled Bavarian plaza. As with most beer halls, hearty platters of German food are available, and there's live music beginning at 7pm. Predictably, the clientele is almost exclusively tourists, but it's convenient if waiting for a train. A half liter of beer costs 5.50 DM ($3.45) during the day, increasing to 6.50 DM ($4.05) in the evenings. It's open Sunday to Thursday from 10am to midnight, Friday and Saturday from 10am to 2am. **U-Bahn:** Kurfürstendamm or Bahnhof Zoo, each just a 1-minute walk.

ZILLEMARKT, Bleibtreustrasse 48a. Tel. 881 70 40.

Located on the same street as Café Bleibtreu and the music house Go-In, this pleasant and airy establishment is named for the antique and curio market that used to be housed here. The building is from the turn of the century and features a brick floor and grillwork. In summer, there's a garden out back with seating, as well as sidewalk seating. Open daily from 9am to 1am, it serves breakfast until a late 4pm. Beer starts at 5.50 DM ($3.45) for a half liter, while a Berliner Weisse is 6.50 DM ($4.05). **S-Bahn:** Savignyplatz, a 1-minute walk.

ZWIEBELFISCH, Savignyplatz 7–8. Tel. 31 73 63.

This bar, with tables outside, has been around for more than 20 years and still enjoys great popularity. Because it stays open later than others in the area, this is where everyone ends up. Open daily from noon to 6am, usually most crowded at 4am. Beer starts at 4.10 DM ($2.55) for .4 liter, a glass of wine is 5 DM ($3.10). **S-Bahn:** Savignyplatz, a 2-minute walk.

BERLIN-MITTE (EASTERN BERLIN)

The first three bars listed below are near Alexanderplatz, in the reconstructed neighborhood known as the Nikolaiviertel. The other three are found on or near Oranienburger Strasse, located near the S-Bahn station of the same name. Berlin's newest alternative nightlife mecca, it has several weird and wonderful bars. Oranienburger Strasse is also the working street of prostitutes in search of customers in cars. A very strange mix.

ZUM NUSSBAUM, Propstrasse, Nikolaiviertel. Tel. 2431 33 28.

A reconstruction of a famous inn built in 1571 but destroyed during World War II—Zum Nussbaum is a cozy bar with wood-paneled walls, low-ceilings, and minuscule rooms. It was a favorite hangout of Heinrich Zille, a famous Berliner artist. There are a few tables outside under a walnut tree that offer a view of the Nikolaikirche. It's open daily from noon to 2am, with beer prices starting at 4.50 DM ($2.80). **U-Bahn:** Alexanderplatz or Kloster-strasse, about 5-minute walk.

ZUM PADDENWIRT, Eiergasse, Nikolaiviertel. Tel. 2431 32 31.

Located behind the Nikolaikirche, this lively place is simply decorated like taverns of former centuries. According to local legend, toads and frogs used to refresh themselves here at a barrel that dripped beer. In addition to platters of German food, it serves beer starting at 5.20 DM ($3.25) for a half liter. Open daily from 11am to midnight. **U-Bahn:** Alexanderplatz or Klosterstrasse, about a 5-minute walk.

ZUR RIPPE, Mühlendamm and Poststrasse. Tel. 2431 32 35.

This tavern was named after a medieval inn first mentioned in documents in 1672. The rib displayed on its facade supposedly belonged to a giant, who was killed by a Berlin fisherman for robbing and abducting a spinster. Zur Rippe offers daily specials of German cuisine, but most people come here to drink, with beer prices starting at 4.70 DM ($2.95) for a half liter. It's open daily from 11am to midnight. **U-Bahn:** Alexanderplatz or Klosterstrasse, about a 5-minute walk.

SILBERSTEIN, Oranienburger Strasse 27. Tel. 28 12 095.

This is the trendiest, hippest, and most sophisticated bar on Oranienburger Strasse, located in the shadows of the newly renovated synagogue. It's decorated in minimalist style, with a bare floor, modern art on the walls, and high-backed chairs that are artsy but uncomfortable (the backs of the chairs are at least six feet tall). The drink menu is written on a slanting wall near the bar. A beer costs 3.50 DM ($2.20) for a third of a liter. It opens at 4pm Monday to Friday and at noon Saturday and Sunday—the closing hour is whenever the staff has had enough, usually the wee hours of the morn. **S-Bahn:** Oranienburger Strasse, less than a 4-minute walk.

TACHELES, Oranienburger Strasse.

This place is so alternative that it doesn't have a street address, a telephone, a sign outside its door, or even regular open hours. In fact, it may not even be around by the time you read this. If it is, you'll know it when you see it. It's located on the ground floor of a massive ruin on Oranienburger Strasse, which became the domain of squatters in 1990 and is famous for its extraordinary state of disrepair and the many artists who work here. Popular with the cutting edge of Berlin's avant-garde, it is a must for a night out on Oranienburger Strasse. Its name comes from Yiddish, meaning "straight talk." **S-Bahn:** Oranienburger Strasse, about a 1-minute walk.

VERKEHRS-BERUHIGTE O[st]ZONE, Auguststrasse.

Located on the corner of Auguststrasse and Oranienburger

Strasse, this bar is a comfortable place for a drink. Its name is a play on words: Verkehrs-Beruhigte Zone means a pedestrian-only street; Ost-zone refers to East Berlin. True to its name, a Trabant (East German car) is part of the bar's decoration, along with newspapers plastered to the ceiling. A .4-liter beer costs 3.50 DM ($2.20). The bar opens daily at 4pm, closing at irregular hours at night. **S-Bahn:** Oranienburger Strasse, a couple minutes' walk.

PRENZLAUER BERG

ALTBERLINER BIERSTUBEN, Saarbrücker Strasse 17. Tel. 282 89 33.

This comfortable German pub is in Prenzlauer Berg, a precinct that borders Berlin-Mitte to the north. One of my favorite bars in eastside Berlin, it's decorated in old Berliner style, with a front room where people drink standing around counters, a back room where people can sit at tables, and outdoor tables from May through October. It's popular with students of all ages and is sometimes so crowded that it is difficult to wade through the crowd to order a drink at the bar, let alone find a seat. The food menu lists typical Berliner fare. Beer prices start at 3.50 DM ($2.80) for a half liter, and it's open daily from noon to 2am. It's located on the corner of Saarbrücker Strasse and Schönhauser Allee, just two subway stops north of Alexanderplatz. **U-Bahn:** Senefelderplatz, a 1-minute walk (take the Saarbrücker Strasse exit).

NEAR WILMERSDORFER STRASSE & BAHNHOF CHARLOTTENBURG

If you find yourself on Wilmersdorfer Strasse after a hard day of shopping, you might wish to reward yourself with a stop at one of these two places.

EXTRA DRY, Mommsenstrasse 34. Tel. 324 60 38.
This café is *for women only* and is certainly one of the best women's cafés in Berlin. It's clean, modern, and nicely furnished and maintains a strict policy against alcoholic drinks, serving instead milk shakes, fruit cocktails, and light snacks. It serves as a meeting place for various women's groups, including those involving battered women and women who have been drug-dependent and need a clean environment in which to socialize. It's also a good place for women traveling alone or tired of the usual bar scene, and is a good place to simply sit and write letters if that's what you feel like doing. The service is friendly. Drinks average about 3 DM ($1.85) or 4 DM ($2.50), and it's open Tuesday through Sunday from noon to 11pm. **S-Bahn:** Charlottenburg, about a 3-minute walk.

WILHELM HOECK, Wilmersdorfer Strasse 149. Tel. 341 31 10.
You'll find two doors at this address. The door on the left leads to a simple family-style restaurant; the one on the right leads to the bar, which has been around since 1892 and has changed little in the past century. The decor features old wooden beer barrels against the wall, old Schnaps bottles on the shelves, and old photographs illustrating the history of the place. If you're hungry, a menu offers home-cooked dishes at modest prices (see Chapter 5, "Where to Eat in Berlin," for more information). A half liter of beer is 3.20 DM ($2). It's open

Monday to Saturday from 8am to midnight, making it the place to come if you want beer for breakfast. **U-Bahn:** Bismarckstrasse, a couple minutes' walk.

NEAR NOLLENDORFPLATZ

CAFE SIDNEY, Winterfeldstrasse 40. Tel. 216 52 53.

A 5-minute walk south of Nollendorfplatz, this modern and breezy café/bar stands on a square called Winterfeldplatz, famous for its morning market on Wednesday and Saturday. Decorated with palm trees and featuring two pool tables and split-level seating, it opens daily at 9am, serves breakfast until 5pm, and closes at 4am. A half liter of beer is 6 DM ($3.75). and a glass of wine is 4 DM ($2.50). **U-Bahn:** Nollendorfplatz, a 5-minute walk.

SLUMBERLAND, Winterfeldplatz. Tel. 216 53 49.

Everyone seems to drop by here after they've been to the Saturday market on Winterfeldplatz. Slumberland is at its most crowded, however, in the very late hours, when many people come here after other bars have closed down. It plays African, Caribbean, reggae, and calypso music, and even has a real sand floor, along with fake banana trees and palms, to set the mood. Beer prices start at 4.50 DM ($2.80) for a half liter, wine at 5 DM ($3.10). It's open daily from 8pm to 4am, and on Saturday it's also open from 11am to 5pm. **U-Bahn:** Nollendorfplatz, about a 5-minute walk.

CAFE SWING, Nollendorfplatz 3–4. Tel. 216 61 37.

Popular with a young, student crowd, this café is about as informal and casual as it gets. It offers outdoor seating in summer, and on Saturday evenings there's free live music starting at 1am. The paintings on the wall are bright and slightly jarring—not the kind of place in which you'd want to nurse a hangover. Beer prices start at 4 DM ($2.50) for a half liter. It's open daily from about 10:30am to 3am. **U-Bahn:** Nollendorfplatz, a 1-minute walk.

IN KREUZBERG

Kreuzberg used to be the insider's tip for Berlin's alternative nightlife scene. Although there's still plenty of that, parts of Kreuzberg have become fashionable and yuppified, as Berlin's professional crowds claim areas of their own. Partyers in search of the radical should head toward Wiener Strasse.

CAFE FONTANE, Fontanepromenade 1. Tel. 691 33 45.

This modern and trendy bar features split-level seating, palm trees, a billiard table, a large window facade, and an outdoor terrace. It's a great place from which to watch the sun set over the treetops of the park across the street. It offers Beck's on tap for 5.50 DM ($3.45) for a half liter; a cup of coffee is 2.60 DM ($1.60). It opens daily at 9am, closing at 4am weekdays and 5am Friday and Saturday nights. **U-Bahn:** Südstern, a 1-minute walk.

CAFE WUNDERBAR, Körtestrasse 38. Tel. 692 11 20.

This is the most casual watering hole in the area, simple and pleasant with blue-and-white walls, a pool table, pinball and video games, and a window facade with a view of a towering church. A half liter of beer is 5 DM ($3.10); a cup of coffee is 2.50 DM ($1.55). It's open Monday to Thursday from 11am to 3am and Friday to Sunday from 11am to 4am. **U-Bahn:** Südstern, a 1-minute walk.

LEYDICKE, Mansteinstrasse 4. Tel. 216 29 73.
Opened in 1877, this bar is one of the oldest drinking establishments in Berlin and features an antique bar and shelving, wainscot, and ceiling. It makes and sells its own wines and liqueurs, produced from fruit brought in from western Germany. Wine by the glass starts at 3.50 DM ($2.20). It's open Monday and Friday from noon to 2pm and again from 4pm to midnight; Tuesday and Thursday from 4pm to midnight; and Wednesday, Saturday, and Sunday from 11am to 1am. **U-Bahn:** Yorckstrasse. **Bus:** 119 from the Ku'damm to Mansteinstrasse stop.

MADONNA, Wiener Strasse 22. Tel. 611 69 43.
Anyone familiar with Berlin's bar scene has either been here or heard of this place, by far the most well-known establishment on Wiener Strasse. It attracts students, the young working class, and punks, and if you want to dress like everyone else here, wear either denim or leather. Although singer Madonna may first come to mind, its namesake is the other Madonna, present in several religious statues that decorate the place, along with fake stained-glass windows. A bottle of Beck's beer, which is all everyone seems to drink, costs 3.50 DM ($2.20). The place is open daily from 11am to about 3am (to 4am on weekends). **U-Bahn:** Görlitzer Bahnhof.

RAMPENLICHT, Körtestrasse 33. Tel. 692 13 01.
Housed in an older building typical of Kreuzberg, Rampenlicht has an artsy, sophisticated atmosphere, with black wainscot, black chairs, and the sparse decoration of a huge Asian fan spreading along one wall. In summer there's outdoor seating on the sidewalk. Breakfast is served until 4pm, and beer costs 5.30 DM ($3.30) for a half liter. It's open daily from 9am to 2am. **U-Bahn:** Südstern, a 1-minute walk.

WIENERBLUT, Wiener Strasse 14. Tel. 618 90 23.
Rustic punk may be the best way to describe this typical Kreuzberg bar, popular with young people who strive for the unkempt, casual look in hairstyles and clothing. Earrings for men are an absolute must. There's nothing refined about this alternative hangout, unless you count the red lights above the bar that cast a bloodlike glow over the place (Wienerblut means Viennese blood, a play on Wiener Strasse). Diversions include a Foosball and a pinball table. Beer prices start at 3.50 DM ($2.20) for a third of a liter. It's open from 2pm to 3am on weekdays, to 5am on weekends. **U-Bahn:** Görlitzer Bahnhof.

BEER GARDENS

LORETTA'S GARDEN, Lietzenburgerstrasse 89. Tel. 882 33 54.
This huge beer garden, located a few minutes' walk south of the Ku'damm in the heart of the city, seats about 6,000 people under a spread of trees. It's open from April to the end of September, daily from 10am to 1am. You fetch your own beer here, with half-liter mugs costing 6.50 DM ($4.05). Stalls sell food ranging from American spareribs and barbecued chicken to crêpes. **U-Bahn:** Uhlandstrasse, about a 5-minute walk.

LUISE, Königin-Luise-Strasse 40. Tel. 832 84 87.
Located in Dahlem not far from the area's many museums, Luise

is a popular watering hole with several hundred seats outdoors. In addition to half-liter mugs of beer selling for 5 DM ($3.10), it also offers Weissbier, a wheat beer. It's open when the weather is fine, from 10am to 11pm. **U-Bahn:** Dahlem-Dorf, a 1-minute walk.

4. MORE ENTERTAINMENT

MOVIES

You won't have any trouble finding a cinema showing the latest movies from Hollywood. However, Berlin's main cinematic attraction lies in its "Off-Ku'damm" cinemas, those specializing in the classics of film history as well as new German and international productions of independent filmmakers. Check *tip* or *zitty* for listings of current films. (*OF*) means that the film is in the original language, and (*OmU*) means that the film has German subtitles. The following are two well-known cinemas.

ARSENAL, Welserstrasse 25. Tel. 218 68 48.

This is the original Off-Ku'damm cinema, and since the 1970s it has been paving the way for alternative programs. Arsenal specializes in retrospectives, film series, and experimental and avant-garde films from around the world.

Tickets: 9 DM ($5.60). **U-Bahn:** Wittenbergplatz. **Bus:** 119, 129, 249, 146, or 185.

ODEON, Hauptstrasse 116. Tel. 781 56 67.

This is the place to go if you want to see the latest Hollywood flick, since it specializes in English-language recent releases. It even has popcorn.

Tickets: 10 DM ($6.25). **U-Bahn:** Innsbrucker Platz.

GAMBLING

If you wish to try your luck at the gambling tables, head toward the Europa-Center on Budapester Strasse, where you'll find the **Spielbank Berlin** (tel. 250 08 90). Since its opening in 1975, it has witnessed an average of 1,000 guests a day, who come to play French and American roulette, blackjack, baccarat, and the one-arm bandits. Admission is 5 DM ($3.10), and a coat and tie are required for men in the winter. It's open daily from 3pm to 3am, and the nearest U-Bahn stations are Kurfürstendamm and Bahnhof Zoologischer Garten, just a couple of minutes away.

CHAPTER 10

EASY EXCURSIONS FROM BERLIN

1. POTSDAM
2. THE SPREEWALD

If you take only one excursion outside Berlin, it should be to Potsdam and Frederick the Great's palace of Sanssouci. In summertime, another great excursion is to the Spreewald, where you can take a boat trip through a unique landscape of waterways.

1. POTSDAM

Located only 15 miles southwest of Berlin, Potsdam was once Germany's most important baroque town, serving both as a garrison and as the residence of Prussia's kings and royal families from the 17th to 20th centuries. The most famous of the Prussian kings was Frederick the Great, who succeeded in uniting Germany under his rule and who built himself a delightful rococo palace in Potsdam, Schloss Sanssouci. His palace still stands, surrounded by a 750-acre estate with several other magnificent structures, including the Neues Palais.

History buffs will also want to visit Cecilienhof, site of the 1945 Potsdam Conference. As for Potsdam itself, although much of it was destroyed during World War II, it still has a delightful Altstadt (Old Town), including a historical Holländisches Viertel (Dutch Quarter) with houses dating from the mid-1700s. Wear your walking shoes, because this is a great town for walking.

ORIENTATION

Schloss Sanssouci can be visited only by joining a guided tour, conducted only in German and often sold out by noon, especially in the summer and on weekends. Try, therefore, to schedule your trip to Potsdam on a weekday and head out early in the morning, allowing at least an hour for the trip from Berlin's center to Potsdam. If you can't get into Schloss Sanssouci, don't despair. I personally think the outside of the palace, viewed from the back below the vineyard terraces, is the most important (and most picturesque) thing to see in Potsdam. In addition, you can always visit the nearby Neues Palais on your own (May to October only). However, if you're worried about getting into the palace and wish to have a tour in English, you're better off joining an organized sightseeing tour from Berlin (see "Organized Tours" in Chapter 6, "What to See & Do in Berlin," for a list of companies offering trips to Potsdam). The disadvantage of the tours, however, is that they don't allow you to explore Potsdam, especially the Altstadt, on your own. An alternative would be to join

9 mi
15 km

❶ Potsdam
❷ The Spreewald

an organized tour and then remain in Potsdam, exploring the city at your leisure and then finding your own way back to Berlin.

The best way to reach Potsdam is by bus 113, which departs approximately every 10 minutes from Wannsee S-Bahn station, reaching Potsdam's city center in less than half an hour. Since Potsdam is considered within Greater Berlin's transportation system, the cost of the entire trip by S-Bahn and bus is 3.20 DM ($2) one way. In Potsdam, get off bus 113 at the last stop, Bassinplatz, which is the city's main bus center. From here it's a pleasant half-hour walk to

Sanssouci palace through the Altstadt and Sanssouci Park (if you don't feel like walking, take bus 695 from Bassinplatz to Schloss Sanssouci, the Neues Palais, and Cecilienhof; note, however, that buses travel infrequently).

You can also reach Potsdam directly from Berlin by taking the S-Bahn (S-3) all the way from Bahnhof Zoo or Alexanderplatz to Potsdam-Stadt station, although the station is not as conveniently located as the Bassinplatz bus depot. You can walk to Sanssouci palace from the station in about an hour; otherwise you're best off taking a taxi.

INFORMATION

For visitor information about Potsdam, contact **Potsdam-Information,** Friedrich-Ebert-Strasse 5 (tel. 0331/211 00), located in the heart of the city and open Monday to Friday from 9am to 8pm and Saturday and Sunday from 9am to 6pm. For information on Schloss Sanssouci, including guided-tour information, call or drop by **Sanssouci-Information,** located in the palace (tel. 0331/22051). It's open during the main tourist season, April through October, daily from 8:30am to 4:30pm.

WHAT TO SEE & DO

Beginning at Bassinplatz, start your day in Potsdam with a stroll through the Holländisches Viertel (Dutch Quarter), located just north of the bus center. The 134 homes of gabled brick, built in the mid-1700s by and for settlers from the Low Countries, represent the largest concentration of Dutch-style homes outside Holland. Nearby is Brandenburger Strasse, Potsdam's most famous street. A quaint pedestrian lane lined with shops and cafés housed in beautifully restored buildings with ornate facades, it leads straight through the Altstadt. At its western end is a large stone portal, Potsdam's own Brandenburger Tor. From here, Allee nach Sanssouci leads to the royal estate. This is the most dramatic way to approach Schloss Sanssouci, since your first view of it includes six grassy terraces with the palace perched on top.

SCHLOSS SANSSOUCI AND PARK, Zur historischen Mühle. Tel. 0331/22051 or 239 31.

IMPRESSIONS

Take, for instance, the Prussians: they are saints when compared with the French. They have every sort of excellence; they are honest, sober, hard-working, well-instructed, brave, good sons, husbands, and fathers; and yet all this is spoilt by one single fault—they are insupportable. . . . The only Prussian I ever knew who was an agreeable man was Bismarck. All others with whom I have been thrown—and I have lived for years in Germany—were proud as Scotchmen, cold as New Englanders, and touchy as only Prussians can be. I once had a friend among them. His name was Buckenbrock. Inadvertently I called him Butterbrod. We have never spoken since.
—HENRY LABOUCHERE, 1871

✪ Although Potsdam was first mentioned in documents in 993 and became the second residence of the Great Elector of Brandenburg in 1660, it was under Friedrich Wilhelm I (Frederick William I) that the city blossomed into a garrison town. Credited with building the great Prussian army, Friedrich Wilhelm I was succeeded by a rather reluctant son, Friedrich II, who first tried to shirk responsibilities by fleeing to England with his friend, Lieutenant von Kette, an army officer. They were caught and tried as deserters and Friedrich was forced to witness the beheading of his friend (some say lover) as punishment. Friedrich II thereafter conformed to his father's wishes, married, and became the third king of Prussia, to be more popularly known as Friedrich der Grosse (Frederick the Great). He doubled the size of the Prussian army and went on to make Prussia the greatest military power on the Continent.

It was Frederick the Great who built much of Sanssouci as we know it today, created in part to satisfy his artistic and intellectual passions. Instead of being able to devote himself to the arts and the period of Enlightenment as he would have liked, it was Frederick the Great's fate to become involved in one war after the other, including the Silesian Wars and the Seven Years' War. He retreated to Sanssouci to meditate, pursue philosophy, and forget the worries of life. In fact, *sans souci* means "without worry."

Schloss Sanssouci (Sanssouci Palace), the summer residence of Frederick the Great, was designed by Georg von Knobelsdorff in the 1740s according to plans drawn up by the king himself. Although it looks comparatively modest and ordinary if approached from the main road and entrance, it is breathtaking if viewed from the park on the other side. For the palace sits atop six grassy terraces, cut into the side of a hill like steps in a pyramid. The terraces were once vineyards, and seem to overwhelm the much smaller one-story palace. It's only after you've climbed the graceful staircases leading up through the terraces that the palace finally reveals itself, like a surprise package. On the top terrace is Frederick the Great's tomb.

Frederick the Great must have liked wine, because the motifs of grapes and wine are carried from the vineyards into the palace itself. Note the figures supporting the roof facing the vineyards—they look a bit tipsy and happy, as though they've just indulged in the fruits of the vine. Inside are statues of Bacchus, god of wine, as well as pictures and reliefs of grapes, vines, and people enjoying themselves. Among the guests who passed through Sanssouci was Voltaire, the great French philosopher. He stayed in Potsdam for three years, during which time he and the king spent many an evening together.

Yet Frederick the Great maintained a rather austere life, preferring to sleep in a camp bed like a soldier rather than in a royal bed. Even the Festival Hall is modestly small, noted for its inlaid marble floor in the pattern of a vineyard. The Concert Room, which contains Frederick the Great's flute, is exquisite—a stucco ceiling in the pattern of a spider web gives the illusion that the room is so light and airy that it can be held together with fragile strands. The Voltaire Room boasts hand-carved wooden reliefs painted in bright yellows, blues, reds, and other colors, as well as a chandelier with delicate porcelain flowers and brass flowers.

Schloss Sanssouci is open only for guided tours, which are conducted only in German, depart every 20 minutes, and last 40 minutes. Remember, if you can't get into Schloss Sanssouci, head for the Neues Palais, described below, which you can tour on your own May through October.

Be sure, too, to walk through the grounds of Sanssouci Park. It's huge, with 750 acres containing a wide range of gardens, ponds, streams, and statues of Greek and mythological figures. There are, for example, the Dutch Garden, the Sicilian Garden, and the Nordic Garden, as well as the Östlicher Lustgarten (Eastern Pleasure Garden) and Westlicher Lustgarten (Western Pleasure Garden). The Orangerie, located in the Westlicher Lustgarten and reached via pathways through the Sicilian and Nordic Gardens, was built according to the style of the Italian Renaissance period to house tropical plants and later became rather elaborate accommodations for guests. Another interesting structure is the Chinesisches Teehaus (Chinese Teahouse), built in the shape of a clover and featuring gilded statues of mandarins.

Admission: 6 DM ($3.75) adults, 3 DM ($1.85) students, children, and senior citizens.

Open: Apr–Sept daily 9am–5pm; Oct, Feb, and Mar daily 9am–4pm; Nov–Jan 9am–3pm. **Closed:** First and third Mon of every month. **Bus:** 695.

NEUES PALAIS, Sanssouci Park. Tel. 0331/22051 or 97 31 43.

The largest building in Sanssouci Park, the Neues Palais was built 20 years after Schloss Sanssouci as a show of Prussian strength following the devastation of the Seven Years' War. Also serving as a summer residence for the royal Hohenzollern family, it is much more ostentatious than Schloss Sanssouci and in comparison seems grave, solemn, and humorless. Wilhelm II, Germany's last kaiser, used it until 1918, his last year in power. When his family fled to exile in Holland, they took 60 wagons full of possessions with them from the Neues Palais.

From November through May, Neues Palais can be viewed only on guided tours, conducted in German and lasting approximately one hour. From the end of May through October, you can elect to either take a tour or walk through on your own—in either case, admission is the same. The Neues Palais is about a 20- to 30-minute walk through the park from Schloss Sanssouci.

Admission: 6 DM ($3.75) adults, 3 DM ($1.85) students, children, and senior citizens.

Open: Apr–Sept daily 9am–5pm; Oct, Feb, and Mar daily 9am–4pm; Nov–Jan 9am–3pm. **Closed:** Second and fourth Mon of every month. **Bus:** 695.

BILDERGALERIE [Picture Gallery], Östlicher Lustgarten, Sanssouci Park. Tel. 0331/226 55.

Located just east of Schloss Sanssouci, the Bildergalerie was built between 1755 and 1763 to house Frederick the Great's art collection. Today it serves as a gallery for works by Italian and Flemish masters.

Admission: 3 DM ($1.85) adults, 1.50 DM (95¢) students, children, and senior citizens.

Open: Apr–Sept daily 9am–noon and 12:45–5pm; Oct, Feb, and Mar daily 9am–noon and 12:45–4pm; Nov–Jan 9am–noon and 12:45–3pm. **Closed:** Fourth Wed of every month. **Bus:** 695.

CECILIENHOF, Neuer Garten. Tel. 0331/225 79.

The Neuer Garten (New Garden) was laid out at the end of the 18th century, alongside lake Heiligensee. It's the home of Cecilienhof, Potsdam's newest palace, built between 1913 and 1916 in mock-Tudor style by Kaiser Wilhelm II. It served as a royal residence of the last German crown prince and his wife, Cecilie, until the end of World War II. Its 176 rooms contain a museum, a hotel, and a restaurant. It also boasts 55 chimneys, each one different.

Cecilienhof gained everlasting fame in 1945 when it served as the headquarters of the Potsdam Conference. It was here that Truman, Stalin, and Churchill (and later Attlee of Great Britain) met to discuss the disarmament and future of a divided Germany. There's a museum here showing the conference room and the round table where the Big Three sat.

Admission: 3 DM ($1.85) adults, 1.50 DM (95¢) students, children, and senior citizens.

Open: May–Oct 9am–5pm; Nov–Apr 9am–4pm. **Closed:** Second and fourth Mon of every month. **Bus:** 695.

WHERE TO EAT

HISTORISCHE MÜHLE, Zur Historischen Mühle. Tel. 231 10.
Cuisine: GERMAN. **Directions:** A 2-minute walk from Schloss Sanssouci.
$ Prices: Soups 2–4 DM ($1.25–$2.50); main courses 10–20 DM ($6.25–$12.50). No credit cards.
Open: Apr–Oct Tues–Sun 10am–6pm; Nov–Mar Wed–Sun 10am–5pm.

Pleasantly situated in a forest of green, this German restaurant is my top choice for a meal in Potsdam and is convenient if you're visiting Schloss Sanssouci. Start your meal with a bowl of Ukrainian Soljanka soup, followed by a main course of Schweinebraten with red cabbage and potatoes, Kasselbraten with Sauerkraut and potatoes, Hungarian Gulasch, Schnitzel with mushrooms and french fries, grilled chicken, duck, Schweinshaxe, or Eisbein. If the weather is warm, you may opt instead for a beer in the restaurant's large beer garden. An alternative is the Jagdhaus, an *Imbiss* on the grounds of the restaurant selling beer and Würste, with outdoor seating.

IHRE FRISCH-BACKSTÜBE, corner of Brandenburger Strasse and Friedrich-Ebert-Strasse. Tel. 48 21 15.
Cuisine: SANDWICHES/SNACKS. **Directions:** A couple minutes' walk from Bassinplatz.
$ Prices: 2.50–5 DM ($1.55–$3.10). No credit cards.
Open: Mon–Fri 6:30am–6:30pm, Sat 6am–2pm, Sun 11am–6pm.

This deservedly popular bakery chain offers freshly baked breads, sandwiches, baguettes, and daily specials ranging from pizza by the slice to noodle casseroles, all on display behind the cafeteria's glass case. There are chest-high tables where you can eat your goodies, or, if you wish, order take-out and eat at one of the benches on Brandenburger Strasse.

There's a smaller branch of Ihre Frisch-Backstübe about halfway down Brandenburger Strasse, in front of Horten department store. It's an outdoor *Imbiss,* with the same open hours.

POTSDAMER BÖRSE, Brandenburger Strasse 35–36.
Tel. 225 05 or 237 03.
Cuisine: GERMAN. **Directions:** A 1-minute walk from the Bassinplatz bus center.
$ Prices: Soups and appetizers 4–8 DM ($2.50–$5); main courses 8–28 DM ($5–$17.50). AE, DC, MC, V.
Open: Daily 11am–10:30pm.

Just a short walk from Potsdam's main bus center in the heart of the Altstadt, this cozy family restaurant served as a distillery and wine merchant's shop in the 18th century. Its menu includes soups, Sauerbraten, omelets, fish, chicken fricassee, smoked pork, roast duck, and Schnitzel. Adjoining the restaurant is the Marktklause, a German-style pub with even cheaper food and snacks, including Gulaschsuppe, Berliner Boulette, Wiener Würste, and scrambled eggs with potatoes, with prices ranging from 2 DM ($1.25) to 12 DM ($7.50).

2. THE SPREEWALD

Approximately 60 miles southeast of Berlin, the Spreewald forms one of middle Europe's most unique landscapes. This is where the Spree River spreads out into countless streams and canals, a labyrinth of waterways through woodlands—a bayou. Little wonder that for decades it's been a lure for city dwellers, who come here for a ride in a punt, a German version of the gondola.

ORIENTATION

The most convenient gateway to the Spreewald is Lübbenau, which you can reach in about an hour by train from Berlin-Lichtenberg Station (be sure to inquire beforehand about train schedules, since there are only a couple of trains daily to Lübbenau and departure times may change). Once in Lübbenau, walk straight out of the train station and continue walking in the same direction on a tree-lined street that leads into town in about 20 minutes. Following signs that read "Kahnfahrten" and "Paddlebooten," you'll pass through the small village to the banks of a small river, where you'll find punts and boatmen ready to take you on rides through the Spreewald.

INFORMATION

For information about the Spreewald and boat trips from Lübbenau, telephone the **Lübbenau Verkehrsamt** at 035 42/3668.

WHAT TO SEE & DO

The best time to visit the Spreewald is from May to October, when boatmen gather at the boat landing in Lübbenau as early as 8am to wait for customers. The price for a boat ride is astoundingly inexpensive—only 2.50 DM ($1.55) per adult and 1.30 DM (80¢) per child for each hour. There are several routes, of varying lengths, from which to choose. One of the most popular is the 3-hour trip to **Lehde,** a Venice-style village of thatched-roof houses. If you wish, you can arrange for a stopover in Lehde, where you can visit an open-air museum consisting of three old farmsteads typical of the

Spreewald. It's open from May to mid-October, Tuesday to Sunday from 9am to 5pm. Admission is 4 DM ($2.50) for adults and 2 DM ($1.25) for students and children. Other boat trips range from 4 to 7 hours. For more information, call 03542/2225.

If you understand German and you hire a gregarious gondolier, you'll probably be regaled with tales about the Spreewald and the people who live here. Most of the inhabitants of the Spreewald are Sorbs, an ethnic minority of swamp-dwelling Slavs who spoke their own language until World War II and are still proud of their traditions and culture. As you glide along the canals, you'll pass rounded haystacks as tall as houses, weeping willows, poplar, and ash, and farmhouses made of logs and brick and surrounded by neat gardens. Since boats are the only means of transportation through the Spreewald, there are fireboats instead of fire trucks, and even children go to school by boat.

In addition to hiring a boat, you can also rent paddleboats if you wish to strike out on your own. Two-seaters cost 4.50 DM ($2.80) per hour, or 30 DM ($18.75) for the whole day.

You can also hike through the Spreewald. True, many paths end abruptly at one of the hundreds of canals, but that shouldn't deter you from hiking. It's only on foot that you'll have the chance to inspect more closely the flora and fauna, as well as see the many water birds that inhabit this special bayou. If you're ambitious, follow the red-marked trail to Lübben, 8 miles away, where you can then catch a train back to Berlin (again, inquire about the train schedule beforehand). Much shorter is the 1-mile educational trail through Schlosspark Lübbenau.

Finally, don't forget to visit Lübbenau's **Spreewald Museum** (tel. 03542/2472), just a short walk from the boat landing. With displays relating to the customs and traditions of the Sorbs, it's open from May to mid-October, Wednesday to Monday from 9am to 5pm. Admission is 4 DM ($2.50) for adults, and 2 DM ($1.25) for students and children.

WHERE TO EAT

The boatmen will suggest cafés and restaurants in the villages you visit. In Lehde, for example, there's the **Fröhlicher Hecht,** former home of a painter who came to the Spreewald 100 years ago and fell in love with it, as well as the more informal **Café Venedig** for coffee and tortes.

In Lübbenau, there are several *Imbisse* between the train station and the boat landing selling Würste and drinks.

Best, however, is to pack a picnic lunch and bring it with you, since this is one of the most idyllic spots for a picnic. Refer to "Picnic Fare and Where to Eat It" in Chapter 5, "Where to Eat in Berlin," for information on where to buy your goodies.

APPENDIX

A. GLOSSARY

Altstadt old town (traditional part of town or city)
Apotheke pharmacy
Art deco stylized art and architecture of the 1920s and 1930s
Art nouveau highly decorative form of art, objects, and interior design with twining, flowing motifs of late 19th and early 20th centuries
Bahn railway, train
    Bahnhof railway station
    Hauptbahnhof main railway station
    Stadtbahn (S-Bahn) commuter railway
    Untergrundbahn (U-Bahn) subway, city underground system
Baroque ornate, decorated style of architecture in the 18th century, characterized by use of elaborate ornamentation and gilding. Also applied to art of the same period.
Bauhaus style of functional design for architecture and objects, originating in the early 20th century in Germany
Biedermeier solid, bourgeois style of furniture design and interior decoration in the middle 19th century
Der Blaue Reiter group of nonfigurative painters, founded in Munich in 1911 by Franz Marc and Wassily Kandinsky
Die Brücke group of avant-garde expressionist painters originating in Dresden around 1905
Burg fortified castle
Dom cathedral
Drogerie shop selling cosmetics and sundries
Expressionism style of painting in early-20th-century Germany characterized by strong use of form and color
Gothic medieval architectural style characterized by arches, soaring spaces, and ribbed vaulting, lasting into the 16th century; also applied to painting of the period
Jugendstil German form of art nouveau
Kaufhaus department store
Kirche church
Kneipe bar, mostly for drinking
Konditorei café for coffee and pastries
Kunst art
Oper opera/opera house
Platz square
Rathaus town or city hall
Schauspielhaus theater for plays
Schloss palace, castle
Secession modernist movement in German art that strongly disavowed expressionism.
Stadt town, city
Strasse street

Tor gateway
Turm tower
Verkehrsamt tourist office
Zitadelle fortress

B. MENU SAVVY

CONDIMENTS & TABLE ITEMS

Brot bread
Brötchen rolls
Butter butter
Eis ice
Essig vinegar

Pfeffer pepper
Salz salt
Senf mustard
Zitrone lemon
Zucker sugar

SOUPS

Erbsensuppe pea soup
Gumüsesuppe vegetable soup
Gulaschsuppe spicy Hungarian beef soup
Hühnerbrühe chicken soup
Kartoffelsuppe potato soup
Leberknödelsuppe beef-liver dumpling soup

Linsensuppe lentil soup
Nudelsuppe noodle soup
Ochsenschwanzsuppe oxtail soup
Schildkrötensuppe turtle soup

SALADS

Gemischter Salat mixed salad
Gurkensalat cucumber salad

Kopfsalat/Grünsalat lettuce salad
Tomatensalat tomato salad

SANDWICHES

Käsebrot cheese sandwich
Schinkenbrot ham sandwich

Wurstbrot sausage sandwich

EGGS

Bauernfrühstück "Farmer's Breakfast"—scrambled eggs with ham or sausage, onion, and potatoes
Eier in der Schale boiled eggs

Mit Speck with bacon
Rühreier scrambled eggs
Spiegeleier fried eggs
Verlorene Eier poached eggs
Soleier pickled eggs

VEGETABLES & SIDE DISHES

Artischocken artichokes
Blumenkohl cauliflower
Bohnen beans
Bratkartoffeln fried potatoes

Erbsen peas
Grüne Bohnen green beans
Gurken cucumbers
Karotten carrots

Kartoffeln potatoes
Kartoffelsalat potato salad
Knödel dumplings
Kohl cabbage
Reis rice
Rote Rüben red beets
Rotkraut red cabbage

Salat lettuce
Salzkartoffeln boiled potatoes
Spargel asparagus
Spinat spinach
Tomaten tomatoes

MEATS

Aufschnitt cold cuts
Bockwurst Berlin sausage
Boulette meatball
Brathuhn roast chicken
Bratwurst grilled sausage
Eisbein pigs' knuckles
Ente duck
Gans goose
Gefüllte Kalbsbrust stuffed breast of veal
Hammel mutton
Hirn brains
Kalb veal
Kaltes Geflügel cold poultry
Kassler Rippchen/ Rippenspeer pork chops
Lamm lamb
Leber liver
Leberkäs German meatloaf
Nieren kidneys
Ragout stew

Rinderbraten roast beef
Rindfleisch beef
Sauerbraten marinated beef
Schinken ham
Schlachteplatte platter of blood sausage, liverwurst, kidneys, and boiled pork
Schweinebraten/ Schweinsbraten roast pork
Schweinshaxen grilled knuckle of pork
Spanferkel suckling pig
Sülze jellied meat
Tafelspitz boiled beef with vegetables
Taube pigeon
Truthahn turkey
Wiener Schnitzel veal cutlet
Wurst sausage

FISH

Aal eel
Brathering grilled herring
Forelle trout
Hecht pike
Karpfen carp

Krebs crawfish
Lachs salmon
Makrele mackerel
Schellfisch haddock
Seezunge sole

DESSERTS

Blatterteiggebäck puff pastry
Bratapfel baked apple
Eis ice cream
Käse cheese
Kompott stewed fruit
Obstkuchen fruit tart
Obstsalat fruit salad

Pfannkuchen sugared pancakes
Pflaumenkompott stewed plums
Rote Grütze cooked fruits with vanilla sauce
Teegebäck tea cakes
Torten pastries

FRUITS

Ananas pineapple
Apfel apple
Apfelsinen oranges

Bananen bananas
Birnen pears
Erdbeeren strawberries

Kirschen cherries
Pfirsiche peaches

Weintrauben grapes
Zitronen lemons

BEVERAGES

Bier beer
Berliner Weisse draft wheat beer with a shot of raspberry or green woodruff syrup
Bier vom Fass draft beer
Bock Bier dark and rich beer
Saft juice
   Apfelsaft apple juice
Sahne cream
Schokolade chocolate
Eine Tasse Kaffee a cup of coffee

Ein Dunkles a dark beer
Ein Helles a light beer
Pils light and bitter beer
Milch milk
Rotwein red wine
Weisswein white wine
Eine Tasse Tee a cup of tea
Tomatensaft tomato juice
Wasser water
Wein Wine
   Sekt champagne
Weinbrand brandy

C. USEFUL PHRASES

German is not a difficult language to learn, especially pronunciation. Unlike English or French, it contains no hidden surprises and everything is pronounced exactly as it's written—according, of course, to German rules. *Ei* is always pronounced as a long *i*; thus, *nein* (which means "no") is pronounced *nine*. A *w* is pronounced *v;* a *v* is pronounced as *f*. As for those two dots over vowels, they signal a slight change in pronunciation.

ENGLISH	GERMAN	PRONUNCIATION
Hello	**Guten Tag**	*goo*-ten tahk
Goodbye	**Auf Wiedersehen**	owf *vee*-der-*zay-en*
How are you?	**Wie geht es Ihnen?**	vee *gayt* ess ee-nen
Very well	**Sehr gut**	*zayr* goot
Please	**Bitte**	*bit*-tuh
Thank you	**Danke schön**	*dahn*-keh shern
Excuse me	**Entschuldigen Sie**	en-*shool-d*-gen zee
You're welcome	**Gern geschehen**	*gehrn* geshai'en
Yes	**Ja**	yah
No	**Nein**	nine
Mr./Mrs.	**Herr/Frau**	hehr/vrow
I don't understand	**Ich verstehe nicht**	ish fer-*steh-he* nisht
I understand	**Ich verstehe**	ish fer-*steh*-he
Where is . . . ?	**Wo ist . . .?**	voh *eest*
the station	**der Bahnhof**	deyr *bahn*-hohf
a hotel	**ein Hotel**	ain *hotel*
a restaurant	**ein Restaurant**	ain res-tow-*rahng*
the toilet	**die Toilette**	dee twah-*let*-tah

a bank	**eine Bank**	ain *bahnk*
a post office	**ein Postamt**	ain *post*-ahmt
the bust stop	**die Bus**	dee
	haltestelle	*bus*-halte-stelle
the tourist information office	**das Verkehrsamt**	dass fer-*kerrs*-amt
To the right	**Nach rechts**	*nakh* reshts
To the left	**Nach links**	*nakh* leenks
Straight ahead	**Geradeaus**	geh-rah-*deh*-ous
Ladies/Gentlemen	**Damen/Herren**	*dah*-men/*heh*-ren
Women/Men	**Frauen/Männer**	*frow*-en/*meh*-ner
How much does it cost?	**Wieviel kostet es?**	vee-*feel kah*-stet ess
Expensive	**Teuer**	*toy*-er
Cheap	**Billig**	*bil*-lich
The check, please	**Die Rechnung, bitte**	dee *rekh*-noong, *bit*-tuh
I would like . . .	**Ich möchte . . .**	ikh *mersh*-ta
stamps	**Briefmarken**	*breef*-mahr-ken
to eat	**essen**	*ess*-en
a room	**ein Zimmer**	ain *tzim*-mer
for one night	**für eine Nacht**	*feer* ai-neh *nakht*
Breakfast	**Frühstück**	*free*-shtick
Lunch	**Mittagessen**	*mi*-tahg-*ess*-en
Dinner	**Abendessen**	*ah*-bend-*ess*-en
Free (vacant)/ occupied	**Frei/besetzt**	*Frahy*/be-*setts*
When?	**Wann?**	vahn
Yesterday	**Gestern**	*geh*-stern
Today	**Heute**	*hoy*-tuh
Tomorrow	**Morgen**	*more*-gen
Sunday	**Sonntag**	*zohn*-tahk
Monday	**Montag**	*mon*-tahk
Tuesday	**Dienstag**	*deens*-tahk
Wednesday	**Mittwoch**	*mitt*-voch
Thursday	**Donnerstag**	*don*-ners-tahk
Friday	**Freitag**	*frahy*-tahk
Saturday	**Samstag**	*zahmz*-tahk

NUMBERS

0 **Null** (nool)	10 **Zehn** (tzayn)	17 **Siebzehn** (*zeeb*-tzayn)
1 **Eins** (aintz)	11 **Elf** (ellf)	18 **Achtzehn** (*akh*-tzayn)
2 **Zwei** (tzvai)	12 **Zwölf** (tzvuhlf)	19 **Neunzehn** (*noyn*-tzayn)
3 **Drei** (dry)	13 **Dreizehn** (*dry*-tzayn)	20 **Zwanzig** (*tzvahn*-tzik)
4 **Vier** (feer)	14 **Vierzehn** (*feer*-tzayn)	25 **Fünfundzwan-zig** (*fewnf* und *tzvahn*-tzik)
5 **Fünf** (fewnf)	15 **Fünfzehn** (*fewnf*-tzayn)	
6 **Sechs** (zex)	16 **Sechszehn** (*zex*-tzayn)	
7 **Sieben** (*zee*-ben)		
8 **Acht** (ahkht)		
9 **Neun** (noyn)		

30	**Dreissig** (*dry*-sik)	70	**Siebzig** (*zeeb*-tzik)	101	**Hunderteins** (*hoon*-dert-ahyns)
40	**Vierzig** (*feer*-tzik)	80	**Achtzig** (*akht*-tzik)	200	**Zweihundert** (*tzvai*-hoon-dert)
50	**Fünfzig** (*fewnf*-tzik)	90	**Neunzig** (*noyn*-tzik)	1,000	**Eintausend** (*ahyn*-tau-zent)
60	**Sechzig** (*zex*-tzik)	100	**Hundert** (*hoon*-dert)		

D. CONVERSION CHARTS

THE MARK & THE DOLLAR

At this writing, U.S. $1 = approximately 1.60 DM (or 1 DM = 62½¢), and this was the rate of exchange used to calculate the dollar values given in this book (rounded to the nearest nickel). This rate fluctuates, and may not be the same when you travel to Berlin. Therefore, the following table should be used only as a guide.

DM	U.S.$	DM	U.S.$
1	.62	30	18.75
2	1.25	35	21.85
3	1.85	40	25.00
4	2.50	45	28.10
5	3.10	50	31.25
6	3.75	60	37.50
7	4.35	70	43.75
8	5.00	80	50.00
9	5.60	90	56.25
10	6.25	100	62.50
15	9.35	125	78.10
20	12.50	150	93.75
25	15.60	200	125.00

METRIC MEASURES
LENGTH

1 millimeter (mm)	=	0.04 inches (or less than $\frac{1}{16}$ in.)
1 centimeter (cm)	=	0.39 inches (or under ½ in.)
1 meter (m)	=	1.09 yards (or about 39 inches)
1 kilometer (km)	=	0.62 miles (or about ⅔ of a mile)

To convert kilometers to miles, take the number of kilometers and multiply by .62 (for example, 25 km × .62 = 15.5 mi).

To convert miles to kilometers, take the number of miles and multiply by 1.61. (for example, 50 mi × 1.61 = 80.5km).

CAPACITY

1 liter (l) = 33.92 ounces or 1.06 quarts or 0.26 gallons

To convert liters to gallons, take the number of liters and multiply by .26 (for example, 50 liters × .26 = 13 gallons).
To convert gallons to liters, take the number of gallons and multiply by 3.79 (for example, 10 gal × 3.79 = 37.9 liters).

WEIGHT

1 gram (g)	=	0.04 ounces (or about a paperclip's weight)
1 kilogram (kg)	=	2.2 pounds

To convert kilograms to pounds, take the number of kilos and multiply by 2.2 (for example, 75kg × 2.2 = 165 pounds).
To convert pounds to kilograms, take the number of pounds and multiply by .45 (for example, 90 pounds × .45 = 40.5kg).

TEMPERATURE

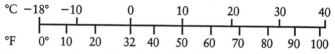

To convert degrees C to degrees F, multiply degrees C by 9, divide by 5, then add 32 (for example, 20°C × 9/5 + 32 = 68°F).
To convert degrees F to degrees C, subtract 32 from degrees F, then multiply by 5, and divide by 9 (for example, 85°F − 32 × 5/9 = 29°C).

Mileage Between Major German Cities (in Miles)

	Berlin	Bonn	Cologne	Düsseldorf	Frankfurt	Hamburg	Munich	Stuttgart
Berlin		375	357	350	343	184	363	392
Bonn	375		17	45	109	282	348	215
Cologne	357	17		24	116	264	335	226
Düsseldorf	350	45	24		141	248	380	251
Frankfurt	343	109	116	141		304	244	127
Hamburg	184	282	264	248	304		483	415
Munich	363	348	355	380	244	483		136
Stuttgart	392	215	226	251	127	415	136	

INDEX

GENERAL INFORMATION

SIGHTS & ATTRACTIONS

BERLIN

NOTE: An asterisk (*) indicates an Author's Favorite.

EXCURSION AREAS

ACCOMMODATIONS

BY AREA

Key to Abbreviations: * = Author's favorite; $ = Super-value choice; B = Budget; M = Moderate; W = Worth the extra bucks.

RESTAURANTS

BY CUISINE

Key to Abbreviations: * = Author's favorite; $ = Super-value choice; B = Budget; M = Moderate; W = Worth the extra bucks.

POTSDAM

Please Send Me the Books Checked Below:

FROMMER'S COMPREHENSIVE GUIDES
(Guides listing facilities from budget to deluxe,
with emphasis on the medium-priced)

	Retail Price	Code		Retail Price	Code
☐ Acapulco/Ixtapa/Taxco 1993–94	$15.00	C120	☐ Jamaica/Barbados 1993–94	$15.00	C105
☐ Alaska 1994–95	$17.00	C130	☐ Japan 1992–93	$19.00	C020
☐ Arizona 1993–94	$18.00	C101	☐ Morocco 1992–93	$18.00	C021
☐ Australia 1992–93	$18.00	C002	☐ Nepal 1994–95	$18.00	C126
☐ Austria 1993–94	$19.00	C119	☐ New England 1993	$17.00	C114
☐ Belgium/Holland/ Luxembourg 1993– 94	$18.00	C106	☐ New Mexico 1993–94	$15.00	C117
☐ Bahamas 1994–95	$17.00	C121	☐ New York State 1994– 95	$19.00	C132
☐ Bermuda 1994–95	$15.00	C122	☐ Northwest 1991–92	$17.00	C026
☐ Brazil 1993–94	$20.00	C111	☐ Portugal 1992–93	$16.00	C027
☐ California 1993	$18.00	C112	☐ Puerto Rico 1993–94	$15.00	C103
☐ Canada 1992–93	$18.00	C009	☐ Puerto Vallarta/ Manzanillo/Guadalajara 1992–93	$14.00	C028
☐ Caribbean 1993–94	$18.00	C123	☐ Scandinavia 1993–94	$19.00	C118
☐ Carolinas/Georgia 1994–95	$17.00	C128	☐ Scotland 1992–93	$16.00	C040
☐ Colorado 1993–94	$16.00	C100	☐ Skiing Europe 1989–90	$15.00	C030
☐ Cruises 1993–94	$19.00	C107	☐ South Pacific 1992–93	$20.00	C031
☐ DE/MD/PA & NJ Shore 1992–93	$19.00	C012	☐ Spain 1993–94	$19.00	C115
☐ Egypt 1990–91	$17.00	C013	☐ Switzerland/ Liechtenstein 1992–93	$19.00	C032
☐ England 1994	$18.00	C129	☐ Thailand 1992–93	$20.00	C033
☐ Florida 1994	$18.00	C124	☐ U.S.A. 1993–94	$19.00	C116
☐ France 1994–95	$20.00	C131	☐ Virgin Islands 1994–95	$13.00	C127
☐ Germany 1994	$19.00	C125	☐ Virginia 1992–93	$14.00	C037
☐ Italy 1994	$19.00	C130	☐ Yucatán 1993–94	$18.00	C110

FROMMER'S $-A-DAY GUIDES
(Guides to low-cost tourist accommodations and facilities)

	Retail Price	Code		Retail Price	Code
☐ Australia on $45 1993–94	$18.00	D102	☐ Israel on $45 1993– 94	$18.00	D101
☐ Costa Rica/Guatemala/ Belize on $35 1993– 94	$17.00	D108	☐ Mexico on $45 1994	$19.00	D116
☐ Eastern Europe on $30 1993–94	$18.00	D110	☐ New York on $70 1992–93	$16.00	D016
☐ England on $60 1994	$18.00	D112	☐ New Zealand on $45 1993–94	$18.00	D103
☐ Europe on $50 1994	$19.00	D115	☐ Scotland/Wales on $50 1992–93	$18.00	D019
☐ Greece on $45 1993– 94	$19.00	D100	☐ South America on $40 1993–94	$19.00	D109
☐ Hawaii on $75 1994	$19.00	D113	☐ Turkey on $40 1992– 93	$22.00	D023
☐ India on $40 1992–93	$20.00	D010	☐ Washington, D.C. on $40 1992–93	$17.00	D024
☐ Ireland on $40 1992– 93	$17.00	D011			

FROMMER'S CITY $-A-DAY GUIDES
(Pocket-size guides with an emphasis on low-cost tourist accommodations and facilities)

	Retail Price	Code		Retail Price	Code
☐ Berlin on $40 1994– 95	$12.00	D111	☐ Madrid on $50 1992– 93	$13.00	D014
☐ Copenhagen on $50 1992–93	$12.00	D003	☐ Paris on $45 1994– 95	$12.00	D117
☐ London on $45 1994– 95	$12.00	D114	☐ Stockholm on $50 1992–93	$13.00	D022

FROMMER'S WALKING TOURS
(With routes and detailed maps, these companion guides point out
the places and pleasures that make a city unique)

	Retail Price	Code		Retail Price	Code
☐ Berlin	$12.00	W100	☐ Paris	$12.00	W103
☐ London	$12.00	W101	☐ San Francisco	$12.00	W104
☐ New York	$12.00	W102	☐ Washington, D.C.	$12.00	W105

FROMMER'S TOURING GUIDES
(Color-illustrated guides that include walking tours, cultural and historic
sights, and practical information)

	Retail Price	Code		Retail Price	Code
☐ Amsterdam	$11.00	T001	☐ New York	$11.00	T008
☐ Barcelona	$14.00	T015	☐ Rome	$11.00	T010
☐ Brazil	$11.00	T003	☐ Scotland	$10.00	T011
☐ Florence	$ 9.00	T005	☐ Sicily	$15.00	T017
☐ Hong Kong/Singapore/ Macau	$11.00	T006	☐ Tokyo	$15.00	T016
☐ Kenya	$14.00	T018	☐ Turkey	$11.00	T013
☐ London	$13.00	T007	☐ Venice	$ 9.00	T014

FROMMER'S FAMILY GUIDES

	Retail Price	Code		Retail Price	Code
☐ California with Kids	$18.00	F100	☐ San Francisco with Kids	$17.00	F004
☐ Los Angeles with Kids	$17.00	F002	☐ Washington, D.C. with Kids	$17.00	F005
☐ New York City with Kids	$18.00	F003			

FROMMER'S CITY GUIDES
(Pocket-size guides to sightseeing and tourist accommodations and
facilities in all price ranges)

	Retail Price	Code		Retail Price	Code
☐ Amsterdam 1993–94	$13.00	S110	☐ Montreál/Québec City 1993–94	$13.00	S125
☐ Athens 1993–94	$13.00	S114	☐ New Orleans 1993–94	$13.00	S103
☐ Atlanta 1993–94	$13.00	S112	☐ New York 1993	$13.00	S120
☐ Atlantic City/Cape May 1993–94	$13.00	S130	☐ Orlando 1994	$13.00	S135
☐ Bangkok 1992–93	$13.00	S005	☐ Paris 1993–94	$13.00	S109
☐ Barcelona/Majorca/ Minorca/Ibiza 1993–94	$13.00	S115	☐ Philadelphia 1993–94	$13.00	S113
☐ Berlin 1993–94	$13.00	S116	☐ Rio 1991–92	$ 9.00	S029
☐ Boston 1993–94	$13.00	S117	☐ Rome 1993–94	$13.00	S111
☐ Cancún/ Cozumel 1991–92	$ 9.00	S010	☐ Salt Lake City 1991–92	$ 9.00	S031
☐ Chicago 1993–94	$13.00	S122	☐ San Diego 1993–94	$13.00	S107
☐ Denver/Boulder/ Colorado Springs 1993–94	$13.00	S131	☐ San Francisco 1994	$13.00	S133
☐ Dublin 1993–94	$13.00	S128	☐ Santa Fe/Taos/ Albuquerque 1993–94	$13.00	S108
☐ Hawaii 1992	$12.00	S014	☐ Seattle/ Portland 1992–93	$12.00	S035
☐ Hong Kong 1992–93	$12.00	S015	☐ St. Louis/Kansas City 1993–94	$13.00	S127
☐ Honolulu/Oahu 1994	$13.00	S134	☐ Sydney 1993–94	$13.00	S129
☐ Las Vegas 1993–94	$13.00	S121	☐ Tampa/St. Petersburg 1993–94	$13.00	S105
☐ London 1994	$13.00	S132	☐ Tokyo 1992–93	$13.00	S039
☐ Los Angeles 1993–94	$13.00	S123	☐ Toronto 1993–94	$13.00	S126
☐ Madrid/Costa del Sol 1993–94	$13.00	S124	☐ Vancouver/ Victoria 1990–91	$ 8.00	S041
☐ Miami 1993–94	$13.00	S118	☐ Washington, D.C. 1993	$13.00	S102
☐ Minneapolis/St. Paul 1993–94	$13.00	S119			

Other Titles Available at Membership Prices

SPECIAL EDITIONS

	Retail Price	Code		Retail Price	Code
☐ Bed & Breakfast North America	$15.00	P002	☐ Marilyn Wood's Wonderful Weekends (within a 250-mile radius of NYC)	$12.00	P017
☐ Bed & Breakfast Southwest	$16.00	P100	☐ National Park Guide 1993	$15.00	P101
☐ Caribbean Hideaways	$16.00	P103	☐ Where to Stay U.S.A.	$15.00	P102

GAULT MILLAU'S "BEST OF" GUIDES
(The only guides that distinguish the truly superlative from the merely overrated)

	Retail Price	Code		Retail Price	Code
☐ Chicago	$16.00	G002	☐ New England	$16.00	G010
☐ Florida	$17.00	G003	☐ New Orleans	$17.00	G011
☐ France	$17.00	G004	☐ New York	$17.00	G012
☐ Germany	$18.00	G018	☐ Paris	$17.00	G013
☐ Hawaii	$17.00	G006	☐ San Francisco	$17.00	G014
☐ Hong Kong	$17.00	G007	☐ Thailand	$18.00	G019
☐ London	$17.00	G009	☐ Toronto	$17.00	G020
☐ Los Angeles	$17.00	G005	☐ Washington, D.C.	$17.00	G017

THE REAL GUIDES
(Opinionated, politically aware guides for youthful budget-minded travelers)

	Retail Price	Code		Retail Price	Code
☐ Able to Travel	$20.00	R112	☐ Kenya	$12.95	R015
☐ Amsterdam	$13.00	R100	☐ Mexico	$11.95	R128
☐ Barcelona	$13.00	R101	☐ Morocco	$14.00	R129
☐ Belgium/Holland/ Luxembourg	$16.00	R031	☐ Nepal	$14.00	R018
☐ Berlin	$13.00	R123	☐ New York	$13.00	R019
☐ Brazil	$13.95	R003	☐ Paris	$13.00	R130
☐ California & the West Coast	$17.00	R121	☐ Peru	$12.95	R021
☐ Canada	$15.00	R103	☐ Poland	$13.95	R131
☐ Czechoslovakia	$15.00	R124	☐ Portugal	$16.00	R126
☐ Egypt	$19.00	R105	☐ Prague	$15.00	R113
☐ Europe	$18.00	R122	☐ San Francisco & the Bay Area	$11.95	R024
☐ Florida	$14.00	R006	☐ Scandinavia	$14.95	R025
☐ France	$18.00	R106	☐ Spain	$16.00	R026
☐ Germany	$18.00	R107	☐ Thailand	$17.00	R119
☐ Greece	$18.00	R108	☐ Tunisia	$17.00	R115
☐ Guatemala/Belize	$14.00	R127	☐ Turkey	$13.95	R027
☐ Hong Kong/Macau	$11.95	R011	☐ U.S.A.	$18.00	R117
☐ Hungary	$14.95	R118	☐ Venice	$11.95	R028
☐ Ireland	$17.00	R120	☐ Women Travel	$12.95	R029
☐ Italy	$18.00	R125	☐ Yugoslavia	$12.95	R030